CHILD SEXUAL EXPLOITATION
Why Theory Matters

Edited by
Jenny Pearce

With a foreword by
Julia Davidson

D1594772

First published in Great Britain in 2019 by

Policy Press
University of Bristol
1-9 Old Park Hill
Bristol
BS2 8BB
UK
t: +44 (0)117 954 5940
pp-info@bristol.ac.uk
www.policypress.co.uk

North America office:
Policy Press
c/o The University of Chicago Press
1427 East 60th Street
Chicago, IL 60637, USA
t: +1 773 702 7700
f: +1 773-702-9756
sales@press.uchicago.edu
www.press.uchicago.edu

© Policy Press 2019

British Library Cataloguing in Publication Data
A catalogue record for this book is available from the British Library

Library of Congress Cataloging-in-Publication Data
A catalog record for this book has been requested

978-1-4473-5141-2 hardback
978-1-4473-5143-6 paperback
978-1-4473-5142-9 ePdf
978-1-4473-5144-3 ePub

The right of Jenny Pearce to be identified as editor of this work has been asserted by her in accordance with the Copyright, Designs and Patents Act 1988.

Cover design by Robin Hawes
Front cover image: iStock/borchee

Contents

List of figures and tables

Figures

Tables

Notes on contributors

Helen Beckett is a reader in Child Protection and Children's Rights and Director of the International Centre: Researching Child Sexual Exploitation, Violence and Trafficking at the University of Bedfordshire. She is an action-oriented researcher, with over 20 years' experience of social research on children and young people's issues. She holds particular expertise in the fields of child sexual exploitation (CSE) and other forms of sexual violence in youth, with an interest in exploring ethical means of researching sensitive issues and facilitating the meaningful engagement of marginalised children and young people in research. She joined the University of Bedfordshire in September 2011 and became the Director of the International Centre in 2016. Prior to coming to the university, she worked in the fields of research and policy across the academic, statutory and voluntary sectors in Northern Ireland for 15 years.

Claudia Bernard is Professor of Social Work and Head of Postgraduate Research in the Department of Social, Therapeutic and Community Studies at Goldsmiths, University of London. Her research interests lie in the areas of social work with children and families, gender-based violence, critical race theory, equalities and social justice. She has written widely on these topics, including a book entitled *Constructing Lived Experiences: Representations of Black Mothers in Child Sexual Abuse Discourses* (2nd Edition, Routledge, 2018), and an edited collection with Perlita Harris, entitled *Safeguarding Black Children: Good Practice in Child Protection* (Jessica Kingsley Publishers, 2016). She is currently writing a book entitled *Intersectionality for Social Workers: Theory and Practice for a Super-Diverse Society*, to be published by Routledge in 2020.

John Coleman is a clinical and developmental psychologist. He was for many years the Director of the Trust for the Study of Adolescence (TSA), and he has been a Senior Research Fellow in the Department of Education at Oxford University (2006–2015). He is the author of many books, including *The Nature of Adolescence* (Routledge, 2011), now in its fourth edition and *Why Won't My Teenager Talk to Me?* (Routledge, 2014). He has served as a Policy Advisor in the Department of Health, and is currently Chair of the Association for Young People's Health (AYPH). He is also a Trustee of Family Lives. His current research interests include the adolescent brain, life skills education, and the impact of the digital world on teenage development. He runs workshops for parents of teenagers, and is the lead for the Hertfordshire 'My Teen Brain' programme. He was awarded an OBE in 2001 for services to youth.

Maddy Coy is a lecturer in the Center for Gender, Sexualities and Women's Studies Research at the University of Florida. She has worked in the field of violence against women and girls for almost 20 years, including with sexually exploited young women in residential and outreach settings. Her PhD explored links between local authority care and sexual exploitation, and she has published widely on women and girls' experiences of sexual exploitation, sexualised sexism in popular culture, and on integrated responses to violence against women and girls. In recent evaluations of specialist projects working with sexually exploited young women and research with young people about sexual consent and pornography, she has focused on the significance of social constructions of gender. Maddy is an associate editor with the Women's Studies International Forum and the editor of *Prostitution, Harm and Gender Inequality: Theory, Research and Practice* (2012, Ashgate).

Pat Dolan is joint founder and Director of the UNESCO Child and Family Research Centre and an academic director of the MA course in Family Support Studies. He also contributes to the wider undergraduate and postgraduate degree programmes of the School of Political Science and Sociology as well as supervising PhD candidates and Masters dissertations in Family Support, Social Work and Community Development. Pat Dolan holds the prestigious UNESCO Chair in Children, Youth and Civic Engagement, the first to be awarded in the Republic of Ireland. Pat has worked with and for families as a practitioner, service manager, and academic for over 20 years. He has completed an extensive body of research on family issues including longitudinal research on adolescents, their perceived mental health, resilience and social support networks and has published in a wide range of academic publications. His major research interests are civic engagement in children and youth, family support, reflective practice and service development, youth mentoring models, adolescents' resilience and social networks.

Carlene Firmin MBE is a principal research fellow at the University of Bedfordshire, where she leads their Contextual Safeguarding and peer-on-peer abuse research programmes. Carlene has spent the past ten years researching young people's experiences of community and group-based violence and advocated for comprehensive approaches that keep young people safe in public places. Her theory of Contextual Safeguarding has informed policy and research agendas for advancing the protection of adolescents, and she has worked with practitioners across the UK to co-create contextual interventions and develop Contextual Safeguarding systems within children's social care. She is a board member for NOTA and the Prison Reform Trust, and also sits on a number of national policy advisory panels for issues including gang violence, violence against women and girls and child protection. Carlene has written on the issues of safeguarding and violence in the national newspaper, the *Guardian*, since 2010, and is widely published in the area of child welfare. Carlene became the youngest black woman to receive an MBE for her seminal work on gang-affected young women in the UK.

Elly Hanson is an independent clinical psychologist and researcher, who specialises in the field of abuse and trauma. She undertakes consultation, training and research with a variety of organisations, including the CEOP Command of the National Crime Agency with whom she has worked since 2008. Other organisations include the NSPCC, local police forces, and the Football Association (informing their approach to recent sexual abuse disclosures). Elly has previously worked in an NHS substance misuse service, an NSPCC service for young people with sexually abusive behaviour, and a residential children's care company.

Kristine Hickle is a senior lecturer in Social Work at the University of Sussex, where she has worked since 2014. Her research interests include child sexual exploitation; human trafficking; trauma-informed approaches to practice; group work and group-based interventions. Kristi also has ten years' clinical practice experience providing trauma-informed group-based interventions with young people and adult survivors of sexual violence. She has written extensively and presented nationally and internationally on her research of sexual exploitation both in the United States and in the UK.

Nick Luxmoore is a freelance trainer, school counsellor, teacher, youth worker, psychotherapist (UKCP registered) and supervisor. He has 40 years' experience of working with young people and with the professionals who support them in a career that has included teaching English and Drama in schools and prisons, teaching counselling at Oxford Brookes University, running a youth centre and youth theatre, setting up and managing a young people's counselling and information service, working as a school counsellor and as a counsellor with young refugees and asylum seekers. He writes a quarterly column for BACP *Children & Young People* magazine, a blog for *Psychology Today* and is the author of eleven books, all published by Jessica Kingsley Publishers.

Caroline McGregor is Professor at the School of Political Science and Sociology with lead responsibility for the discipline of social work. She is Director of the Masters in Social Work Programme and teaches a range of subjects, including social work with vulnerable children and families, childhood and children's rights, law and human rights, and cultural competence in social work. She is also a Senior Research Fellow at the UNESCO Child and Family Research Centre. Formerly Dr Caroline Skehill of Queen's University, Caroline also has experience of research and publication in relation to child protection practice and policy, history-of-the-present methodologies, socio-legal studies and young people in and leaving care. Her current project work is focused on outcomes for young people leaving care, public awareness of child protection and welfare, youth mentoring and youth development, family support services and policy, and the interface between child protection and family support practices in child welfare.

Jenny Pearce OBE is Professor of Young People and Public Policy at the University of Bedfordshire, UK, where she is was Founder and Director of the International Centre: Researching Child Sexual Exploitation, Violence and Trafficking (2006–2016). She is a visiting professor at Goldsmiths College, London, and International Senior Research Fellow with the UNESCO Child and Family Research Centre, NUI Galway, Ireland. She is the Independent Chair of the Local Safeguarding Children Board for Hammersmith and Fulham, Westminster and the Royal Borough of Kensington and Chelsea. She has researched and published on topics related to child sexual exploitation and has advised local and national inquiries and reviews into Child Sexual Abuse and exploitation.

Jo Phoenix currently works with the Open University. She has extensive experience of writing and researching about sex, sexuality and discourses of prostitution and violence against women. She was commissioned by the Howard League for Penal Reform to undertake research into the policing and criminalisation of sexually exploited girls and young women.

Emilie Smeaton established Paradigm Research in 2009 to provide research, evaluation, training and consultation services to statutory and third sector agencies and has recently worked with Calderdale Community Safety Partnership to identify critical risk to community safety and with the Centre of Expertise on Child Sexual Abuse to deliver a participation project with young people to inform the work of the Centre. She began her career as a practitioner working with homeless young people, street children and adults and children who exchanged sex both in the UK and India. Emilie developed a particular interest in working with children and young people who are not known to services and/or services often find difficult to engage. Emilie has completed national research studies addressing the relationship between running away and CSE and meeting the needs of young people with learning disabilities who experience, or are at risk of, CSE.

Editor's acknowledgements

The idea for this book emerged as I developed training on how theory informs our work with children affected by sexual exploitation. I want to thank all the fantastic course participants who took part in the stimulating conversations about why we might be interested in or do this work, about why particular approaches had emerged at particular times and what current theoretical approaches influenced our practice. I also want to thank my inspiring PhD students who keep the search for new and innovative knowledge at the forefront of our thinking. Catherine Gray from Policy Press helped to develop the thinking behind the book and has encouraged me to keep going at every step of the way, and her colleagues Shannon Kneis and Vaarunika Dharmapala have provided very welcomed guidance and support at each stage of the process.

The International Centre (IC), researching child sexual exploitation, violence and trafficking has, with its many partners and colleagues, been at the forefront of developing and integrating research and theory into practice with children and young people affected by sexual violence and other forms of harm. I am very grateful to all the past and current IC staff. My thinking and understanding has been guided by these leaders in their fields who have maintained groundbreaking applied research, developed in partnership while placing the voice of the child at the centre of their work. This includes thanks to all the resourceful, resilient, challenging and inspiring children and young people who challenge and fight back from experiences of CSE. With them, practitioners and researchers can keep asking why a particular approach may be useful or helpful or not.

I also want to thank all of the researchers, policy leads and practitioners with whom I have worked over the years. This book would not have been possible without the opportunities for me and others to share experiences across research, policy and practice. I have been so lucky to have the opportunity to work with colleagues across disciplines and professions, sharing areas of expertise as we challenge and support each other.

Finally, I want to thank my daughters Anne-Marie and Rosie along with all of my full extended family for continual inspiration to think as well as act. Special thanks to my husband, John, who provides my foundation through wise counsel, support and lovely humour. Thank you!

Foreword

Julia Davidson

This book provides a unique and current overview of the role of theory in understanding and responding to child sexual exploitation (CSE). As practitioners, academics and policymakers we do not necessarily consider the important and central role that theory plays in underpinning and informing our work in the area of CSE and child sexual abuse (CSA). It is unfortunately the case that theory has become somewhat separate from practice all too often 'remain(ing) in books and not jumping off the page into use', theory is perhaps seen as something that academics 'do' that has little relevance for those working directly with children affected by CSE. This view may be exacerbated by education and training across social sciences and other relevant disciplines, that has traditionally separated theory, research and practice rather than promoting a more integrated understanding of the ways in which theory might usefully underpin and enable practice.

This book eloquently challenges the assumption that theory has no relevance in practice with young people affected by CSE, illustrating ways in which theoretical definitions, constructs and models from many different disciplines should not only inform practice, but should also cause us to continually question our own assumptions, considering the ways in which these assumptions might have an impact upon our work with and about young people. These assumptions may force us to continue working in ways that are based on the received wisdom in which our disciplines are steeped. For example, the contributors in this book challenge the use of language and terms questioning current narratives and 'collective agreements' regarding the meaning of CSE, criticising the way in which young people are cast as victims. This essentially denies their agency and the choices they make. The development of effective child protection systems is seen to be hampered by a focus on the role of parents in shaping children's behaviour with no consideration of peer, community and other social influences. Cyberlibertarian ideology is held to account for resulting in an internet that is under-regulated and not designed with children in mind, thus becoming a space where CSE has freedom and licence, resulting in a form of 'ethical drift'. Authors cite useful examples of theoretical approaches drawing upon psychoanalysis, trauma-informed practice in fostering safety, trust, choice and empowerment, advocating a strong child rights approach in responding to CSE. Emphasis is placed upon the value of theory-informed practice and the importance of seeking to understand and act upon young people's lived experience. Intersectionality, for example, is considered as a means of understanding the experience of black adolescents affected by CSE in the context of structural inequalities and the social model focuses upon support and training for professionals to enable an understanding of the needs of children and young people with disabilities affected by CSE.

This important book has many key messages and it is clear that a cross-disciplinary approach to the understanding and application of theory in practice would benefit not only those who work and study in this area, but would also ultimately benefit the children and young people whose lives are undeniably devastated by CSE.

Bringing theory home: thinking about child sexual exploitation

Jenny Pearce

Introduction

I want this book to be an opportunity to ask why theory matters to our work with children affected by sexual exploitation. Following revelations of some of the painful realities facing children affected by child sexual exploitation (CSE), there has been a welcome recognition that CSE is one of three main national threats to the country (Gov.uk 2015) and is a form of child sexual abuse (CSA) (see DfE 2017). Alongside this, we have seen a plethora of work exploring the evidence base for interventions looking at what works to prevent and respond to CSE and CSA (see later in the chapter). This focus on 'how' to prevent and respond to CSE is essential. I hope here to engage with the equally important question of 'why?' What is informing the way that we approach the work and target our interventions?

Whether readers are considering working with children affected by sexual exploitation and related issues, or are firmly embedded in years of practice, I want the book to help ask about the rationale for their interest in this area of work. The answer may appear straightforward. It is to stop children being exploited and to work with those affected to recover in whatever way possible. But even this universal aim of stopping children being exploited may, to some extent, be socially constructed and influenced by political persuasions of the time (see Beckett, Phoenix and Hanson in this volume). Within this universal aim, there may be nuances specific to particular individuals' interests and expertise. It may be that someone is particularly motivated to challenge patriarchal domination or other power imbalances expressed through violence against children (see Coy, Bernard, and Smeaton in this volume), or/and is wanting to explore the impact of insecure early attachments that may lead children to be exploited through promises of love (see Luxmoore in this volume). Even though we have long-established theories about CSA, noting how sexualised trauma impacts so negatively on children affected (Finkelhor 1984), I am keen for us to further apply this (see Hickle in this volume) and other various nuances from different perspectives into our work.

I hope the book will provide some background into our work with children affected by CSE to put this work in context and perhaps to help ask if individuals' rationales are the same or different to theoretical position(s) adopted by teams or others with whom they work. For example, are teams, or individuals, or both, assessing different 'social fields' within which their young people inhabit, leading to the full incorporation of Contextual Safeguarding (see Firmin in this volume and Firmin, 2017), and/or is the team, or individuals within it, drawing on theories of lifespan development which address the impact of new research on adolescence and brain development (see Coleman in this volume), or theories of empathy (see Dolan and McGregor in this volume) or trauma-informed approaches to engaging with children (see Hickle in this volume), or all of these? If these, and other, theoretical underpinnings are transparent, are they influencing the way that service(s) are delivered? Are these questions being considered and discussed and if not, does that matter?

I argue that it does matter: our understanding of the reasons why we do the work has significant impact on how we engage in practice. If a CSE intervention is purposefully underpinned by one or more theoretical approaches, with its staff trained to understand the principles and any associated methods, the practice (and therefore experience received by the child) may be very different from a CSE project drawing on various, perhaps unarticulated theoretical understandings at different times with different service users. My aim is not to set up a hierarchy of one form of intervention being any better than another (see the comments later in the chapter about evidence-based practice). My aim is to suggest a series of questions for discussion about what theories inform approaches to the work. While this book does not, and could not, cover every theoretical approach that could influence the way that we work with children and young people affected by CSE, I hope that the chapters included will provide some initial background thinking to some of these questions.

Context

To unpick this, we have to demystify 'theory' and bring it home to our everyday work and activity. Theory is, according to the *Oxford English Dictionary* (https://en.oxforddictionaries.com/definition/theory):

A supposition or a system of ideas intended to explain something, especially one based on general principles independent of the thing to be explained.
For example: 'Darwin's theory of evolution'

It is:

1.1 A set of principles on which the practice of an activity is based
For example: 'a theory of education'
1.2 An idea used to account for a situation or justify a course of action
For example: 'my theory would be that the place has been seriously mismanaged'
1.3 *Mathematics:* A collection of propositions to illustrate the principles of a subject.

For our purposes here, theory is explained as 1.1 and 1.2: it is about the principles that underpin our practice and the ideas used to justify what we are doing. Theory both informs and emerges from practice and as such is 'owned' just as much by those working with children affected by CSE as by those researching and writing about the work. In terms of social work, Payne notes that:

> Social work theory in general, and practice theory in particular, is socially constructed in interactions between clients and practitioners in their agencies and in wider political, social and cultural arenas. This makes clear that we build both practice and theory through our experiences operating in the real world; they are not given to us from on high. (Payne 2014:3)

In this way, theories both inform our work with CSE affected children and arise from this work. Payne goes on to say:

- Theory is different from knowledge – theory involves thinking about something; knowledge is a description of reality. Reality is a picture of the world that is accepted as true.
- Theory is different from practice – theory is thinking about something, practice involves doing something. (Payne 2014:5)

While most 'thinkers' try to keep a broad and open mind, David Howe (2008) notes that there can be fierce debates between champions of particular views from a range of subjects, including the humanities, sociology, philosophy and political theory.

Inevitably those interested in training for, and working in different professional disciplines such as, for example: policing, healthcare, youth and community work and social work may be influenced by different theoretical positions. As safeguarding children affected by CSE is a genuinely multi-agency activity, there is no guarantee that staff approach the work from these different professions with a shared understanding of which particular theoretical approaches inform their work. Theories of prevention under a public health model may differ from theories of prevention influencing police work with potential 'victims' or 'young offenders', if, indeed, the two categories can be distinguished from each other. This may vary again from how prevention is understood by welfare workers informed by radical social work traditions (see Bailey and Brake 1975; Lavalette 2011) and again from those informed by psychodynamic traditions.

Trying to help students to chart these potentially different perspectives, Howe goes on to explain how he has taught theory for social workers drawing on Burrell and Morgan (1979) work on sociological paradigms and organisational analysis. He remodelled their approach under two axes: one considering human nature along the subjective (humanities) versus the objective (scientific) axis, and the second examining society in terms of social order versus social conflict and change (Howe 2008:viii). He develops five unique positions in the human nature/science debate that could be helpful for readers applying thinking about where their particular approaches to protecting children may be positioned.

The works of Howe and others (see Healey 2005 for example) explore the different impacts academic disciplines can have on how we think about theory. It is also important for us to consider the impact that different political agendas can have on supporting or neglecting particular theoretical approaches: both in terms of international and national politics which might give overarching credibility, kudos and potential funding. This bears significance on our own actions and the resulting impacts these have on children's lives. Corby et al (2012) give a helpful introduction to some theoretical approaches explaining the 'causation of child abuse' (pages 130–153), addressing some of the global perspectives affecting understandings of child abuse and neglect (pages 202–210). In their book about rethinking social work in a global world, Harrison and Melville (2010) note that while 'globalisation' is a contested concept, the international movement of skilled social work labour, the domination of international neoliberal perspectives of welfare and the relationship between poverty and inequality at local, national and international levels have all been influenced by globalisation. This is further explored by Davidson and Bifulco (2019) who focus on the impact of globalisation on understandings of child abuse and protection, paying particular attention to the increased impact of organised international criminal networks on children being trafficked and on the relationship between the digital world, online abuse and child safety (see Hanson in this volume for further debate about online abuse). These texts and others note that theories about social work and about child protection in particular are influenced by the international context within which they are developed and explored.

At a UK national level, Parton (2014) explores the changing impact of the political arena on our understanding and approaches to child protection. He takes us through the 'growing crisis' of child protection in the 1980s, to The Children Act 1989 which, he explains, was generally welcomed but was affected by the political climate as it was 'Being introduced in a "hostile climate", out of step with the philosophy and aims of most of the other social and economic policies of the Conservative government of the time' (Parton 2014:24).

Parton notes the discrepancy between the Act's onus on working with the best interests of the child and other neoliberal philosophical approaches of the time that prioritised self-interest in market economies. He continues to chart the development of child protection policy and practice as influenced by the political agendas of the 'Third Way', 'New labour and modernization', ideas about 'social exclusion', 'risk factors and risk vulnerabilities' and the way this was embraced within the safeguarding children agenda, 'every child matters' and the Children Act 2004 (Parton 2014:1–10). Continuing this discussion to the current political climate we see the delegation of responsibility to local authorities for scrutiny of their safeguarding arrangements. Rather than continuing a national requirement for each local authority to have and evidence partnership working through a safeguarding board, revisions to 'Working together to safeguard children' (DfE 2018) commit leadership of safeguarding children to three providers: the local authority; a clinical commissioning group; and the chief officer of police for an area any part of which falls within the local authority area. In the face of current austerity, it will be interesting to see if this reduction in the nature of required partnership arrangements might reduce previously wider ranging approaches to safeguarding all children. Will this take us back to a core focus on child protection for those deemed to be at risk of serious harm as opposed to generic safeguarding of every child, and if so, what will be the impact on early preventative work and diversionary interventions? Time itself will tell. While this is yet to unfold, it will be of interest to review how these changes impact on ways of thinking about safeguarding and child protection, including preventing and responding to CSE.

In their description of a 'social model' to understanding the protection of children, Featherstone et al (2018) are concerned about any reduction of focus to the individual case level. They want us to shift away from the individualist focus in child protection and ask us to become:

> preoccupied by
> • understanding and tackling root causes;
> • rethinking the role of the state;
> • developing relationship(s) – based practice and co-production; and
> • embedding a dialogic approach to ethics and human rights in policy and practice. (Featherstone et al 2018:8)

Warrington (2013) has explored many of the complexities of engaging with children affected by sexual exploitation. This addresses Featherstone et al's call to understand the root cause of child abuse and how to tackle it, and about the ethical issues involved with genuine relationship-based practice that engages with co-production of knowledge. If we do try to integrate these ideal 'theories' into everyday thinking about our approaches to working with children we need to understand the political influences within which they are developed and delivered. Turner (2017) reiterates this theme when he refers to theory as a resource. Referring to a number of theoretical approaches he explains how they may relate to social work interventions. He says that:

> although in an earlier day we presented groups of theories in a scholarly comparative manner, we have now become more comfortable in also seeing them as groups of therapeutic resources. That is, we are leaning to present groups such as this volume as a discussion of resources on which a practitioner can draw. (Turner 2017:23)

Turner is advocating using theory as a 'hands on' resource: as we discuss why our thinking is influenced one way or another, we become more familiar with how it has an impact on our work. Developing this, Bay (2014) cited in Young et al (2014) is concerned that we do not fall into a 'tick box' approach to thinking about what influences our practice. Noting concern that the bureaucratisation of service provision has undermined scope for such exploration, Young et al (2014) refer to Bay's work to note concern that the increasing use of 'tools' to guide, monitor and assess practice interventions places the focus on the ticking of a box and away from talking about what we are doing and how it feels:

> De-professionalisation, new public management technologies distancing decisions and policy from the lived experiences of both clients and workers, and the increasing use of standardising and quantifying tools for information management in child protection have all affected the practice of social work with child protection. As Bay states: "One of the concerns is that what newer practitioners learn is how to become good at ticking boxes rather than critically thinking about their practice." (Bay 2014 in Young et al 2014:912)

Much has helpfully been done to encourage awareness of Munro's similar concerns about how the prioritisation of bureaucratic procedure, which focused on recording interventions and events, had dominated over the use of time for supervised reflection and critical discussion of how and why these events and interventions were taking place (Munro 2011). Cooper's work on child protection policies and procedures explores this further, noting how bureaucratisation can act as a barrier to engaging with the 'tragedy' of child neglect and abuse. Cooper (2014) argues that the child protection system has two functions: one to protect children and the second to contain society's anxiety about child abuse. He argues for the importance of a societal recognition of the 'tragic perspective' of child maltreatment to counter the idealisation that the child protection system can, on its own, protect children (Cooper 2014). He argues that for change to come about, it is not only social workers and, in our case here, CSE workers, who need to be supported to recognise pains caused by abuse, but others outside the child protection networks. Thinking along these lines encourages us to see that addressing the question of why we do this work is shared between academics, students, practitioners, children, their families and communities. If left to academics and/or practitioners alone, the thinking about protecting children is confined to the child protection systems.

This work mentioned earlier suggests that the political and economic agendas can have an impact on what theoretical approaches are in favour, and on the climate within which we might implement them. It looks at how theory might be influenced by global, national and local economic policies. Before we move to looking in more detail about how we can bring theory home into our everyday practice, it is important to question just a little more the relationship between theory and evidence-based practice.

Theory and evidence-based practice

If, as this book is suggesting, we see theory as central to our work with children affected by CSE, the inevitable questions emerge of 'How do we evidence which theories impact well in practice? How do we know what works?' While these questions about evidence-based practice are important (see for example Fisher 2013), they are not the core questions for this particular book. Before moving on though, it is helpful to touch on some initiatives that do address evidence-based practice so that readers have access to the plethora of important work on what's known to be effective in protecting and responding to CSE.

Although not specifically focused on what works to prevent and respond to CSE, Fonagy et al's (2015) collection of 'What works for whom' provides an excellent overview of what's known about the origin and impact of 'treatments' for children and adolescents. Following the high-profile cases of CSE going through courts and the Jay report on the failure of detecting the abuse (Jay 2014) there has been increased focus on 'what works' to prevent and respond to CSE. Major UK children's charities have all invested in trying to assess and evaluate their services while the central UK government funded CSA Centre of expertise (www.csacentre.org.uk) is looking at the evidence base informing practice and providing directories of services. Information sharing and networking activities are being undertaken by the National Working Group network (www.nwgnetwork.org) and through a new DfE funded partnership led by The Children's Society, Research in Practice and Bedfordshire University (DfE 2019). The College of Policing is working to improve evidence-based policing on police approaches to Child Sexual Exploitation and related vulnerabilities (College of Policing 2019). The Independent Inquiry into Child Sexual Abuse has summarised evidence of the impact of CSA/E (see Fisher and Soares 2017), and what can be learnt from other jurisdictions (outside England) about evidence of best practice for institutions in preventing, identifying and responding to child sexual abuse (Radford et al 2017). A randomised control trial has taken place to assess therapeutic services with children affected by sexual abuse (Carpenter et al 2016); and a recent overview of the voluntary sector engagement with CSE cases has given findings from a 'Realist Evaluation' of 16 services reaching into 35 local authority areas (Harris et al 2017). These outputs explain different methods to access data and review findings about 'what works'. A recent overview of the evidence base of 'what works' in CSE has been undertaken (Scott et al 2019) while the Social Care Institute for Excellence has helpful overviews of the evidence base both in work with children and in safeguarding (www.scie.org.uk). The 'What Works for Children's Social Care' centre (https://whatworks-csc.org.uk) is developing new initiatives working with the children's services sectors, generating, using and sharing evidence about (among other topics) safeguarding children. The DfE, OFSTED and HMIC websites have published findings from a number of evaluations and inspections of CSE services and DMSS Research who have also undertaken a specific evaluation of the Barnardo's CSE project 'ReachOut' in Rotherham drawing on a theory of change approach (McNeish et al 2019). This plethora of work is exciting and essentially useful to projects working with children affected by CSE.

The foregoing covers work taking place in the UK, occurring within a global context where 'evidence' is being generated and assessed. It has been acknowledged by Radford et al 2017, Brodie and Pearce (2017) and Bovarnick et al (2018) that global initiatives aimed at raising awareness and sharing expertise about violence against children, including specifically sexual violence, has an over-reliance on evidence from the 'global north' where academic credibility is given to the 'scientific' production of knowledge through controlled conditions such as randomised control trials. Less is known about how violence affects children in countries where, because of economic or socio-political pressures, there has been less investment in the provision of services and the evaluation of their effectiveness. The 'Know Violence' (www.knowviolenceinchildhood.org) and the 'End Violence' (www.end-violence.org) initiatives, each global alliance aiming to improve knowledge and information about the levels and types of violence experienced by children, are trying to address this imbalance. The changing nature and context for social work in a global world is explored by Harrison and Melville (2010) and in Cloward's book on what we know about early and forced child marriage (E&FCM) and female genital mutilation (FGM). This text considers the questions of how globally agreed norms and values are communicated around the world. Titled 'When Norms Collide' Cloward (2016) explores the schisms between what she calls 'international moral entrepreneurs': invariably practitioners and academics educated within the 'global north' and local community members, particularly women and girls, in areas targeted for change. Without underestimating the harm caused by FGM and E&FCM she illustrates the gaps between knowledge as understood by the moral entrepreneurs and the lived experiences of girls and women in local communities across the world. Harrison and Melville (2010:29) also look at the way that 'Social work cannot be imagined in terms of a core set of values that are transferable across the globe. Local practices are impacted by their own historical, social and cultural conditions which, in turn, produce "situated" clients'.

Exploring schisms between different approaches to understanding child protection gives us a stronger insight into both the generation of 'evidence' and its use in practice. There is so much more to be done exploring these issues, including how they have an impact on the theories of child sexual abuse that we think we know about and understand.

In addition to these initiatives that aim to address the question of what works, some academics have focused on how this has changed, addressing historical perspectives, understandings and responses to CSE. Publications on 'critical perspectives' on CSE and related trafficking (Melrose and Pearce 2013); 'Making Sense of Child Sexual Exploitation' (Hallett 2017); and understanding and responding to CSE (Beckett and Pearce 2018) have looked at the changes in how CSE is understood and worked with. As noted earlier, the comprehensive and contemporary work of Davidson and Bifulco (2019) explore, among other issues, how the impact of global changes and the digital world have an impact on our understanding of child abuse. Alderson (2016) looks at how our understanding of risk has influenced the development of theory informing CSE. Firmin has widely published on theoretical perspectives informing Contextual Safeguarding and how this affects our understanding and responses to CSE (see Firmin in this volume). These texts help us to think about the relationship between some theoretical perspectives, their historical and global context and how we understand CSE. There have also been publications giving important insight into personal experiences of abuse through CSE or about how to work to prevent it (see Jackson 2010; Senior 2016; Gladman and Heal 2017). These texts are all helpful in encouraging us to engage with questions about how 'evidence' is generated, from where and why, with an analysis of the relationship between the credibility of individual narrative, financial restraints, political interests, global differences and the generation of evidence.

There are many different theoretical perspectives that this book does not explore in detail. For example, although many chapters refer specifically to children's rights based approaches (see Beckett, Bernard, Coy) we do not have a chapter covering the important work that has developed on the child's right to participate in decisions affecting them and in the way CSE services are developed and delivered. Warrington's work in this field is groundbreaking and important (Warrington 2017; 2013). Although the book considers the contexts within which harmful sexual behaviors develop (see Firmin and Luxmoore in this volume), it does not have a dedicated chapter on theories of why children might develop and perpetrate harmful sexual behaviours which is addressed in current work elsewhere (see Hackett and Smith 2018 and https://www.csacentre.org.uk/research-publications/perpetrator-research). Neither is there a chapter on theories about 'emerging adulthood' addressing questions of transition from adolescence to adulthood (see the Sage journal entitled *Emerging Adulthood* and Arnett et al 2014) and questions of revictimisation and recovery (Ullman and Peter-Hagene 2016). Important as this is, the focus of the book here is on preventing and responding to children less than 18 years of age affected by abuse. The book notes, but does not have a chapter dedicated to the important work informed by systems theories promoted from the Munro review (see Munro 2011 and Parton 2014, pp 122–129). Systemic practice and the implications of the Munro review are taught in most social work training programmes, refreshed through continuing professional development. An impact of this work post Munro (2011) is explored by Blyth (2014).

The overarching, original questions of whether child sexual exploitation services are aware of and engaged with questions about which theoretical perspectives inform their work and why remains. Why is our practice with children affected by sexual exploitation taking place and what principles underpin our work?

Bringing theory home

I want to explore a little further how we might bring thinking about how theory has an impact on our approaches to CSE by bringing it home: connecting it with our thinking about what we do and why.

Some of us might have put time aside to think about why we are interested in working in a particular way with children affected by CSE, why we lean towards one set of theoretical approaches as opposed to others. We might have been encouraged to consider this in terms of our own motivation and the motivation of any of the teams we are working in or with. We might be able to personalise theory like this. Others however may not have done this for a variety of reasons. There may not be time in our busy response to the heavy caseloads we carry; we might actively avoid looking at these questions for fear that they are too exposing, touching into parts of ourselves that we have not explored or have purposefully hidden for fear of being seen as biased, confused or unclear; or, alternatively, we might have 'done' theory when we were training and have now moved into the 'real' world where changing life circumstances require rapid responses in short timescales. All of this might well be the case, but I want to ask if it might, perhaps, also feel safer for us to see theory as something that is in a textbook and not in our everyday work as Payne (2014) notes earlier. I argue that if theories remain in books and are not jumping off the page into use, they remain limited: they are not connecting into our experiences of working with children and young people affected by CSE.

To explore this connection, I explain my own trajectory with how, why and when I understood that for me, theory was something with personal meaning. By doing this I am not suggesting that we only connect with different theoretical approaches as a direct result of life events. There are a variety of reasons that individuals will be responsive to one particular theoretical position over another, some of which might be based on life experiences and others on questions of capacity, access and curiosity. I am, though, suggesting that our capacity to listen, hear and be open to ideas from different perspectives may be personal, may be influenced by what is going on for us at the time.

When I was training as a teacher, I became angrier about the impact of gendered and racialised social and economic divisions in the treatment of and responses to different children in the schools where I was training. I was increasingly drawn to writers who explored divisions in society and the impact on school experience and achievement, on the impact of social and economic divisions on gendered youth cultures and on achievements according to social class (see Willis 1977, Lees 1986 and McRobbie 1991). Sociology of education classes taught a wide range of sociological theories but I latched onto ones that drew on the impact of structural and economic inequalities on children's educational achievements. My understanding of children affected by CSE (at that time called children involved in prostitution: see Phoenix and Beckett in this volume) was that they were responding to and affected by inequalities arising from race, gender and economic divisions. My focus was on the social structures that 'forced' and indeed condoned the sale of sex as a commodity, and then blamed children for engaging with this very same sex market. Courses on psychology and education, which looked at childhood development (see Coleman in this volume) and learning theories, did not attract my attention, despite being jumped upon with enthusiasm by fellow practitioners and students. I was concerned that a focus on the individual hid the impact that social division had on children. Although I was introduced to writers working on social psychotherapy and psychoanalysis (see Luxmoore and Dolan in this volume), I was pulled towards critiques that these approaches placed the onus on the individual, not the system, to change. With others, I shouted out against the way that some of these perspectives appeared to 'blame' individual mothers for the behaviours of their children.

Later, when I became a mother of two children, my attitude shifted. Taking the responsibility for being 'good enough' as a mother gave me a new interest in what a 'good' attachment was, how my role as mother involved trying to sometimes reflect and sometimes contain my children's feelings. Suddenly I was that individual mother assuming societies responsibilities for childcare that I had read about and critiqued (see McRobbie, 2009 for more discussion on this). I tried to live up to an ideal of sharing caring roles with partner, friends and extended family. I tried to remain politicised, avoiding feelings of blame for everything and anything 'wrong' my children were perceived to do, but I carried a new sense of my own responsibilities. This did not shift my fundamental interest in social division; but how attachments work, what that meant to me as a mother and the impact this had on my children suddenly became real. I started reading more about child development and about some of the concepts explored in psychoanalytical thinking. This influenced the way that I thought about my role as a worker with different young people affected by CSE giving me a better understanding of the importance of a trusted and secure relationship. I better understood some of the ways that abusers manipulated children through promises that are not kept of secure attachments and how I held responsibility, as a practitioner, to help contain some of the young people's feelings and try to reflect them back in a manageable format. Not being a therapist, I did not try to deliver 'therapeutic' interventions but my practice was better informed by understanding the principles behind these interventions. I am not suggesting that you have to be a mother to gain an interest in attachment: there are many different reasons that the interest may emerge. I am purely trying to illustrate a connection between some personal experiences and an emerging interest in particular theoretical positions.

Accompanying this, and as result of other life events, I began to question some of those master narratives that I had so firmly believed in earlier. I became more interested in lessons from postmodernism and became more aware of the multiple identities that we all carry. I further explored the reasons behind some identities becoming our own definition of 'self' in relation to 'others' while some other identities remained hidden or submerged. While I have never lost my desire to work towards a more equal and just social structure, I was interested how in the way we were each 'situated' had an impact on what we thought we knew and understood. I was motivated by Haraway who noted that she wanted to 'argue for a doctrine and practice of objectivity that privileges contestation, deconstruction, passionate constructivism, webbed connection, and hope for transformations of systems of knowledge and ways of seeing' (Haraway 1991:191–192).

I am not suggesting that in order to understand a theory you have to have lived experiences that bring it to light. While this was my experience, as noted earlier, there are a variety of reasons why individuals are pulled towards particular theoretical perspectives. So for example, I am absolutely not advocating that an interest in attachment theories only arise from parenting: in fact, parenting could repel some from thinking about attachment. What I am suggesting is that there may be certain reasons that we are able to absorb the meaning of some approaches over others at particular times and as result of particular circumstances in our lives. As noted earlier, this may be influenced by a number of factors, including the support that we have been given to embrace theoretical ideas, by our situated personal economic and geographical positions and by what theories are 'approved' at the time. Looking at it this way, we can explore why we, and/or our service employer connects with theory; we can bring it home. It becomes something that is important to talk about, even if we are not quite sure that we have understood what it means. In fact, the more we are supported to say that we don't know what it means, the better: the more we will explore why we are working with CSE cases ourselves, what motivates us and how we justify this work.

Figure 1.1 offers a structure to start some of these discussions. Whether or not readers are working in a team or alone with children affected by CSE, they might find it helpful to think through the questions outlined in Figure 1.1, remembering that this is not a test, or a competition about who knows the most! It is a tool to facilitate

Figure 1.1: Bringing theory home

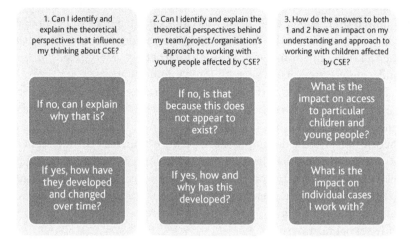

discussion and sharing of ideas and knowledge about if and what theory has an impact on our work.

The structure of the book

Throughout the discussion earlier I have noted specific references to chapters contained within this book. I give an overview later of how the chapters are arranged within the text to provide continuity of reading from and between different perspectives.

Following this introductory chapter, we start the book with chapters that raise questions about definition and meaning: the creation of a body of knowledge and assumed truths about CSE. Beckett explores the way that structuration theory can help us unpick essential questions of victimhood and agency, addressing how these have influenced both the way we think about CSE and the policies that have framed and structured our interventions. Phoenix then provides a critique of our accepted truths about CSE, advocating use of discourse analysis to encourage us to question our assumptions about 'normal' adolescent behaviour and how these assumptions may be shaped by wider societal norms. Firmin then explains the influence of Bourdieu's theories on the way that we understand the environments which children inhabit and create. Looking at ideas about the 'social field', 'capital' and 'habitus' she looks at the changing contexts children inhabit as they move from a predominantly home-based lifestyle in early years to entering out into other 'social fields' through adolescence. She draws on this background to explain the development of Contextual

Safeguarding as an approach that engages with the safeguarding responsibilities of those providing services in the public sphere. This is followed by a chapter by Hanson who looks at the impact of neoliberal economic theory on the development of the internet. She argues that the lack of regulation and control of internet providers' freedom has undermined attempts to keep children safe from abuse.

From here, we move to look at how some psycho-social theories can help us to explore the relationship between the individual child and the society within which they function. Coleman looks at theories of lifespan development to help us understand adolescence as a stage within the lifecourse. He explores the changes taking place through puberty and refers to new learning from studies about brain development that can help us to understand specific vulnerabilities which some young people may experience in their early sexual relationships.

Luxmoore then takes us though a number of concepts developed in psychodynamic thinking to address how early childhood experiences may have an impact on how a child or young person may behave or understand themselves. He looks at how, through their development, children are forever exploring their own sense of agency, often arguing for their sense of sexual agency to be recognised as important and significant. In her chapter on trauma-informed CSE practice, Hickle describes the origin and meaning of trauma-informed practice and explores how it can contribute to understanding the issues faced both by children and young people affected by CSE and the practitioners engaging with them. Dolan and McGregor look at ideas about empathy, arguing for an increased awareness of the significance of moving from passive to activated empathy. As with Firmin, mentioned earlier, they refer to ecological theory as a helpful approach to maximise potential for informal and formal support mechanisms for children and families and communities affected by CSE. They continue to link the significance of understanding empathy as a key component to activating change.

To bring learning from all of the foregoing, we engage with questions posed by theoretical approaches that look at discrimination, advantage and disadvantage. Bernard looks at how theories of intersectionality can help us understand the experiences of black children and how this has an impact on both their experiences of social care systems and on practitioners' understanding of their needs. Coy asks questions about the gendered nature of sexual violence in general and CSE in particular. She looks at how violence against women and girls is understood and the impact this has on children's experiences of abuse.

We then move to Smeaton's chapter which draws on social theories of disability to show that there remains an invisibility of the impact of learning disabilities on CSE affected children. This remains despite research suggesting that a disproportionally high number of children with learning difficulties are sexually exploited.

Together these chapters introduce a range of ways of thinking about and understanding CSE. As noted earlier in this chapter, the idea of introducing these different approaches is to encourage us to think about our interest in and work on preventing and addressing CSE. It is not to set up a hierarchy of one approach being any more important than another. I hope that by reading these chapters and exploring the ideas at an individual and/or team level, those interested in the work will continue to ask 'why', and consider how the answers to 'why' may influence practice and ultimately, the experiences of children and young people. Now is an opportune time to be asking these questions. Increasingly we are looking at multiple vulnerabilities faced by and with children (College of Policing 2019). Also, children affected by other forms of potential criminality are being better understood. For example, the notorious shift from seeing children who were sexually exploited away from being perpetrators of crimes to being victims of abuse is now being used as a model for understanding young people's engagement in some organised drug related crimes. Arguments are presented that children and young people distributing or selling drugs are not perpetrators of drug related offences but are victims of abuse by organised criminal networks (HMIP et al 2018). As these bigger questions about the complex relationships between ideas of childhood, agency and victimhood are being asked, it is hoped that chapters contained in this volume will provide a variety of ways of thinking about and debating the use of theory, bringing it home into our everyday thinking and practice.

References

Alderson, K. (2016) 'Child sexual exploitation', *Journal of Forensic Practice*, 18(4): 292–295, https://doi.org/10.1108/JFP-07-2016-0036

Arnett, J.J., Zukauskiene, R. and Sugimura, K. (2014) 'The new life stage of emerging adulthood at ages 18–29 years: Implications for mental health', *Lancet Psychiatry*, 1(7): 569–576, doi:10.1016/s2215-0366(14)00080-7

Bailey, R. and Brake, M. (1975) *Radical Social Work*, London: McGraw Hill

Bay, U.U. (2014). *Social Work Practice: A Conceptual Framework*, Melbourne: Palgrave Macmillan

Beckett, H. and Pearce, J. (eds) (2018) *Understanding and Responding to Child Sexual Exploitation*, Routledge: London

Blyth, M. (ed) (2014) *Moving on from Munro: Improving Children's Services*, Bristol: Policy Press

Bovarnick, S. with Peace, D., Warrington, C. and Pearce, J. (2018) *Being Heard: Promoting children and young people's involvement in participatory research on sexual violence: Findings from an international scoping review*, Luton: Bedfordshire University, accessible on www.beds.ac.uk/ic

Burrell, G. and Morgan, G. (1979) *Sociological Paradigms and Organizational Analysis*, Aldershot: Gower

Carpenter, J., Jessiman, T., Patsios, D., Hackett., S. and Phillips, J. (2016) *Letting the Future In: A Therapeutic Intervention for Children Affected by Sexual Abuse and Their Carers: An Evaluation of Impact and Implementation*, Online report, https://research-information.bristol.ac.uk/files/73876820/LTFI_Final_Report_11.02.16b.pdf

Cloward, K. (2016) *When Norms Collide: Local Responses to Activism against Female Genital Mutilation and Early Marriage*, Oxford: Oxford University Press

College of Policing (2019) *Vulnerability and Violence Crime Programme*, https://whatworks.college.police.uk/Research/Pages/Vulnerability.aspx

Cooper, A. (2014) 'A short psychosocial history of British child abuse and protection: Case studies in problems of mourning in the public sphere', *Journal of Social Work Practice*, 28(3): 271–285

Corby, B., Shemmings, D. and Wilkins, D. (2012) *Child Abuse: An Evidence Base for Confident Practice*, Maidenhead: McGraw-Hill

Davidson, J. and Bifulco, A. (2019) *Child Abuse and Protection: Contemporary Issues in Research, Policy and Practice*, Abingdon: Routledge

DfE (Department for Education) (2017) *Child Sexual Exploitation: Definition and a Guide for Practitioners*, DFE-00056-2017, Crown copyright, London, HM Government

DfE (Department for Education) (2018) *Working Together to Safeguard Children*, DFE-00195-2018, Crown copyright, London: HM Government

Featherstone, B., Gupta, A., Morris, K. and White, S. (2018) *Protecting Children: A Social Model*, London: Routledge

Finkelhor, D. (1984) *Child Sexual Abuse: New Theory and Research*, New York: Free Press

Firmin, C. (2017) *Abuse Between Young People: A Contextual Account*, Abingdon: Routledge

Fisher, M. (2013) 'Beyond evidence-based policy and practice: Reshaping the relationship between research and practice', *Social Work and Social Sciences Review*, 16(2): 20–36

Fisher, C. and Soares, C. (2017) *The Impacts of Child Sexual Abuse: A Rapid Evidence Assessment. Key Research Findings*, www.iicsa.org.uk/key-documents/1536/view/impacts-child-sexual-abuse-a-rapid-evidence-assessment-key-research-findings.pdf

Fonagy, P., Cottrell, D., Phillips, J., Bevington, D., Glaser, D. and Allison, E. (2015) *What Works for Whom: A Critical Review of Treatments for Children and Adolescents* (2nd edn), New York: Guilford Press

Gladman, A. and Heal, A. (2017) *Child Sexual Exploitation after Rotherham*, London: Jessica Kingsley

Gov.uk (2015) 'PM unveils tough new measures to tackle child sexual exploitation', www.gov.uk/government/news/pm-unveils-tough-new-measures-to-tackle-child-sexual-exploitation

Hackett, S. and Smith, S. (2018) *Young People who Engage in Sexual Exploitation Behaviours*, Durham: University of Durham and CSA Center of Expertise on Child Sexual Abuse, www.csacentre.org.uk

Hallett, S. (2017) *Making Sense of Child Sexual Exploitation*, Bristol: Policy Press

Haraway, D. (1991) *Simians, Cyborgs and Women: The Reinvention of Nature*, New York: Routledge

Harris, J., Roker, D. with Shuker, L., Brodie, I., D'Arcy, K., Dhaliwal, S. and Pearce, J. (2017) *Evaluation of the Alexi Project 'Hub and Spoke' Programme of CSE Service Development: Final Report*, November, Luton: Bedfordshire University, www.beds.ac.uk/__data/assets/pdf_file/0004/568912/Final-Report-Alexi-Project-evaluation.pdf

Harrison, G. and Melville, R. (2010) *Rethinking Social Work in a Global World*, Basingstoke: Palgrave Macmillan

Healey, F. (2005) *Social Work Theories in Context: Creating Frameworks for Practice*, Basingstoke: Palgrave Macmillan

Howe, D. (2008) *An Introduction to Social Work Theory: Making Sense in Practice*, Farnham, Ashgate

Jackson, E. (2010) *Exploited*, London: Ebury Press

Jay, A. (2014) *Independent Inquiry in to Child Sexual Exploitation in Rotherham: 1997–2013*, Rotherham: Rotherham Metropolitan Borough Council

Lavalette, M. (ed) (2011) *Radical Social Work Today: Social Work at the Crossroads*, Bristol: Policy Press

Lees, S. (1986) *Losing Out: Sexuality and Adolescent Girls*, London: Hutchinson

McNeish, D. and Scott, S. with Lloyd, S., DMSS Research and Pearce, J. (2019) *Barnardo's ReachOut: Final Evaluation Report*, www.dmss. co.uk and www.beds.ac.uk/ic

McRobbie, A. (1991) *Feminism and Youth Culture: From Jackie to Just Seventeen*, Basingstoke: Macmillan

McRobbie, A. (2009) *The Aftermath of Feminism: Gender, Culture and Social Change*, London: Sage

Melrose, M. and Pearce, J. (eds) (2013) *Critical Perspectives on Child Sexual Exploitation and Related Trafficking*, Basingstoke: Palgrave Macmillan

Munro, E. (2011) *The Munro Review of Child Protection. Final Report: A Child Centered System*, London: The Stationery Office

Parton, N. (2014) *The Politics of Child Protection: Contemporary Developments and Future Directions*, Basingstoke: Palgrave Macmillan

Payne, M. (2014) *Modern Social Work Theory*, Basingstoke: Palgrave Macmillan

Radford, L., Richardson Foster, H., Barter, C. and Stanley, N. (2017) *What Can be Learnt from Other Jurisdictions About Preventing and Responding to Child Sexual Abuse?*, www.iicsa.org.uk/key-documents/1372/view/april-seminar-uclan-part-1.pdf

Scott, S., McNeish, D., Bovarnick, S. and Pearce, J. (2019) *What Works in Responding to Child Sexual Exploitation*, Basingstoke: Barnardos

Senior, J. (2016) *Broken and Betrayed: The True Story of the Rotherham Abuse Scandal by the Women who Fought to Expose It*, London: Pan Books

Turner, F. (2017) *Social Work Treatment: Interlocking Theoretical Approaches* (6th edn), Oxford: Oxford University Press

Ullman, S. and Peter-Hagene, L. (2016) 'Longitudinal Relationships of Social Relations, PTSD, and Revictimisation in Sexual Assault Survivors', *Journal of interpersonal violence*, 31(6): 1074–1094

Warrington, C. (2013) 'Partners in care? Sexually exploited young people's inclusion and exclusion from decision making about safeguarding', in M. Melrose and J. Pearce (eds) *Critical Perspectives on Child Sexual Exploitation and Trafficking*, Basingstoke: Palgrave Macmillan, pp 110–124

Warrington, C. (2017) *Young Person-centred Approaches in CSE – Promoting Participation and Building Self-Efficacy: Frontline Briefing*, Totnes: Research in Practice

Willis, P. (1977) *Learning to Labour: How Working Class Kids Get Working Class Jobs*, Dorchester: Saxon House

Young, S., McKenzie, M., More, C., Schjelderup L. and Walker S. (2014) 'Practicing from theory: Thinking and knowing to "do" child protection work', *Social Science*, 3: 893–915, doi:10.3390/socsci3040893

2

Moving beyond discourses of agency, gain and blame: reconceptualising young people's experiences of sexual exploitation

Helen Beckett

Introduction

Child sexual exploitation (CSE) (as currently defined within the United Kingdom) is a form of child sexual abuse (CSA), typified by the presence of exchange, whereby the victim and/or perpetrator receives something in return for the sexual activity. It is this exchange dynamic that distinguishes CSE from other forms of CSA within current UK and many other nations' definitions. It is also this exchange dynamic, where the young person is the one deemed to be benefiting from the exchange that raises particular questions about the exercise of agency within abusive situations; the focus of this chapter.

Drawing on a decade of primary and secondary research in the field, I explore the relationship between victimhood and agency, and the unhelpful binary ways in which it has often been conceptualised within CSE discourse and practice to date. I observe how adherence to dichotomous conceptualisations of those experiencing CSE, and associated narrow understandings of CSE victimhood, have served to diminish our responses to particular populations and particular manifestations of harm; namely those typified by any degree of observable agency on the part of the child.

Both my own research and the wider body of literature clearly articulate the need for 'a new sexual abuse narrative' (Woodiwiss 2018:163) if we are to address the evidenced shortcomings in CSE practice. This narrative must be capable of accommodating the co-existence of choice and constraint, benefit and harm, and victimhood and agency that I and other researchers have observed to be present in many young people's experiences of CSE (Pearce 2010;

Beckett 2011; Melrose 2012, 2013; Beckett et al 2013; Warrington 2013; Hallett 2017; Woodiwiss 2018). It is my contention that Gidden's (1976) structuration theory, widely utilised in other fields but not yet in relation to CSE, offers a helpful framework around which such a narrative can be developed.

Reframing young people's experiences of CSE through the lens of structuration theory offers a much-needed way to move us beyond the observable simplistic binary conceptualisations of victimhood versus agency. It helps us to better understand and respond to the widely variable and complex dynamics and contexts of CSE. Specifically, re-conceptualising young people as 'reflexive agents' operating within a 'structure of constraint' offers us a means of concurrently recognising the range of biographical and contextual factors at play in any given situation, and allows us to move beyond exclusionary 'idealised' victim-based patterns of identification and response.

Though explored primarily with reference to CSE within the UK, both the theoretical insights and the practical implications of the alternative conceptualisation I propose hold relevance for other forms of harm (sexual and other) typified by the concurrent presence of harm and gain, both within the UK and other jurisdictions.

What is the problem?

A wide body of literature, emanating from research, serious case reviews and inspections, has documented evidenced failures to appropriately identify and respond to some cases of CSE (see for example, Jay 2014; Ofsted 2014; Bedford 2015; HM Government 2015; Ofsted 2016; Hallett 2017; Research in Practice 2017). The underpinning premise of this chapter is that a key contributory factor to these documented shortcomings has been a failure to recognise, and work with, the potential co-existence of both agency and constraint; both harm and gain. While applicable to all circumstances where the young person can be seen to be in receipt of something they want or need in return for sexual activity, these challenges are particularly acute in cases where the young person is the one initiating the exchange (offering sexual activity in return for something they need or want) and/or is seen to be resistant to being 'rescued' by services.

Such cases challenge the dominant discourses around CSA, which emphasise themes of (sexual) innocence, victim passivity and perpetrator control/manipulation. As explored later in the chapter, such conceptualisations leave no place for agency, initiative or choice, with the consequence that those who fail to fit this predominant construction have, by default, been excluded from our idealised constructions of victimhood (Pearce 2010; Melrose 2012, 2013; Beckett et al 2013; Warrington 2013; Beckett et al 2017; Hallett 2017; Woodiwiss 2018).

Practically speaking this has had a negative impact on both the identification of the harm these young people experience and the level and nature of response they, and those who perpetrate the abuse, have received. While few professionals question the need to act when faced with the groomed and manipulated 'puppet on a string' victim (Barnardo's 2011), repeated serious case reviews, inspections and research observe a failure to act in cases of CSE where the young person is seen to be exercising some degree of choice or initiative, even where this is clearly occurring within less than ideal circumstances (Research in Practice 2017). Deemed to be 'making active lifestyle choices', those perceived to be exercising any degree of initiative or choice can be seen as somehow less deserving of support because of this; with little, if any recognition, of the influence of external constraints upon their actions. As Research in Practice (2017:23) concludes in their CSE Evidence Scope:

> Overplaying the extent to which young people are exercising informed rational 'choices' is a theme that emerges in many CSE-related SCRs [serious case reviews]. What can be interpreted as 'risky lifestyle choices' may more accurately and more helpfully be understood as (mal)adaptations to earlier trauma, or as attempts to meet unmet needs (Hanson and Holmes, 2014)…Understanding how previous experiences might (for some young people) underpin behaviours is important for practitioners, and demands a more sophisticated interpretation of 'choice'.

This documented failure to engage with these complexities contributes to a partial and overly-simplistic construction of CSE victimhood. This, in turn, can result in the overlooking of harm for those who fail to adhere to the expected behaviours of the passive victim stereotype (Beckett et al 2017; Research in Practice 2017; Woodiwiss 2018). It also serves to suggest a homogeneity among CSE victims and the contexts of their abuse (and therefore the required response) that is not supported by the research evidence base (Beckett and Walker 2018).

Changing this requires a dismantling of the dominant binary CSE discourses of 'puppet on a string' versus a free agent 'making active lifestyle choices'. It requires the adoption of an alternative theoretical lens that moves beyond such simplistic binary conceptualisations and associated judgements to more accurately accommodate the complex reality of young people's lives. Applying structuration theory (Giddens 1976, 1993, 1994) to the field of CSE, I argue, offers a helpful framework around which a new narrative of CSE can be constructed. Also applicable to other exploitative situations with similar dynamics around concurrent harm and gain, adopting such a lens can not only address evidenced shortcomings in the identification of such abuse, but also help us better tailor our responses to the realities of young people's lived experiences of such harm.

The origins of the debate: actors on a stage or creators of our own destiny?

This question as to the relative influence of individuals and their external circumstances, and the ways in which these intersect and interact, is one that can be traced back to the foundations of sociological discourse and can be variably observed throughout sociological debate ever since. So too can the associated issues of culpability and blame, determinism and potential for change. While in reality the various positions within this sociological debate exist along a conceptual continuum, showing at least some degree of concern with both social action and social structure, the frequent prioritisation of one over the other has led many commentators to conceptualise the debate in terms of a formal dichotomy between structure and action perspectives (Archer 1982; Jenks 1998; May 1998).

Though somewhat differing in their particular emphasis and conceptual vocabulary, structural perspectives tend to portray people's lives as patterned, if not wholly determined, by social forces outside of their control. In this view society is, metaphorically speaking, a puppet theatre in which individuals are little more than 'puppets jumping about on the end of their invisible strings, cheerfully acting out the parts that have been assigned to them' (Berger, cited in Haralambos and Holborn 2000:9). Far from being creative agents capable of exercising independent thought or action, they (like the CSE puppet on a string conceptualisation) are purely passive participants in an externally determined existence.

Located at the other extreme of this conceptual divide are social action or agency perspectives. Paramount within these perspectives is 'the idea of conscious, thinking subjects, actually planning and carrying out courses of action' (Jenks 1998:265) Such perspectives place the individual actor firmly at centre stage, crediting them with 'creating subjectivity and the capacity for voluntary self-directing action' (Parker 2000:54), and relegating the role of external structures of opportunity and constraint.

Neither extreme has been deemed to have presented an adequate and accurate conceptualisation of the complex organic relationship between the individual and their external environment. Critiques of this binary divide have highlighted the limits of focusing on one influence to the exclusion of the other. Structural perspectives have been criticised for being overly deterministic; positioning individuals as helpless dopes with no ability to influence their lifecourse. Agency perspectives have been subject to the alternate charge of surrendering too much to the rational self-determination of individual actors, and failing to recognise externally determined limits on their self-determination (as summarised in Beckett 2004).

These dichotomous theoretical conceptualisations hold clear implications for how we then view individuals and their actions and experiences. If, as structural perspectives emphasise, our life experiences are externally determined, the blame for negative outcomes lies with society and not the individual. If on the other hand, we locate the axis of power and control with the individual, it follows that negative outcomes must therefore be the result of something they did (or did not do), and therefore their fault.

'Puppet on a string' or 'making active lifestyle choices'?

These extreme conceptualisations, and the associated patterns of culpability and blame, are clearly observable within both historical and recent discourse around CSE and its child prostitution origins. As highlighted earlier, it is my contention that this is, in large part, due to the predominant influence of a deterministic idealised (child) victim profile, that equates victimhood with passivity and an inability to exert any degree of influence over one's experiences.

Though not the only such conceptualisation, this dynamic is most starkly demonstrated in both the visuals and language associated with the now-retired Barnardo's (2011) puppet on a string CSE campaign. As can be seen from Figure 2.1, victims of CSE were portrayed in this campaign as having their every move controlled by an abuser, who pulls the strings to make them do what they want, when they want. The (white female) victim is helpless to do otherwise. She is entirely at the mercy of her all-controlling abuser(s) and in need of rescue. We, in turn, are portrayed as their rescuers, with a call to 'cut them free' from these manipulative controlling abusers.

Figure 2.1: Front cover image of Barnardo's (2011) *Puppet on a String* report

Source: Shutterstock/Marcus Lyon

The adoption of such a simplistic portrayal of CSE is understandable given both the public-facing and campaigning nature of the publication, and the dominance of such discourses at the time of its use. It is also understandable given the desire to challenge legacy issues around accountability and blame, emanating from previous child prostitution discourses (see Phoenix in this volume).

The flipside of such conceptualisations however is that they have contributed to, and compounded, a particular articulation of CSE victimhood that, while reflective of the experience of some, is by default exclusive of the experience of many others. Unfortunately, while the charity, like many of us, has embraced a more nuanced conceptualisation of CSE as our understanding of the issue has increased, the legacy of such conceptualisations remains. This holds serious implications for how children and young people's experiences are conceptualised and responded to.

While there is no doubt that some sexually exploited young people may experience the conditions of the abuse as something over which they have no control, there is increasing evidence from both research and practice to show that this is by no means the case for all (Pearce 2010; Beckett 2011; Melrose 2013; Dodsworth 2015; Warrington 2013; Hallett 2017). As illustrated in the case study presented later in this chapter, there are many young people who, finding themselves in less than ideal circumstances, 'choose' – in the absence of any preferable option – to utilise the resource of their sexuality to meet a need or want. As Beckett and Walker (2018:17) observe of the puppet on the string model and other such conceptualisations:

> While this degree of external control is indeed present in some cases of CSE, we know that there are many other cases in which the axis of power and decision-making is much more subtle and complex (Melrose, 2010; Pearce, 2010; Beckett, 2011; Beckett et al, 2013; Pitts, 2013; Hallett, 2015; Beckett et al, 2017). Practice evidence shows that the reality of many young people's experiences of CSE are not necessarily driven by threat or force, but may be driven more by need or want or, akin to many domestic violence situations, loyalty to, or love for, the perpetrator. Although also provided for within the definitions of CSE, these are the cases that we are less likely to recognise as abusive, and where the child/young person can be misconstrued as 'making active lifestyle choices' (Jago and Pearce, 2008; Griffiths, 2013; Pearce, 2013; Jay, 2014; Bedford, 2015;

Research in Practice, 2015). This dynamic of 'choice' or 'agency' – and the presence of victim gain often observed within CSE – complicated and uncomfortable as it may be, is not one that can be avoided or denied. Indeed it is the very presence of such gain that both distinguishes cases of CSE from other cases of sexual abuse and adds an additional layer of complexity in responding to such cases.

As highlighted in this quotation, these young people are those whom we see misconstrued as 'making active lifestyle choices', 'prostituting themselves' and 'putting themselves at risk', with no recognition of the circumstances in which they are making such choices. Such harmful narratives result from an inability/unwillingness to recognise the potential concurrent presence of gain and harm and an associated acceptance that the exercise of agency does not necessarily negate the abusive or exploitative nature of an act. Where agency is observed it is done so at the virtual exclusion of recognition of external constraint, including consideration of unmet needs that may actually be contributing to the conditions for abuse (Phoenix 2002; Melrose 2004; Pearce 2010; Beckett 2011; Warrington 2013; Hallett 2017). Despite this shortcoming being highlighted by academic commentators for over 15 years now, an acceptable integrated conceptualisation seems to continue to elude policy and practice (Beckett et al 2017). It is to this that we now turn.

An alternative conceptualisation

As highlighted earlier, the relative influences of agency and structure have been well rehearsed in sociological discourse, and it is there we return for insights as to an alternative conceptualisation for CSE. Over the years various theorists, including Giddens, Archers, Bourdieu and Bhasker, have sought to offer an alternative integrated framework, that moves beyond an 'either–or' approach, to recognise that structure and agency are, in short, mutually related not mutually exclusive. Here is not the place for a detailed analysis of each particular approach; suffice it to say that while there are several significant points upon which these contemporary theorists diverge there is also much that unites them. Of particular relevance to this argument is the fact that all are premised on an understanding that agency and structure not only co-exist, but continually intersect and interact in the day to day practice of people's lives. Social life is, according to these theorists, the outcome of a complex interplay between contextually bound individual actions and interactions and individually-mediated structural opportunities and constraints (Beckett 2004).

I explore this recursive relationship further through the particular lens of Giddens' structuration theory; proposing this as a framework through which we move beyond simplistic understandings of agency and victimhood and more helpfully understand the lived realities of those young people who – operating in less than ideal circumstances – may 'choose' to exchange sexual activity for something they need or want.

Structuration theory

Structuration theory first appeared 40 years ago in Giddens' 1976 text *New Rules of Sociological Method*.[1] It draws upon a myriad of theories and theorists, integrating the wisdom of existing structure and agency perspectives, while at the same time abandoning the extreme bias that served to undermine their validity and usefulness. Giddens (like Archer, Bhaskar and Bourdieu) focuses on the interconnected and mutually influencing nature of the structure–agency relationship. Agency and structure are seen as two interconnected parts of a larger whole, or two ways of looking the same thing, that thing/whole being 'social practices ordered across space and time'.

Within the context of this recursive relationship, individuals are understood to possess the capacity to proactively negotiate their lives within an externally determined structure of opportunity and constraint. Translating this to a less abstract level, people are not free to do what they want when they want, irrespective of context or circumstance; their lives are unavoidably context-bound, both in terms of the obstacles they face and the resources at their disposal.

This is not to say, however, that individuals are devoid of any power or autonomy or that their lives are entirely determined by external forces outside of their control. Individuals are rarely completely constrained by circumstance; they nearly always have the opportunity to 'do otherwise', to exert some degree of choice. They may not like the choices with which they are faced, they may not be what Giddens terms 'feasible' options and/or they may be limited in number, but they are options nonetheless and individuals retain the capacity to choose between them.

As 'reflexive knowledgeable agents' Giddens sees individuals as having the capacity to evaluate circumstances, identify goals and preferred options (albeit from a possibly limited palette) and implement steps to pursue these. They consequently also possess the capacity to influence their lifecourse and bring about change, however difficult this may be or however small the chance. Though the options open to them may be externally determined, both in terms of number and nature, what they choose to do with these is not.

This approach holds much in common with the concept of survival strategies, observable in related literature on adult sex work, poverty and homelessness. As Jones (1995:7) describes in her work on youth homelessness, 'some young people's actions may clearly be seen as informed choice strategies, arising from opportunity, and others as survival strategies, arising from constraint'. Or as Phoenix (2002:362) similarly describes: 'people involved in prostitution are like many other impoverished individuals; they make choices, but not in conditions of their own choosing'.

What does this mean for CSE?

As noted earlier, questions around the relative influence of individuals and their external circumstances are well rehearsed in terms of adult sex work. They are however complicated with regard to children and the social construction of childhood, and by definitions of CSE/CSA devoid of reference to developmental appropriateness.

To expand, constructed cultural expectations around childhood innocence, dependency and asexuality add complexity to debates about agency and sexual abuse when applied to 'children' (those under the age of 18, UNCRC). The history of CSE, both within the UK and internationally, is one that has sought to highlight the 'otherness' of children and, in doing so, divorce discussions about children exchanging sexual activity for money or any other benefit, from discourse on adult prostitution. Such efforts have succeeded to a large degree, and while observable benefits have been seen in this regard, key challenges remain. These challenges have their roots in simplistic binary understandings of victimhood predicated on the mutual exclusivity of agency and control, and harm and gain. Core to these are the continued alignment of abuse with passivity, receptivity and sexual innocence, and associated judgements and overlooking of harm where such traits are not observed.

This is a tension that can be observed throughout the history of this issue. As the history of CSE, and its relationship to child prostitution, is well rehearsed elsewhere (see, for example, Hallett 2017 and Phoenix in this volume) the detail will not be repeated here. What is, however, important to explore are the ways in which young people who experienced these forms of harm have been constructed and the strong undercurrent of a deserving/undeserving discourse within this, depending on the degree to which they were perceived to be manipulated or in control.

The pendulum swing away from the 'active child prostitute' to 'abused passive child' has left little space for nuanced developmentally-informed discussion around the complex lived realities of young people's lives. Indeed, as Melrose (2012:158) observes, the dominance of the 'pimping and grooming' model has meant that 'the idea that at least some young people may exercise agency (albeit in severely constrained circumstances) and become involved under their own volition has become unimaginable within the parameters of debate established by this discursive formation'.

This is a binary divide that we need to challenge and a conversation we now need to have if we are to engage with complex lived realities of the harm that children and young people experience. This is particularly pertinent when considering CSE and other forms of sexual harm experienced in the teenage years; a phase of childhood characterised by developing sexual interest, broadening social networks and increasing capacity and self-determination.

As recognised by authors such as Melrose (2013), Dodsworth (2015) and Warrington (2015), challenges around childhood innocence, passivity and asexuality present uniquely in relation to adolescents, whom research shows to be the primary population affected by CSE. Although debates continue around the socially constructed nature of childhood, there is widespread recognition that adolescence is somehow distinct from pre-pubescence, both biologically and in terms of the social construction of these life phases (Hanson and Holmes 2014). And yet, although there are a myriad of observable ways in which pre-pubescence and pubescence are distinguished (including legal age of consent to sexual activity) responses to CSE and other child protection issues are based on the developmentally-blind application of childhood ideals to those recognised in other areas of life to be on a trajectory towards adulthood (see Coleman in this volume for further analysis of this point).

Accommodating both agency and constraint

Viewing CSE through the lens of structuration theory, and paying cognisance to issues of lifecourse development, allow us to move beyond the predominant discourses of puppet on a string versus active lifestyle choices to recognise that young people's experiences of CSE are rarely as simplistic as either of these. As Warrington (2013:51) observes, in her application of structuration theory within doctoral research on young people's decisions around service engagement: 'Gidden's approach allows for a perspective that moves beyond deterministic accounts of victimhood and ideas about the passive client. It allows for the possibility of creative reflexive welfare subjects while acknowledging the constraints imposed by the intersection of structural disadvantage, personal biography and interventions.'

For most young people who experience CSE, there is the potential to exercise some degree of agency or choice but, and this is the critical point, within circumstances that are far from ideal and rarely of their own making. These constraints operate at multiple levels and are uniquely experienced according to the biography of the individual and the contexts of opportunity and constraint within which their lives are negotiated. As such the exercise of choice does not necessarily equal culpability or accountability. Nor does it in any way sit at odds with the concurrent presence of harm and abuse or necessarily negate the abusive nature of an act. The choice we see in many situations of CSE is one that is highly constrained and externally influenced. It does however exist, and a failure to recognise this will lead to continued overlooking of potential harm in situations where the young person may appear and/or feel themselves to be in control.

Seen as 'reflexive knowledgeable agents', such young people are not simply puppets on a string, acting out the part life has given them, but individuals whose agency can be seen to be a resource through which they can seek to minimise harm and maximise benefit, within the complex and difficult situations in which they find themselves. To at least some degree, they can assess the situation – the opportunities and constraints – and decide how to respond. As Giddens notes, they retain the capacity to evaluate circumstances, identify goals and preferred options (albeit from a possibly limited palette) and implement steps to pursue these.

Though the options open to them may be externally determined – both in terms of number and nature – what they choose to do with these is not. That is not to say that the 'choice' they make is one they would choose to make were the options available to them different or more expansive; a theme we see replicated throughout young people's accounts of their experiences (Phoenix 2002; Beckett 2011; Beckett et al 2013; Hallett 2017). However, as we can observe in both practice and research, not all individuals react in the same way to the same circumstances, or end up with the same outcomes, a fact that illustrates the capacity for individual action even within severely constrained circumstances.

Adopting an alternative lens

So what might this look like in practice? In this section we explore the concept of constrained choice in relation to a specific case example of a 14-year-old female who exchanged sexual activity for tangible gain.

The case study derives from a major study that explored the prevalence and nature of CSE in Northern Ireland (Beckett 2011).[2] The research was the first of its kind to be conducted there, and remains one of the most extensive studies in the UK CSE field. The research included the quantitative analysis of 1102 CSE risk assessments, completed by social workers on 12–17-year-olds on their caseload, and qualitative analysis of data around the nature of CSE concerns in the 147 cases where the social workers documented such concerns. The research also included 29 social care case files for young people who had experienced CSE, in-depth qualitative interviews with five young people who had experienced CSE and 110 professionals, from a range of disciplines, working in the field. The case study was shared by one such police professional, whose staff had managed the case.

Though the data was generated in the context of understanding the different ways in which CSE may manifest, the detail of the case is re-examined through the lens of reflexive biographies operating in a structure of constraint, and included here to illustrate how this can move us beyond face-value judgements and enhance our understanding of the needs of the young person involved:

> She met this man outside a pub and she basically offered him a blowjob for a tenner. She took him into an alley way, performed oral sex on him, got a tenner, went to the off licence and bought four litres of cider. Her and her friend decided they wanted to come back to the area where she was from but needed to get a taxi, so again she needed money. So she went to a pub and approached two other men and offered them sex for the price of the taxi home, which she did. On the way home in the taxi she decided she wanted to keep the money she had earned from having sex with the other two so she offered the taxi driver sex for the fare. (Case of 14-year-old female, cited in Beckett 2011)

This scenario is one typical of those where a young person may be labelled as 'making active lifestyle choices', 'prostituting him/herself' or 'placing him/herself at risk'. While it is true that this 14-year-old girl is initiating every exchange of her own volition, and as such making choices, a concurrent consideration of the circumstances in which she is making these choices demonstrates that she is clearly doing so from a limited rather than expansive palette of options; as a survival rather than an informed choice strategy.

Sexually abused by her father from a young age, who subsequently charged others to sexually abuse her from the age of nine, this young person was receiving treatment for alcohol misuse by the time this encounter occurs. Consuming alcohol is her means of blocking out (at least temporarily) the ongoing debilitating impacts of her prior abuse. It is doubtful that given alternative circumstances, with a different life history and different current needs and priorities, this young person would have chosen to spend her evening doing this, but given the context in which she found herself (constraint) she did what she could (agency) to 'made the best of a bad situation'.

To take license and place myself in this young person's shoes for a moment, what we as professionals may judge to be risk-taking destructive behaviour may actually be the most resourceful and self-protective action she could take within the circumstances she found herself. She needed alcohol to block out her trauma. Aged 14, she will clearly not be given this by the professionals who work with her so, having learnt that people will pay money to 'have sex with her', she used what limited 'capital' she had – her sexuality – to meet her needs and make it through the day. She assessed her (limited) options, through the lens of her life experiences and learning, and decided that 'selling sex' to source alcohol was preferable to not being able to block out her emotions. As insightfully explained by another young person with a similarly abusive background:

> Sometimes people's been through that [abusive background] and they just put on a brave face like nothing's happened but really deep inside they're hurting and they don't know what to do. People that's been through so much like that, you can't blame them for turning to drink or drugs because it's the only thing; it's givin them'ins like a big buzz and it's takin away their problems. But then you get up and then it's happenin again, so you take more. (17-year-old female, in Beckett 2011:63)

What does this mean for practice?

As noted in the introduction, the current binary construction of puppet on a string versus free agent making active lifestyle choices

– and the failure to recognise the concurrent presence of agency and harm – is having an impact on our practice. It affects: (a) our ability to recognise abusive situations, (b) young people's propensity to disclose and (c) the ways in which we need to work with them (Beckett et al 2017).

The exercise of any agency, is (whether consciously or unconsciously on our part) disqualifying some young people from access to 'victim status' and the support and response that such designation brings. As highlighted earlier, these are the cases that appear in serious case reviews, with observations of abusive experiences being interpreted as problematic behaviours on the part of the child (Jay 2014; Bedford 2015; Beckett et al 2017). This is particularly pertinent in instances where the young person's 'choices' do not align with what we think we would do in such circumstances. The presence of choice (albeit from severely constrained options) means that there is always the opportunity to do otherwise. This presents the danger that when we approach the situation from our own adult perspectives and experiences we can think 'that's not what I'd have done'; thoughts that can inadvertently result in judgement-driven exclusionary and alienating responses. As I and my colleagues explain in the 2017 extended government guidance on CSE:

> If we do not recognise the constrained circumstances within which victims make 'choices', we will see them as being 'in control' and not recognise their need for intervention. This can lead to judgements about the victim ('they could have done otherwise') and the use of blaming language (such as putting themselves at risk, making lifestyle choices, or promiscuous or sexualised behaviour) that hides the abuse and shifts responsibility for what they have experienced onto the victim. (Beckett et al 2017:18)

Such an approach has obvious implications for how a young person may experience our responses. If we talk about them placing themselves at risk or engaging in risk-taking behaviour, we are clearly locating the responsibility of the abuse with the child. Intentional or not, the message which that gives the young person is 'this happened because of something you did', 'you are somehow responsible for what happened to you' and therefore you are less deserving of our support.

Core to shifting this harmful and distancing discourse is an ability to see beyond the observable actions of the young people, and recognise the constrained circumstances within which their choices are being made. This requires effort on our part, as the reasons for seemingly 'irrational' choices are not always immediately obvious, for example, the young woman who 'chooses' to leave the foster-home where she is safe and get in a car with two men she knows plan to rape her. This is a seemingly irrational choice to the foster carer and other professionals, until they learnt that her exit from the home was preceded by a text threatening to rape her young sister if she did not come out to meet them (unpublished research data, available from author). A very rational choice, however, to that young person who, assessing her options, decided to sacrifice her own safety to protect her younger sibling.

Similarly, the 15-year-old male who finds himself homeless, may 'choose' to take up the offer of having sex with someone in return for a place to stay for the next week, rather than 'take their chances' on the street; fearing that the harm they may experience there may be worse. In deciding to do so, he exercises what control he can in intensely challenging and constrained circumstances, choosing to opt for the 'known' rather than 'unknown' even if this entails him doing something he would never choose to in other circumstances.

The confusion around culpability and blame that professionals may experience is also observable in young people themselves; a fact we need to pay cognisance to if we are to understand what they need from us and tailor our responses appropriately. Research repeatedly shows that failing to recognise the abusive nature of their experiences and/or seeing themselves as somehow responsible for what has happened to them – or thinking we will view them in this way – can prevent children and young people from seeking and/or receiving support (Beckett 2011; Beckett et al 2013; Warrington 2013; Research in Practice 2017).

A young person may feel in some way responsible for what happened to them ('if only I hadn't…then this wouldn't have happened') and/or anticipate similar blame-based responses from us. They may think that the fact that they are getting something they want or need (whether money, drugs, love or attention) in return for the sexual act means that it is not abusive; a dynamic frequently observed in cases where the young person believes themselves to be in a loving relationship with the perpetrator.

In recognising that harm and gain can concurrently co-exist, it may be that the young person does recognise the exploitative nature of his/her situation but is not ready or able to give up the particular 'gain' (money, drugs, love, attention and so on) that is underpinning the exchange dynamic. It may also, of course, be the case that they are indebted to, or under threat by, the perpetrator. In the same way that we need to challenge our own unhelpful assumptions around passivity and victimhood, we need to clearly give young people the message that they are not to blame; that neither the exercise of agency nor the presence of gain renders them culpable for harm experienced or place them outside of our support.

In terms of how we work with young people whose experience of CSE is typified by some form of perceived gain on their part (which may or may not obscure the abusive nature of the situation) it is critical to recognise the complex multi-faceted dynamics at play. This includes recognition of their potentially conflicting feelings around the concurrent presence of gain and harm, and their views of/feelings towards those who are exploiting them. Akin to the complex dynamics observable in domestic abuse, a young person may, for example, retain strong positive feelings for a perpetrator, despite the fact that they simultaneously cause them harm. For reasons of emotional engagement and/or reluctance to forego whatever want or need is being met through the abusive situation, they may not want to be 'rescued' by us and be resistant to our efforts to protect them.

This does not mean that they do not need our support, but it may be that young people's resistance to engage with us is indicative that the approach we are taking, or the timing/pace of our efforts, are not reflective of their needs. It may also be that we insufficiently understand that our offer of help falls short when viewed through the lens of the reflexive young person who assesses relative risks and benefits from their point of knowledge and understanding.

To expand, research repeatedly shows that choosing to engage with services can hold a range of risks and challenges for young people (Pearce 2010; Beckett 2011; Beckett et al 2013; Warrington 2013; Hickle and Hallett 2015; Hallett 2017) They may, for example, be at physical risk from a perpetrator who fears the implications of disclosure. They may experience negative reactions from professionals or a loss of control over the direction of their lives. Indeed, they may experience negative inter-personal dynamics with professionals – dismissal of their views, being told what to do and when to do it – that replicate those of their abuse (Beckett and Warrington 2015; Warrington 2013; Hallett 2017). Engagement with services may involve a radical re-conceptualisation of self and one's experiences; the significance of which should not be underestimated. It may mean giving up something that they are not yet ready to forego, or dismantling coping mechanisms around which they have built their daily functioning. When we recognise all of these potential challenges and risks – and the concurrent pull of 'gain' and familiarity on the other hand – we can better understand the difficult and complex challenge we present a young person with when we seek to intervene.

Last, but of critical importance, applying a lens of reflexive biographies within a structure of constraint also usefully takes our focus beyond the individual child to consider the contextual constraints which impinge upon their capacity to exercise choice. At an individual case level, this involves moving beyond a singular deficit-based focus on the individual child to contextually consider all the interconnected conditions of abuse when identifying and responding to harm (Beckett 2011, Walker and Beckett 2017). At a more macro level, it demands active consideration of 'the socio-cultural context and the existential conditions in which [young people's] choices and non-choices are made' (Pitts 2013:31) and the challenging of harmful discourses and decisions which serve to limit, rather than expand, young people's choices; to disenfranchise rather than empower the exercise of individual agency.

Notes

[1] It is important to note that Giddens' theory of structuration has, over the years, been subject to both validation and commendation, and criticism and concern. These are well rehearsed elsewhere (and summarised in Beckett 2004), and so will not be repeated here, but it is the author's contention that the criticisms levelled at the approach do not serve to undermine its usefulness as an ontological lens through which to view life.

[2] Further information about the methodology/analysis for this, and all of the author's studies cited in the chapter, are available in the original research reports (all available online). Beckett (2011) is downloadable from: www.barnardos.org. uk/cym/13932_not_a_world_away_full_report.pdf

References

Archer, M. (1982) 'Morphogenesis versus structuration: On combining structure and action', *The British Journal of Sociology*, 33(4): 455–483

Barnardo's (2011) *Puppet on a String: The Urgent Need to Cut Children Free from Sexual Exploitation*, Barkingside: Barnardo's

Beckett, H. (2004) *An Ethnography of Youth Homelessness*, Doctoral thesis, the Queen's University of Belfast

Beckett, H. (2011) *Not a World Away: The Sexual Exploitation of Children and Young People in Northern Ireland*, Belfast: Barnardo's NI

Beckett, H. and Warrington, C. (2015) *Making Justice Work: Experiences of Criminal Justice for Children and Young People Affected by Sexual Exploitation as Victims and Witnesses*, Luton: University of Bedfordshire

Beckett, H. and Walker, J. (2018) 'Words Matter: Reconceptualising the conceptualisation of child sexual exploitation', in H. Beckett and J. Pearce (eds) *Understanding and Responding to Child Sexual Exploitation*, Abingdon: Routledge

Beckett, H., Holmes, D. and Walker, J. (2017) *Child sexual Exploitation: Definition and Guide for Professionals*, Extended text, Luton: University of Bedfordshire

Beckett, H. with Brodie, I., Factor, F., Melrose, M., Pearce, J., Pitts, J., Shuker, L. and Warrington, C. (2013) *'It's Wrong...But You Get Used To It': A Qualitative Study of Gang-associated Sexual Violence Towards, and Exploitation of, Young People in England*, London and Luton: Office of Children's Commissioner and University of Bedfordshire

Bedford, A. (2015) *Serious Case Review into Child Sexual Exploitation in Oxfordshire: From the Experience of Children A, B, C, D, E and F (overview)*, Oxfordshire: Oxfordshire Safeguarding Children Board

Dodsworth, J. (2015) *Pathways into Sexual Exploitation and Sex Work: The Experience of Victimhood and Agency*, London: Palgrave Macmillan

Giddens, A. (1976) *New Rules of Sociological Method: A Positive Critique of Interpretive Sociologies*, London: Hutchinson

Giddens, A. (1993) *New Rules of Sociological Method: A Positive Critique of Interpretive Sociologies* (2nd edn), Cambridge: Polity Press

Giddens, A. (1994) 'Elements of the theory of structuration', in A. Giddens, D. Held, D. Hubert, D.I. Seymour and J. Thompson (eds) *The Polity Reader in Social Theory*, Cambridge: Polity Press

Hallett, S. (2017) *Making Sense of Child Sexual Exploitation: Exchange, Abuse and Young People*, Bristol: Policy Press

Hanson, E. and Holmes, D. (2015) *That Difficult Age: Developing a More Effective Response to Risks in Adolescence*, Evidence Scope, Totnes: Research in Practice

Haralambos, M. and Holborn, M. (2000) *Sociology: Themes and Perspectives* (5th edn), London: HarperCollins Publishers

Hickle, K. and Hallett, S. (2015) 'Mitigating harm: considering harm reduction principles in work with sexually exploited young people', *Children and Society*, 30(4): 302–313

HM Government (2015) *Tackling Child Sexual Exploitation*, London: Crown Copyright

Jay, A. (2014) *Independent Inquiry into Child Sexual Exploitation in Rotherham 1997–2013*, Rotherham: Rotherham Metropolitan Borough Council

Jenks, C. (1998) 'Active/Passive', in C. Jenks (ed) *Core Sociological Dichotomies*, London: Sage

Jones, G. (1995) *Leaving Home*, London: Open University Press

May, T. (1998) 'Reflections and reflexivity', in T. May and M. Williams (eds) *Knowing the Social World*, London: Open University Press

Melrose, M. (2004) 'Young people abused through prostitution: Some observations for practice', in *Practice*, 16: 17–29

Melrose, M. (2010) 'What's love got to do with it? Theorising young people's involvement in prostitution', in *Youth and Policy*, 104: 12–30

Melrose, M. (2012) 'Twenty-first century party people: Young people and sexual exploitation in the new millennium', in *Child Abuse Review*, 22: 155–168

Melrose, M. (2013) 'Young people and sexual exploitation: A critical discourse analysis', in M. Melrose and J. Pearce (eds) *Critical Perspectives on Child Sexual Exploitation and Related Trafficking*, London: Palgrave Macmillan

Ofsted (2014) *The Sexual Exploitation of Children it Couldn't Happen Here, Could It?*, London: Ofsted

Ofsted (2016) *Time to Listen: A Joined Up Response to Child Sexual Exploitation and Missing Children*, London: Ofsted

Parker, J. (2000) *Structuration*, London: Open University Press

Pearce, J. (2010) 'Safeguarding young people from sexual exploitation and from being trafficked: Tensions within contemporary policy and practice', *Youth and Policy*, 104: 1–11

Pearce, J. (2013) 'A social model of "abused consent"', in M. Melrose and J. Pearce (eds) *Critical Perspectives on Child Sexual Exploitation and Related Trafficking*, London: Palgrave Macmillan

Phoenix, J. (1999) *Making Sense of Prostitution*, London: Palgrave

Phoenix, J. (2002) 'In the name of protection: Youth prostitution policy reforms in England and Wales', *Critical Social Policy*, 71: 353–375

Pitts, J. (2013) 'Drifting into trouble: Sexual exploitation and gang affiliation', in M. Melrose and J. Pearce (eds) *Critical Perspectives on Child Sexual Exploitation and Related Trafficking*, London: Palgrave Macmillan

Research in Practice (2017) *Working Effectively to Address Child Sexual Exploitation: Evidence Scope*, Totnes: Research in Practice

Walker, J. and Beckett, H. (2017) *Child Sexual Exploitation: How Public Health can Support Prevention and Intervention*, London: Public Health England

Warrington, C. (2013) *'Helping me Find my Own Way': Sexually Exploited Young People's Involvement in Decision-making About Their Care*, Doctoral thesis, Luton: University of Bedfordshire

Woodiwiss, J. (2018) 'From one girl to "three girls": The importance of separating agency from blame (and harm from wrongfulness) in narratives of childhood sexual abuse and exploitation', in *Pastoral Care in Education*, https://doi.org/10.1080/02643944.2018.1464593

3

Child sexual exploitation, discourse analysis and why we still need to talk about prostitution

Jo Phoenix

Introduction

> A critique is not a matter of saying that things are not right as they are. It is a matter of pointing out on what kinds of assumptions, what kinds of familiar, unchallenged, unconsidered modes of thought the practices that we accept rest. (Foucault 1988:155)

It is nearly 20 years since the UK started 'doing something' about child sexual exploitation (CSE). From our vantage point of the early twenty-first century, it seems self-evidently true that CSE is a form of child sexual abuse (CSA) and, as such, statutory social services (and the police) are the best agencies to deal with it. It also seems self-evident that social work professional knowledge and expertise is required in order to assess individual cases, understand the aetiology of CSE and individual's circumstances, devising and managing programmes of intervention that will produce the best possible outcome for the abused child.

If we scratch below these taken-for-granted truths, though, we may see that our contemporary practices rest on what is, in effect, certain 'unsayable' things. What is 'normal' adolescent behaviour? How is it shaped by wider social structures of race, gender, ability and age-based inequalities? What are the connections between CSE and prostitution? They may be 'unsayable' because the assumptions we work with seem in themselves 'self-evident' (the difference between 'normal' and 'not normal'). They may be unsayable because of the way that we define and act upon CSE. As CSE is currently constituted, to acknowledge that there might be a connection between CSE and prostitution is seen as implying that the children harmed have somehow, in some way, consented to their harm. Yet, these 'discursive erasures' have not always existed. The connections were once acknowledged, understood and discussed *without* the sole recourse being to statutory social services and child protection practices and *without* anyone denying the harm and damage that was done to young people.

This chapter provides a discourse analysis of the emergence of CSE as a social problem in order to uncover the unchallenged modes of thought that dominate our practices and assumptions about what CSE is and how to deal with it. The first section describes discourse analysis and suggests the sort of questions that such an approach raises. The second section describes the discursive field out of which emerged the discourse of CSE as a particular type of social problem. The third section describes the discourse of CSE and the subjects of regulation that it creates. In the chapter conclusion, I reflect on the discursive erasures within the discourse and why it is important to still talk about prostitution.

Discourse analysis as a framework for understanding the construction and regulation of social problems

This section describes the epistemological position in social sciences that is associated with social constructionism before moving on to describe discourse analysis, as framed by Foucault's concepts of discourse, power/knowledge and subjectivity.

What is social constructionism?

The basis of a social constructionist approach to studying social problems is the recognition that the social world does not have an independent existence. It is constructed by and within the processes we have of making sense of it. The implications of this for the study of social problems are profound. It means that there is no ultimate 'truth' about social problems that social science can uncover. Instead, there are only truths that are true in particular contexts at particular moments in history.

Within criminology, social constructionism opened up new ways of thinking about 'crime'. It shifted the concerns of the discipline away from positivistic questions of aetiology or causation to questions of context, meaning and power. For example, it asked how and under which social, ideological, economic and political conditions are particular types of social problems categorised and classified as 'crime' and to what effect? Social constructionism is particularly apposite for the study of CSE given that a significant dimension of policy reform of the last two decade has been the struggle over definition and meaning – as even the most cursory look at the literature will demonstrate (see Chapter 2 for a history of the contested definitions of CSE).

To move beyond a contest of meanings requires an analytical line of demarcation to be drawn between, on the one hand, the experiences and lived realities of the commercial sexual exchanges that young people endure, resist and survive and, on the other, how and in what ways 'CSE' is constituted as knowable and thus a governable thing. In other words, it requires that we treat young people's *experiences* of exchange-based sexual relationships (which have existed for millennia) as a different object of knowledge than governmental efforts to make sense of, define and regulate them (which similarly have existed for millennia). Doing so also importantly acknowledges that there will be no eventual state of enlightenment when governments and practitioners will have 'got it right' and will understand and comprehend 'the true nature' of the social phenomenon. Truth *per se* is bracketed off.

What is discourse analysis?

Discourse analysis provides a powerful tool to examine how social problems are defined, regulated and governed. Although there are many varieties of discourse analysis,[1] the one adopted here follows from Foucault's observations about discourses and the connections between knowledge/power. Discourses are:

> Ways of constituting knowledge, together with the social practices, forms of subjectivity and power which inhere in such knowledge and relations between them. Discourse are more than ways of thinking and producing meaning. They constitute the 'nature' of the body, unconscious and conscious mind and emotional life of the subject they seek to govern. (Weedon 1987:108)

For Foucault, discourses are organised, systematic and have rules. They 'delimit what can be said, while providing the spaces – the concepts, metaphors, models, analogies for making new statements within a specific discourse' (Henriques 1984:105). Discourses are not *just* language and meaning. They can be thought of as systems of knowledge along with any accompanying social practices, all of which contain within them power relations. Foucault conceptualised power as a set of force relations that are *productive* and not merely, or only, repressive. Power is not possessed, but practised. It is not an attribute, but an exercise. The question that power poses is not a question of why or what it is, but how it works. For Foucault, there is an important connection between power/knowledge nexus and subjectivity. He argued that the formation of subjects is part and parcel of power's productivity. The term 'subject' has many different meanings. The subjects of knowledge/power are the people who become subjected to those forms of knowledge/power and regulation. They are also, however, the subject positions that are created via knowledge/power and regulation. The subject of how we regulate CSE is, at the moment, a social services subject, an abused child historically located as female. She was in the recent past a subject of epidemiological knowledge: a needy, occasionally victimised, usually vulnerable girl or young woman in prostitution. These constructions create specific subject positions by which individuals are known and processed via specific organisations. They also, however, create positions by which those subjected may come to 'know' themselves and around which they communicate to others who they are, what their problems are and what they need. What discourse analysis offers us is not just a way of excavating these subjects of regulation, but a way of tracing the operation of power by thinking about who and what is excluded from dominant modes of thought and practice.

Foucault's ideas about discourse, power/knowledge and the creation of subjectivities come together to form a powerful framework in which to think about the work of governments in regulating social problems. It opens the space to pose questions about what is speakable (and unspeakable) within a discourse, as well as who can speak and how it can be said. It poses questions about meaning and about the subject positions discourse creates and, what is important, *closes off*.

A discourse analysis of CSE demands that we pay attention to what the modes of thought are that sit underneath current dominant discourses of CSE, who is 'authorised' to produce knowledge about CSE, how that knowledge circulates and what or who are excluded. A social constructionist approach might open up the space to analyse the contested, confusing and contradictory definitions of CSE and how these map on to the messiness of individuals' lived experiences. A discourse analysis opens the space to ask how systems of thought and practice render knowable (and by whom) the lived realities and experiences of young people and exploitative commercial sexual exchanges. What subjectivities are produced (or excluded)?

Prostitution, public health and political modernisation

This section traces the emergence of the discourse of CSE. The first part outlines the shifts in the discourse and regulation of prostitution[2] which eventually opened the space for CSE to emerge as a unique age differentiated problem of prostitution, rooted in the potential of young people to be exploited by abusive and/or criminal men. It shows how epidemiological and public health discourse, originally intended to deal with HIV/AIDS transmission, generated new knowledges about welfare and health issues faced by many women (of any age) in prostitution. This new knowledge coalesced with the rise of political discourse about modernisation which shaped central governmental policies concerning children and concerning the regulation of sex and started a process of fragmenting older undifferentiated categories of 'young person', 'victim' and 'prostitute'.

Prostitution as posing problems of criminal nuisance and public health

Throughout most of the twentieth century in the UK prostitution has been constituted (and regulated) as a criminal justice problem – specifically as a criminal nuisance caused by the visibility of street-based sex workers. This approach – which dates back to medieval times – was consolidated in the Report of the Committee on Homosexual Offences and Prostitution (1957) which subsequently formed the basis of the Street Offences Act 1959 in England and Wales. The Wolfenden Report drew a sharp line of distinction between matters of sexual morality and the role of criminal law in 'preserving public order and decency' and protecting individuals from the 'injurious' or 'offensive' behaviours of others. It recommended that regardless of how immoral other people may believe any specific sexual practice to be (like homosex or prostitution), consenting adults could do what they wanted to do with each other and without interference from the law as long as they did it in private. The Committee was clear in stating that it was the place of the law to regulate, via criminal justice, the nuisance and offence caused by the *visibility* of street prostitution. The approach suggested by the Committee was that police ought to arrest, prosecute and convict women working from the streets while simultaneously operate tolerance towards less visible forms of prostitution (such as indoor work).[3] In terms of day to day regulation, prostitution was and remains governed by the priorities of the local police constabularies as part of their general policing responsibilities. Thus, in addressing prostitution, the dominant concern of government was (and remains) dealing with the offenders: those who loiter or solicit in public places for the purposes of selling sex as well as those who loiter or solicit in public places for the purposes of buying sex (kerb crawling).

Much changed with the discovery of a new killer sexually transmitted disease in the 1980s and 1990s. HIV/AIDs caused widespread fear and governments reacted. In the UK, these fears also drew on longstanding popular stereotypes of prostitution as a conduit of disease from the undeserving, immoral, diseased few to the healthy, moral many. The fears drew on stereotypes of prostitutes as immoral women and reservoirs of disease. At the time, the public debate was vituperative. Calls were made, for instance, to imprison and incarcerate, indefinitely, those who sold sex until it could be established that they were not infected. Despite this, medical discourses ended up dominant and framed the complex issues as an epidemiological problem. The spread of HIV/AIDS happened because of 'risky' behaviours and lifestyles (promiscuity, intravenous drug use, anal sex) rather than because of 'risky' categories of people (sellers of sex, gay men). Significant funds were made available for new services to develop. These services were modelled on a harm minimisation (Kinnell 2013:304). This was a new approach that sought to minimise the potential health risks posed to those who sold sex by providing, for instance, free condoms.

Throughout the 1990s, the Department of Health expanded these types of services via local hospitals genito-urinary clinics and sexual health and drugs outreach projects. In practice, the service users of these new projects were predominantly women who sold sex, particularly those with drug and alcohol problems. That said, there were some services that specialised in dealing with gay men and men and boys involved in selling sex to other men. The outreach services were pragmatic and adopted a broad definition of harm in which everything from general and sexual health concerns, drugs and alcohol abuse and misuse, housing problems and homelessness, and domestic violence were addressed. That same pragmatism marked the relationships that many of these services developed with the local police constabularies. Projects such as the SAFE project in Birmingham, POW in Nottingham and the Praed Street Project in London began to identify violence from men (as clients, as partners and as exploiters) as being a critical threat to the health of many of the women (young and adult) with whom they worked and pressed their local police to 'do something' about these men. So, for instance, the Ugly Mugs scheme was pioneered at the SAFE project in Birmingham in the 1990s as a means of sharing and disseminating information between women in prostitution of potentially violent clients. This also inadvertently highlighted the woeful lack of protection accorded by the police to women in prostitution.

An enormous wealth of new empirical data and information was generated during this period, particularly in relation to the links between prostitution and poverty, homelessness, growing up in local authority care, domestic violence and abuse, high levels of drug and alcohol problems, and the endemic levels of violence and harassment that adult and young women in prostitution, particularly those working from the streets, experienced (see McKeganey and Barnard 1996; Church et al 2001; O'Neill 2001; Phoenix 2001; see also Balfour and Allen 2014). Arguably, this gave rise to what some have called 'sex work studies' or the new sociologies of sex work (Hardy and Kingston 2016). This information also found its way into central governmental debates about what 'the problems' of prostitution were and what ought to be done about them, as the next section will demonstrate.

Before moving on, it is appropriate to return to the question of subjects and subject positions and note three things. First, despite the new knowledge about the health and welfare needs of women (as opposed to men) in prostitution, the problem of prostitution continued to be seen mostly as a problem of criminal nuisance. The main subject of regulation remained the criminal, offending woman. Regardless of new working arrangements on the ground, local police constabularies continued to focus on the visibility of women working from the streets. Arrests and prosecution of women, aged 16 or over, for soliciting and loitering for the purposes of prostitution remained in the 1000s each year (reaching their peak at just over 10,000 in 1989) until well into the twenty-first century. In comparison, arrests (of men) for other prostitution related offences, including the then new kerb-crawling offence and those connected with violence and exploitation, numbered fewer than a few hundred each year. Second, issues of violence and exploitation faced by vulnerable, usually impoverished girls and young women with histories of being in local authority care were seen as being no different to the violence and exploitation faced by those older women in prostitution who did not come into local authority care or were less vulnerable. This enabled a powerful critique to be developed about prostitution and its regulation. The exploitation, abuse, coercion and violence experienced by the individuals with whom many of these sexual health outreach agencies came into contact was gender-based violence against women that was *unaddressed* and occasionally made worse by unjust and sexist police policies and laws. All the while this was underpinned by the effects of women's and girl's poverty relative to men. Third, at the time, girls and young women were simply absorbed into the newly formed outreach projects, which operated on a non-judgemental voluntary basis. The age of the person was not seen as being a particular type of problem that required *separate* systems of intervention (see Kinnell 2013 for both the history of sexual health outreach projects and the critique of gender-based violence that was offered).

New labour, new modes of governing and the creation of new subjects of regulation

In 1997, New Labour gained electoral success by positioning itself as a young, newly formed, modern Labour party and the only political party capable of creating a modern government, enacting modern laws to face a modern age. To that end, and in relation to major areas of social policy, New Labour initiated what has been referred to a 'responsibilising' mode of governance (Garland 1996, 2002). This became part of the more general project, started by the New Right and specifically the Conservative governments headed by Margaret Thatcher, of dismantling the post-war social democratic welfare state. Responsibilisation, in this context, refers to those political processes, and rhetoric, by which the delivery of public goods – for instance social security and criminal justice – are devolved (or seen as needing to be devolved) from statutory central authorities, to local authorities, local individuals and local third sector organisations. In this way the state's role in providing public services is lessened. While responsibilisation could take many different forms, the form it took at the end of the twentieth and in the early twenty-first century was contradictory as it was also framed by more centralising and controlling strategies and rhetoric of managerialism (see Clarke and Newman 1997). This meant that local authorities were seen as being the site through which local organisations and communities could be responsible for ensuring the provision and delivery of public goods necessary for their communities. Yet, local authorities were also held to account (often financially) by central government for ensuring that the delivery of services and goods were cost effective and done according to key performance indicators set by central government.

A political recognition of the need to differently govern youth and childhood seemed to be hardwired into the discourse of modernisation on which New Labour based its electoral success. The new policy mantra was: intervention, intervention, intervention (Haines and Case 2015). This was not intervention for its own sake though. The political project was a programme of interventions designed to create young citizen-subjects who would be prudentialised: that is who would calculate the risks and benefits of any particular course of action and act in ways that avoid negative outcomes. These would be young people who would assess the risks and benefits of, for instance, staying on in education, taking menial jobs, acting in law-abiding ways and make the *correct* calculation, thereby becoming adults capable of fitting into the social and economic landscape of Britain's new place in the world of global (and globalising) consumer capitalism. Being prudentialised, they had only their faulty risk calculations to blame if they did not fit into this new world (see also Kemshall 2008)! In relation to criminal justice policy, this approach clearly underpinned the Crime and Disorder Act 1998 and the creation of a new national youth justice system whose aim was to reduce reoffending by holding more and younger young people to criminal account for their misdeeds. New Labour also placed greater emphasis on more general interventions in younger and younger lives – including presiding over the expansion of youth inclusion and prevention (of criminality) projects, the introduction of a citizenship curriculum targeted at young people and reforms to the key performance targets governing the provision of general welfare for children and young people (see *Every Child Matters* (DCFS 2003) and *Youth Matters* (DCFS 2005)).

These policy initiatives had the effect of fragmenting the catch-all subject position of 'child' or 'youth' of previous generations and creating new ways of differentiating young people and holding them responsible for their own fate. Take, for instance, the youth justice reforms. Young people coming into youth justice were to be assessed according to the risk they posed of reoffending and sentences and programmes of interventions were designed that related to the severity of risk. Local authorities were held responsible by central government for demonstrating how they were identifying and working with new categories of 'troublesome' youth, including those 'at risk' of being 'at risk' of offending. The point here is that the lives into which local authorities were intervening were, arguably, no different than prior to New Labour's election. What was different was that these lives were now categorised by children's and youth services and youth justice as being a particular type of life that required a particular type of intervention. New subjects of regulation were created. The economic, social and wider conditions which shaped their offending, however, were left unaddressed.

Where sex was concerned the same drive to create new categories in need of regulation and intervention characterised dramatic changes to law and policy that marked the first seven years of New Labour.

The reforms drew directly upon two decades of (often feminist) research about sex, prostitution and sexual violence. The raft of reforms included: the *Safeguarding Children Involved in Prostitution* (DH and HO 2000)[4] which was rapidly followed by a *National Plan for Safeguarding Children Involved in Commercial Exploitation* (DH 2001). Shortly afterwards, the Sexual Offences Act 2003, criminalised (for the first time in UK history) the 'commercial sexual exploitation' of a child (that is, someone under the age of 18 years old), the facilitation of purchase of sex from someone under the age of 16 years old and all sexual activities with someone under the age of 16 years old or between individuals less than 16 years old. The Home Office published *Paying the Price* (HO 2004) and *Tackling Street Prostitution* (Hester and Westmorland 2004) which formed the basis of *A Coordinated Strategy on Prostitution* (HO 2006) which inaugurated a new system for dealing with prostitution that became known as 'enforcement plus support'. In 2007, the government published its first *UK National Action Plan on Tackling Human Trafficking* (HO 2007) that included the categories of 'internal trafficking' and child victim of trafficking. In the main, these documents addressed themselves to the responsibilities of local authorities and police constabularies in identifying, assessing and managing the various problems of prostitution and sexual exploitation.

In ten years, then, there was a significant shift in the official construction and regulation of prostitution from solely focusing on women who caused a criminal nuisance to one whose effect was to add to that a seemingly endless catalogue of 'newly' discovered victims and vulnerable people (children abused through prostitution, victims of human trafficking, child victims of human trafficking, vulnerable women who needed the compulsion of enforcement, plus support, to 'exit' prostitution, young people who are sexually exploited) and 'newly' discovered categories of offenders: coercive men, exploiters, traffickers, sex abusers, predatory child sex abusers.

Safeguarding reforms: the incorporation of CSE into CSA and the creation of new subjects of regulation

The discourse of CSE as a form of CSA emerged with the splitting of services for young people involved in commercial sexual exchanges from those of adults. This split created new organisational and institutional arrangements which then generated their own knowledge base about the challenges of working with young people and sexual exploitation – including challenges presented by the policies – which in turn then shaped new constructions of what 'the problem' was that needed addressing.

By the end of 2004, redefining young people's involvement in prostitution and commercial sexual exploitation as a child protection issue had an effect on the organisation of services at the local level and the types of services available to young women. In the first years after *Safeguarding Children Involved in Prostitution* (DH and HO 2000), local level voluntary sexual health outreach projects found themselves having to confront the statutory powers (and responsibilities) of child protection legislation and agencies. In practice, this meant that such organisations became less confident that they could, as a matter of course, guarantee the level of anonymity and confidentiality to the young people with whom they worked, or indeed to adopt the same harm minimisation approach they had with adults. The challenge, it seemed, was that statutory social services and police constabularies operated with different understandings of risk, need and protection (see Phoenix 2002, 2012). At the local level, this unresolvable contradiction in working methods became the rationale for the creation of an entirely new set of specialist child welfare and protection oriented services.[5] The result was new services that established ways of working with young people involved in commercial sexual exchanges that prioritised the statutory child protection concerns of social services and the police (including in the early days, the desire to place young people in secure accommodation in the name of protection) (see Phoenix 2002). The working practices and issues of these new organisations were shared by a new network, the National Working Group (www.nwgnetwork.org), which established a network of agencies, organisations and professionals interested in this area of practice and policy. The longstanding work with children who were affected by sexual exploitation undertaken by major charities (such as The Children's Society, Barnardo's and the NSPCC) hitherto described through a number of different headline titles (going missing, sexually abused, impacted by prostitution, sexually exploited) became commissioned services to address the 'new' categories of 'abused' as explained earlier.

The effect of this expansion was the creation of new professional knowledge that constituted the new subject of intervention (child victim of sexual exploitation) and discussed the challenges of working with this 'newly emerging' category of victims. So, for instance, many agencies reported that the realities of young people's experiences and what they could do about these realities simply did not fit into the new policy framework. They reported that young people's experiences of exchanging sex for economic reward were far more complex, varied and informal than the policies assumed. Young people were swapping sex for (loosely defined) economic reward, such as drugs, alcohol or accommodation (Pearce et al 2003). The policy framework invoked simple notions of victimhood and agency whereas the experience of service providers and professionals lead them to argue that there were very complex issues around what consent and coercion meant (Melrose 2002, Melrose and Barret 2004). Part of the new professional knowledge was also that CSE, for many young people, was shaped by the force of necessity (Phoenix 2002), and that rather than being wholly and archetypically 'victims' many young people demonstrated high levels of resilience and managed the risks they encountered in active ways (Thom et al 2007). Thinking about the wider social context, new professional knowledges also developed about the links between CSE and violence in relation to gangs (Firmin 2011).

This new professional knowledge was framed loosely by social work discourses of protection, tutelage and intervention. This meant that the common starting point was the implicit assumption that the 'problem' that they were addressing was distinct from and unrelated to prostitution. Indeed, as others have noted, foundational to the new discourse of CSE was a complete rupture of the link between it and prostitution. This rupture was embedded within the very definition of 'the problem'. What defines involvement in prostitution is consent. Where that involvement is exploitative, coercive or violence, then that involvement is, by definition, abuse. Hence, CSE is *conceptually* distinct. Thus to suggest a link to prostitution is to deny that young people are abused in these sexual exchanges.

A decisive moment came with the Department for Children, School and Families *Safeguarding Children and Young People from Sexual Exploitation: Supplementary Guidance* (DCFS 2009). This guidance defined sexual exploitation in the following way:

> Sexual exploitation of children and young people under 18 involves exploitative situations, contexts and relationships where young people (or a third person or persons) receive 'something' (for example, food, accommodation, drugs, alcohol, cigarettes, affection, gifts, money) as a result of them performing, and/or another or others performing on them, sexual activities...In all cases, those exploiting the child/young person have power over them by virtue of their age, gender, intellect, physical strength and/or economic or other resources. Violence, coercion and intimidation are

common, involvement in exploitative relationships being characterised in the main by the child or young person's limited availability of choice resulting from their social/ economic and/or emotional vulnerability. (DCSF 2009:10)

With that, the problem that policy and agencies were to address was not young people's involvement in prostitution but rather the much more generalised category of risky, abusive, exploitation sexual relationships and behaviours. At least in terms of official discourse, sexual exploitation was by definition not prostitution. It was now its own special category of age-related problems of pathological, inappropriate, abusive forms of sex that involve young people.

The effect has been that sexual exploitation is now completely subsumed within the dominance and hegemony of social work professional discourse about child abuse. By 2017, most specialist services dealing with CSE have been incorporated into statutory social services who hold a near monopoly on the provision or commissioning of services. Expertise about 'the problem of sexual exploitation' has become the sole preserve of the professional knowledge base of social work. In 2017, the Department for Education formalised this by explicitly defining CSE as 'a form of child sexual abuse' (DfE 2017:5) and by adding that:

[it] can be difficult for those working with children to identify and assess. The indicators for child sexual exploitation can sometimes be mistaken for 'normal adolescent behaviours'. It requires knowledge, skills, professional curiosity and an assessment which analyses the risk factors and personal circumstances of individual children to ensure that the signs and symptoms are interpreted correctly and appropriate support is given. (DfE 2017:6)

With that, the targets (or subjects) of social work expertise in this area are sexual relationships and behaviours of young people defined as 'at risk'. The net of social work governance and regulation (as well as liability) has been widened (see also Melrose 2013). Professional social workers have become those *exclusively* authorised to speak the Truth about CSE. To put it more prosaically, they become the professionals who are, at least officially, seen as qualified to assess and manage it and as the responsible agencies for addressing it – a responsibility which also brings with it the realities of professional liability 'should things go wrong' (see Armitage et al 2016). At the risk of repetition, the 'it' that is now the preserve of social work is not young people's involvement in commercial sexual exchanges (or prostitution) but rather the risky, potentially abusive, sexual relationships of young people. The subjects of intervention have shifted from young victims of CSE to, potentially, any young person who displays any of the risk factors and/or whose general behaviour departs from what is considered 'normal adolescent behaviours'.

Conclusion: why we still need to talk about prostitution

By way of concluding this chapter, I want to offer some thoughts on possible implications of the unchallenged assumptions on which our practices concerning CSE rest and from there move on to why I think it is still important to talk about young people's involvement in prostitution. I have not discussed the problems that exist in implementing the broad definition that has been adopted for sexual exploitation as it is the subject of much discussion elsewhere.

One of the key effects of erasing 'youth prostitution' is that it is no longer possible to talk about how economic necessity and poverty may shape the sorts of choices girls and young women (and indeed boys and young men) make in relation to sex. Yet, we also know that sex is nevertheless an economic commodity. Creating a policy and regulatory framework based on notions of child abuse does not and has not altered that empirical reality. Thus prostitution remains a plausible option as it always has done for young women, or young men, with few other means of economically resourcing themselves. This is particularly true in the context of austerity Britain where services and support for young people have been dramatically cut and young people's social and economic security lacks stability and predictability.

This discursive erasure – the unsayability of young people in prostitution – can have devastating consequences when it comes to what we do in the name of justice. To date, there has been no change in criminal law that stops the arrest, prosecution, conviction and punishment of a young person over the age of criminal responsibility (that is, 10 years old) for prostitution-related offences. If for no other reason, we must continue to be concerned about young people's involvement in prostitution. More, an unchallenged discourse of CSE as a form of CSA leads to an unchallenged assumption that justice for victims is provided through prosecution of offenders. Yet, nearly 50 years of robust empirical research into the prosecution of sexual offences tells a woeful tale of what this means for women (regardless of age) living in societies structured by profound economic and gender-based inequalities. Attrition rates for sexual offences are the highest of all offences with successful prosecution of rape numbering around 10 per cent and for CSA being less than 16 per cent. At every stage in the process, extra-legal factors, such as the 'believability of the victim', stereotypes of female sexual chasteness, sexist rape myths and so on, become determining factors in whether a case proceeds and how it is adjudicated (see Temkin 1995; Starmer 2014; Hohl and Stanko 2015). Indeed, research has shown that young women's experiences of the criminal justice system is re-traumatising and undermining (Beckett et al 2016). Women (young or adult) in prostitution are seen as the least believable of all victims of sexual offences because of the way that the discourse of prostitution works to imply consent to whatever happens afterwards. So, against the laudability of social work discourse are the realities of legal practice and discourses that trade in the absolute binaries of 'guilty', 'not guilty', 'victim', 'offender' and do so in ways that are shaped by gender-based structural inequalities, stereotypes of female chastity as indicating blamelessness and ideologies of male sexuality in which violence is turned into 'natural' sexual urges gone wrong. We need to talk about young people in prostitution because we need a frame of reference in which to address the question of what *justice* in the context of the harms of commercial sexual exchange means and how it can be achieved.

For those readers who feel that this chapter has lead us to an impossible place and suggest that bringing 'prostitution' into the debate might undermine what is deemed as current good practice, I will leave the final words to Foucault:

> My point is not that everything is bad, but that *everything is dangerous*, which is not exactly the same as bad. If everything is dangerous, then we always have something to do. So my position leads not to apathy but to a hyper- and pessimistic activism. I think that the ethico-political choice we have to make every day is to determine which is the main danger. (Foucault 1983:231)

Notes

1   The term discourse analysis can refer to any study of language and discourse from textual analysis to linguistics. Within the social sciences the term refers to a variety of different methodologies and epistemological stances that all take language as their starting point. When studying social policies, there is also 'critical discourse analysis' which is slightly different to Foucauldian discourse analysis. For a discussion of the differences please see Fairclough (2013).

²   One of the challenges of talking about the commercial exchange of sex is that the language we use is over-burdened with meaning. There are no politically neutral terms. Prostitution and prostitutes are seen as being normative, implying moral taint and/or imposing a political position that assumes, *a priori* that such work is always and already violence. The terms 'sex work' and 'sex workers' are seen as less stigmatising and acknowledge that sex work is an economic choice for adults. In this chapter, however, I use the term 'prostitution' and 'prostitutes' specifically. The term 'prostitution' denotes a social institution, regulated through criminal justice, comprised of a variety of relationships (between those selling and buying sex, including agencies and organisations working with those individuals, or third parties such as pimps and/or minders or managers as well as any other individuals). 'Prostitute' refers to the subject of regulation within that institution.

³   See Edwards (2002) for a discussion of the sexist ideologies that are permissive of an approach whereby those who sell sex are policed and not also those who buy it.

⁴   I am not reviewing the reforms of policy and practice that took place in the first decade of the twenty-first century. Please see Melrose (2002, 2013) and Melrose and Barrett (2004).

⁵   It is important to note that what was happening during the late 1990s in the run up to SCIP (*Safeguarding Children Involved in Prostitution*) (DH and HO 2000), was complex. Several sexual health outreach organisations ran subprojects specifically for young people – see for instance the Leeds Genesis project. There were even projects set up through Barnardo's that worked with sexually exploited young people – see for instance Barnardo's BASE in Bristol or SECOS in Middlesbrough. What is interesting to note is that these services also worked with child protection police officers and social services. In many senses, what they offered was not particularly different to contemporary working practices. However, at the discursive level, the issues, challenges and problems faced by the young people with whom these projects worked, as well as the young people themselves, were not constituted as a specific type of social problem, requiring specialist (social work) regulation and intervention. There were no broader 'subjects' of governance. There were only local individual young people whom these projects sought to help in their own particular ways and as guided by the funding they received.

References

Armitage, V., Kelly, L. and Phoenix, J. (2016) 'Janus-faced youth justice work and the transformation of accountability', *The Howard Journal of Crime and Justice*, 55(4): 478–495

Balfour, R. and Allen, J. (2014) *A Review of the Literature on Sex Workers and Social Exclusion*, London: UCL Institute of Health Equity

Beckett, H., Warrington, C., Ackerley, E. and Allnock, D. (2016) *Children's voices research report. Children and young people's perspectives on the police's role in safeguarding: a report for Her Majesty's Inspectorate of Constables*, Luton: University of Bedfordshire

Church, S., Henderson, M., Barnard, M. and Hart, G. (2001) 'Violence by clients towards female prostitutes in different work setting', *British Medical Journal*, 322: 524–525

Clarke, J. and Newman, J. (1997) *The Managerial State*, London: Sage

DCFS (Department for Children, Schools and Families) (2003) *Every Child Matters,* CMND 5860, London: The Stationery Office

DCFS (Department for Children, Schools and Families) (2005) *Youth Matters*, London: The Stationery Office

DCFS (Department for Children, Schools and Families) (2009) *Safeguarding Children and Young People from Sexual Exploitation*, London: HM Government

DfE (Department for Education) (2017) *Child Sexual Exploitation: Definition and Guide for Practitioners*, London: HM Government

DH (Department of Health) and HO (Home Office) (2000) *Safeguarding Children Involved in Prostitution. Supplementary Guidance to Working Together to Safeguard Children*, London: HM Government

DH (Department of Health) (2001) *National Plan for Safeguarding Children from Commercial Sexual Exploitation*, London: The Stationery Office

Edwards, S. (2002) *Sex and Gender in the Legal Process*, London: Blackstone

Fairclough, N. (2013) *Critical Discourse Analysis: The Critical Study of Language* (2nd edn), Abingdon: Routledge

Foucault, M. (1983) 'On the genealogy of ethics: An overview of work in progress', Afterword, in H.L. Dreyfus and P. Rabinow (eds) *Michel Foucault: Beyond Structuralism and Hermeneutics* (2nd edn), Chicago, IL: University of Chicago Press.

Foucault, M. (1988) 'Practising criticism', in L. Kritzman (ed) *Michel Foucault: Politics, Philosophy, Culture*, London: Routledge

Garland, D. (1996) 'The limits of the sovereign state', *British Journal of Criminology,* 36(4): 445–471

Garland, D. (2002) *The Culture of Control*, Oxford: Oxford University Press

Hester, M. and Westmorland, N. (2004) *Tackling Street Prostitution: Towards a Holistic Approach*, London: Home Office Research, Development and Statistics Directorate

Haines, K. and Case, S. (2015) *Positive Youth Justice: Children First, Offenders Second*, Bristol: Policy Press

Hardy, K. and Kingston, S. (2016) *New Sociologies of Sex Work*, London: Routledge

Henriques, J., Hollway, W., Urwin, C., Venn, C. and Walkerdine, V. (1984) *Changing the Subject: Psychology, Social Regulation and Subjectivity*, London: Routledge

Hohl, K. and Stanko, E. (2015) 'Complaints of rape and the criminal justice system: Fresh evidence on the attrition problem in England and Wales', *European Journal of Criminology*, 12(3): 324–341

Home Office (HO) (2004) *Paying the Price: A Consultation Paper on Prostitution*, London: The Stationery Office

Home Office (HO) (2006) *A Coordinated Strategy on Prostitution*, London: The Stationery Office

Home Office (HO) (2007) *National Plan on Tackling Human Trafficking*, London: The Stationery Office

Kemshall, H. (2008) 'Risk, rights and justice: Understanding and responding to youth risk', *Youth Justice*, 8(1): 21–37

Kinnell, H (2013) *Violence and Sex Work in Britain*, London: Routledge

McKeganey, N.P. and M. Barnard, M. (1996) *Sex Work on the Streets: Prostitutes and their Clients*, London: Open University Press

Melrose, M. (2002) 'Labour PAINS: Some considerations of the difficulties in researching juvenile prostitution', *International Journal of Social Research Theory, Methodology and Practice*, 54: 333–352

Melrose, M. (2013) 'Twenty-first century party people: Young people and sexual exploitation in the new millennium', *Child Abuse Review*, 223: 155–168

Melrose, M. and Barrett, D. (2004) *Anchors in Floating Lives: Interventions with Young People Sexually Abused Through Prostitution*, Ware, Lyme Regis: Russell House Publishing

O'Neill, M. (2001) *Prostitution and Feminism: Towards a Politics of Feeling*, London: John Wiley and Sons

Pearce, J.J., Galvin, C. and Williams, M. (2003) *It's Someone Taking a Part of You: A Study of Young Women and Sexual Exploitation*, London: Jessica Kingsley Publishers

Phoenix, J. (2001) *Making Sense of Prostitution*, Palgrave: London

Phoenix, J. (2002) 'Youth prostitution policy reform: New discourses, same old story', in P. Carlen (ed) *Women and Punishment: The Struggle for Justice*, Uffculme: Willan Publishing

Phoenix, J. (2012) *Out of Place: The Policing and Criminalisation of Sexually Exploited Girls*, London: The Howard League for Penal Reform

Starmer, K. (2014) 'Britain's criminal justice system fails the vulnerable: We need a victims' law', *Guardian*, 3 February, www.theguardian.com/commentisfree/2014/feb/03/britain-criminal-justice-system-victims-law-public-prosecutions

Temkin, J. (1995) *Rape and the Criminal Justice System*, London: Routledge

Thom, B., Sales, R. and Pearce, J.J. (eds) (2007) *Growing Up With Risk*, Bristol: Policy Press

Weedon, C. (1987) *Feminist Practice and Poststructuralist Theory*, London: Blackwell Publishing

4

Contextual Safeguarding: theorising the contexts of child protection and peer abuse

Carlene Firmin

Introduction

When young people are sexually harassed or assaulted by their peers they experience an intrusion and, in varying ways, are harmed (Turner and Ormrod 2008; Barter 2009; Firmin 2017a). To this extent peer-violence is abuse. The absence of adequate protections from (sexual) abuse is considered a breach of a child's rights – and as such, as a 'child protection issue', requires a statutory intervention (UN 1989; DfE 2018b). In response, a number of countries have established child protection systems that invariably seek to reduce the likelihood of abuse and increase safety through intervention with, or support to, families (Corby et al 2012; Parton 2014). Yet peer abuse rarely occurs within families and therefore sits beyond contexts that are overseen, or influenced, by child protective services (Firmin 2017a; Barter 2009; Smallbone et al 2013). In short: child protection systems have developed to protect children who experience abuse within families, or by adults connected to their families – while peer abuse, which is also a child protection issue, largely manifests within peer relationships which themselves form in school, community and online contexts that exist beyond traditional child protection systems. In this chapter, the extra-familial dynamics of peer abuse are presented against the familial parameters of child protection. Analysed through the constructivist structuralist concepts offered by Pierre Bourdieu (1992), cumulative data from a multi-study programme into extra-familial abuse provides a roadmap towards identifying the components of a contextual account of, and response to, peer abuse. Through this process, it is possible to bridge the gap between the field of child protection and the social fields of peer groups by theorising and testing a new approach to extra-familial child protection – Contextual Safeguarding. In so doing the chapter explains a framework through which peer abuse can be both perceived, and responded to, as a child protection issue.

The theory: constructivist structuralism – social field, capital and habitus

The findings of this chapter have been produced by examining peer abuse and child protection systems through a lens of Bourdieu's Constructivist Structuralism (Bourdieu 1992). According to Constructivist Structuralism there is a reflexive relationship between structure and agency. The agency of individuals (habitus) is informed by the social rules at play within a range of environments (fields), and these same environments (and the rules at play within them) are shaped by individual action. Social fields are distinguished by their sphere of influence, and individuals may navigate a range of social fields at any given time – such as their peer groups, their families and other social contexts. In addition, Bourdieu recognises fields of practice and behaviour – such as the field of education – of which the rules are informed and enforced by a range of structures, institutions and practice.

According to Bourdieu individuals draw upon four types of capital – social, cultural, economic and symbolic – to engage with the rules of any given social field to achieve status. The desire for status is such that some individuals will engage with social rules even if it is to their detriment – a process Bourdieu called symbolic violence.

Sociologists have drawn upon these concepts to explore young people's experiences of violence in intimate relationships (Powell 2010) and street gangs (Pitts 2013) – evidencing the ways in which young people may display behaviours which reinforce the ability of others to exploit them, as these behaviours are in keeping with the wider status-quo or rules at play within peer groups, school or neighbourhood communities.

Background: extra-familial dynamics of peer-on-peer abuse

Young people's exposure to abuse within their peer relationships increases as they move from early childhood into adolescence (Barter 2009; Hackett 2014; Sidebotham et al 2016). During this time young people have an increased: desire for autonomy (Coleman 2011; Hanson and Holmes 2015); ability to form relationships independently of parental supervision or selection and; opportunity to spend social time in community contexts (Sidebotham et al 2016). This combined sense of growing independence occurs at a time of biological changes associated with emotional regulation, motivation by short-term (rather than long-term) gain and a limited ability to utilise consequential thinking (Casey et al 2008; Coleman 2011). As a result, adolescence is a time in which individuals navigate community and peer contexts with a new sense of freedom and autonomy while being particularly emotionally and socially vulnerable in those settings.

Meta-reviews of serious case reviews in the UK have demonstrated that during adolescence risk of significant harm shifts from familial to community contexts for a number of young people (Firmin 2017b; Sidebotham et al 2016). This is not to say that young people no longer experience abuse within families – in fact neglect is thought by some to peak during this period (Gorin and Jobe 2013; Hanson and Holmes 2015; Ofsted 2018). Rather, community risks to which younger children are rarely exposed, such as gang-affiliation, abuse in intimate relationships, sexual and criminal forms of exploitation, street-based substance abuse, become a feature in the school, neighbourhood and online contexts that some young people navigate. Many of these issues occur within their peer relationships – for example, a third of child sexual exploitation cases in the UK are thought to be peer-on-peer rather than examples of adults abusing children (MOPAC 2018). In some instances of peer abuse young people will experience severe acts of physical harm including rape and murder (Losel and Bender 2006; Barter and Berridge 2011; Firmin 2017b). The social and psychological impacts of peer abuse have also been documented – and the cumulative impact that such experiences can have on young people's access to education, their mental health and their involvement in offending. Considering this evidence base, safeguarding professionals, researchers and policymakers are increasingly recognising that peer abuse can cause significant harm to young people and as such is a child protection issue (Turner and Ormrod 2008; Barter 2009; BBC 2015; Hanson and Holmes 2015; DfE 2018a). This is despite it often occurring in public/community contexts (rather than private/familial contexts) and being perpetrated by other young people (rather than parents, carers or professionals with a duty of care).

While it causes significant harm and is therefore arguably a child protection issue – peer abuse is not an issue to which many child protection systems were ever designed to respond. Like many other parts of the western world, in the UK the notion of child protection (and social work) is relatively young (Corby et al 2012; Parton 2014) and was introduced to provide a mechanism through which the state could intervene with families who were failing to protect, or actively causing harm to, their children. The systems and operating model designed to meet this purpose, therefore, are intended to either improve levels of safety and care within families or remove children from familial settings in which they cannot be kept safe. As will be explored later in this chapter, this has taken the form of referral, assessment and intervention models that are primarily focused on parenting and broader cultural practices that view protection as starting and ending with action taken by parents. In terms of safeguarding young people from peer abuse, therefore, the child protection system is limited in intention, design and function: for example – it could assess and intervene with the parents of a young person who is being sexually abused by peers at school despite this not reaching the context in which abuse occurred. It is such a tension/limitation that this chapter explores. When one theorises about peer abuse by exploring the extra-familial dynamics of the issue, it brings to the fore a fundamental mismatch between the location and perpetration model of the abuse in question verses the location and perpetration model to which the child protection system has influence and reach. Therefore, stating that peer abuse is a child protection issue which safeguarding professionals must address is insufficient for protecting young people from it – the child protection system requires a radical cultural and procedural transformation if professionals are to be equipped to act upon such a statement.

Methodology

This chapter takes a cumulative approach to theory development – drawing upon the findings from multiple studies into peer abuse and safeguarding practices conducted from 2011 to 2018. It explores the challenges of using traditional models of child protection to safeguard young people from extra-familial risk. All studies form part of the ongoing Contextual Safeguarding research programme at the University of Bedfordshire in which researchers are working alongside practitioners to interrogate and develop safeguarding approaches to address abuse within extra-familial contexts.

Study overviews

The studies drawn upon for this chapter are as follows:

- 19 reviews of cases into peer abuse from 2008 to 2016 across 12 local authority areas in England (both rural and urban). Cases were reviewed in four phases – nine were reviewed from 2011 to 2014, a further nine were reviewed in 2015 and a final one in 2016. In total the cases featured 216 young people, and included instances

66

of murder (n=3), severe physical injuries (n=5), rape and other forms of contact sexual offences (n=9), online sexual exploitation (n=2), physical abuse within intimate relationships (n=3), and all involved a multi-agency response from professionals;

- audits of responses to peer abuse within 14 local authority areas in England (both rural and urban) in two phases. The first 11 were audited from 2013 to 2014 and a further three were audited in 2016. Audits included reviews of local strategic documents, observations of multi-agency meetings, focus groups with professionals and young people and summary case reviews;

- action research to develop responses to extra-familial risk within 11 local authority areas who engaged in the audit programme outlined earlier. Actions were conducted from 2014 to 2016 and featured practitioners working alongside researchers to identify and test opportunities to engage with the social rules at play within peer, school and community settings when responding to peer abuse;

- an examination of the personal, familial and contextual profiles of 49 young people, across four local authority areas in London, referred into children's services or youth offending services for having displayed harmful sexual behaviour towards another child or young person. Information was drawn from a contextual assessment framework – designed by researchers and completed by practitioners when holding multi-agency meetings to discuss young people who were the subject of the referral;

- a qualitative study of the enablers and barriers for preventing harmful sexual behaviours between young people at schools (including further education colleges, alternative and special school provisions) (2016–2018). Data was collected from seven schools in four local authority areas (both rural and urban), and from the safeguarding partnerships operating in those local authority areas. Within-schools researchers: reviewed policies and procedures relevant to behaviour, safeguarding and equalities; observed practice (including the start and end of the school day, lessons and transition between classes); reviewed 'behaviour incident logs' to identify how responses to harmful sexual behaviour were recorded; and held focus groups with staff and students. This approach was mirrored within each local authority where researchers reviewed relevant policies and procedures, reviewed case example to consider partnership working with schools when a case was referred, observed multi-agency meetings and held focus groups with professionals;

- an action research study in the London Borough of Hackney to create a Contextual Safeguarding system within their children and families service. The study commenced in 2017 and runs until March 2020. It involves the research team being embedded within a local practice team, working alongside professionals to use the theoretical and empirical evidence base for Contextual Safeguarding to reform and test child protection practices for responding to risk outside of the family home.

Data collection methods

These studies used a range of methodological approaches to data collection that have been designed, and continue to be developed, by the research team. Primary approaches include:

- Contextual case review: the completion of a case review template – drawing data from social care, policing, education and other relevant multi-agency paperwork to build an account of an incident and professional response. The case review template is split into three sections – the incident and the individual young people involved; the nature of the contexts associated with the individuals involved (homes, peer groups, schools and neighbourhoods); the response – actions taken, their target (individuals/contexts), and their outcomes.
- Observation: using observation templates designed to capture the nature of conversation at multi-agency professional meetings, documenting the issues that were discussed, the actions agreed upon by professionals and their approach to describing/assessing the risks faced by young people.
- Strategic document content analysis: qualitative analysis of published strategic documents to assess the extent to which consideration is given to the extra-familial dynamics of abuse, the nature of adolescent development and the interconnected challenges faced when responding to abuse in community, school or peer contexts.
- Focus groups: using a semi-structured interview schedule to complement the aims of any given study, and in line with agreed ethical approvals, an opportunity to discuss local responses to different forms of peer-on-peer abuse – as perceived by young people or professionals. Interactive methodologies employed at times including the use of vignettes to explore responses to incidents, as well as colour-coding maps of areas or buildings to identify where young people feel safe and/or vulnerable.
- Side-by-side learning and co-creation: Researchers spending time physically situated alongside practitioners who are developing

extra-familial models of safeguarding practice. Researchers provide theoretical and empirical evidence which is applied by practitioners in the design/delivery of assessment and intervention. These approaches are then reviewed against the research base for Contextual Safeguarding in reflective workshops to capture the learning during implementation for evidencing the practical reality of contextual operating models.

With the exception of the Contextual Safeguarding project in Hackney, the detailed methodologies and findings from all of these studies are published elsewhere (Firmin et al 2016; Firmin 2017a; Firmin 2017b; Lloyd et al 2017). In this chapter they are brought together for the first time to consider what they offer cumulatively for advancing how we theorise about peer abuse and the most effective ways to safeguard those affected by the issue. The emerging learning from the work in Hackney is also published for the first time, and provides the most current source of knowledge for considering the practical, structural and cultural consequence of seeking to reform child protection to better engage with the extra-familial dynamics of peer abuse.

Ethics and limitations of the dataset

All studies in the research programme have received approval from the two-stage ethics procedures at the University of Bedfordshire. All studies that collected data in local sites received further oversight from local area research steering groups, and all case reviews were delivered under, and reported to, local safeguarding board governance structures. In-keeping with the ethical requirements for the programme, no information is published from any study which would lead to the identification of a young person, family or professional – with learning from case reviews combined to create composite examples where necessary for anonymity preservation.

   In keeping with the programmes commitment to ethical publication it is also critical to acknowledge the limitations posed by the data presented within this chapter. All studies are limited by the fact that they examine abusive incidents and professional responses of which they were made aware. There may be other examples of abuse or practice in any given site that were not the subject of an observation or case review – and no study used a sampling approach intended to capture a statistically representative sample of reviews or observations. These limitations are managed by a) considering the cumulative knowledge amassed over multiple years and projects (rather than reviewing findings in isolation), and b) presenting and discussing findings with reference to wider international evidence on the nature of peer abuse and/or the limitations of child protection systems. For the purposes of this chapter the data from these studies is used to demonstrate and extend how we theorise about child sexual abuse, and for these purposes the evidence base, and approach to analysis, is well-suited and proportionate.

Analysis: theoretical framework for cumulative learning

The Bourdieusian social concepts of field, habitus and capital, as well as symbolic violence, have provided the theoretical foundations for analysing both the nature of peer abuse and professional responses to the issue within the research programme. In every study outlined earlier, researchers have sought to identify the extent to which processes, practices and interventions change the rules at play within social fields in which young people experience peer abuse; and consider what this means for service design and development.

In this chapter the learning from across these studies has been further extended using this same Bourdieusian framework. Re-analysing the data through the concepts of field, habitus and capital it is possible to conceive of 'family' and 'peer group' as two distinct social fields – with differing sets of social rules in which differing forms of capital present value. Using this lens it is possible to theorise about the distinct practice and policy structures that have influence over the rules at play within these two social fields and what this means for safeguarding young people at risk of peer abuse. While our child protection system is designed to change the rules at play within families, peer abuse is informed by the rules at play within peer groups. In order to avoid peer abuse being perceived as a matter beyond the reach of social work a system is required that can engage with the differing social fields that inform abusive behaviours. The remainder of this chapter works through this theoretical exploration to build the bases of a contextual account of peer abuse and safeguarding practices, before considering the cultural, structural and practical reform required to make that conceptual narrative a reality.

Findings

The learning from the studies outlined earlier can be disaggregated into three distinct, but connected, themes which communicate the contextual nature of peer abuse, and the required response. First, the conceptual intentions and practical parameters of child protection will be presented – acknowledging that the system was introduced to safeguard young people abused by parents (or adults connected to their parents), and the legal framework, institutions, practices and language which characterise that system are aligned with these parameters. Second, the peer groups and relationships in which young people encounter peer abuse sit outside of that aforementioned system – and the rules at play within peer relationships are not assessed or governed by frameworks, institutions or practices that are familiar to child protection. Third, and finally, therefore a Contextual Safeguarding system offers a bridge to address the divide between the field of child protection and the fields associated with peer sexual abuse. Extending and reframing key concepts (particularly language and structures) that are familiar to child protection processes, has provided the initial steps to creating a system that is equipped to address abuse regardless of the context in which it manifests. Action-research to operationalise the approach has helped to illuminate how the system needs to adapt to address the social conditions in which peer abuse occurs as well identify and work with the individuals affected by it. Considering this process of cumulative learning and system design provides the foundations for discussing the cultural, structural and practical reform required to safeguard young people from peer abuse.

Safeguarding young people in the field of the family

Like in many western countries, England's child protection system is relatively young. Emerging around the late 1800s (Corby et al 2012), it was created to protect children who faced abuse by those who had primary responsibility for them. The Children Act 1989 cemented the formal, structural and procedural parameters for the system that we have today – providing the legislative foundations for social work practices that could intervene to keep young people safe when either a) they were abused by a parent or carer or b) their parent or carer did not have the capacity to keep them safe from abuse (Corby et al 2012; Parton 2014; Lloyd and Firmin in press). The work of social workers as the principal actors in this system, supported by partnerships with the police, health and other services, has been further articulated through *Working Together to Safeguard Children* (DfE 2018b). This document – which is regularly updated and reviewed – provides the guidance and regulatory framework for practicing the intentions of the Children Act 1989 (and legislation that followed in 2004 and 2017) and states that:

All children have the right to a safe, loving, and stable childhood. While it is parents and carers who have primary care for their children, local authorities have overarching responsibility for safeguarding and promoting the welfare of all children and young people in their area. They have a number of statutory functions under the 1989 and 2004 Children Acts, which make this clear, and this guidance sets these out in detail. (DfE 2018b:6)

Through this document social work, and children's social care more broadly, are positioned as the profession that leads the child protection response to vulnerable young people. Furthermore, the mantra that 'safeguarding is everybody's business' is first and foremost realised through the duty placed on a range of services to: refer their concerns about children into children's social care; provide information on children and their families to children's social care when social workers are conducting assessments: and attend meetings that are called by children's social care to discuss, agree or review a plan designed to reduce the risk of abuse.

The emphasis on both the role of the social worker (to lead and coordinate the response) and the target of their concern (the child and their family) is further enshrined in the language, structures and tools that are outlined in this statutory guidance. The 'Common Assessment Framework' and 'Assessment Triangle' that are used by social workers to assess the level of need that a child is in are both primarily focused on assessing a child and their family. If a child is thought to be at risk of significant harm, then the nature of the enquiries that social workers can make direct other agencies to provide information that they hold about the child and family. And finally, should a 'child protection conference' (a statutory multi–agency meeting to discuss the findings of the assessment) be held to discuss assessment findings and agree a plan, then guidance clearly states that:

Social workers should convene, attend and present information about the reason for the conference, their understanding of the child's needs, parental capacity and family and environmental context and evidence of how the child has been abused or neglected and its impact on their health and development…[and] prepare a report for the conference on the child and family which sets out and analyses what is known about the child and family and the local authority's recommendation. (DfE 2018b:52)

The language used to both describe the social work role and the processes/structures they use, position the child protection system as one designed to intervene with families in order to safeguard young people. Far from being a conceptual set of parameters, data from the studies in question provide multiple illustrations of a practical adherence to this framework.

In all 19 cases that were reviewed social work professionals described through conversation, or displayed through actions, that their role was to assess risk within families or the capacity of parents to be protective – rather than the cause/location of abuse which in most cases was the young person's peer relationships. For example, in the case of a young man who was sexually and physically abused by a group of his peers, he was put on a child protection plan on the grounds of neglect – because his parents had failed to get him to all the medical appointments required to address the injuries that he sustained during the assault. Four of those who abused him were opened to children's social care because they had been remanded in custody, and automatically became 'looked-after' young people by virtue of their incarceration. The two who were not remanded were not allocated a social worker, and case notes routinely demonstrated how social workers of the four who were remanded told families that this was a matter of procedure alone, and that as there were no concerns about parenting there wasn't a more practical role that they would play in reducing the risks faced, or posed, by the young people in question. In a different case, an email debate was recorded between a social worker and sexual health nurse – the nurse wanted social care to conduct an assessment of the risks being faced by an 11-year-old girl who disclosed that she was being sexually exploited by a group of 14–15-year-old boys. Social care stated that as the abuse was not being perpetrated by a family member (or someone connected to the family) this was a 'policing matter' only and social work did not have a role in reducing risk.

Such narratives were reinforced during practice observations in action research studies, where social work interventions offered in response to allegations of peer abuse primarily consisted of 1:1 support and advice to the young person who had been abused, and family intervention intended to equip families to support young people who had been abused by, or abused, their peers. Interventions to engage with the peer group dynamics associated with the abuse, or with the environmental factors that characterised such behaviours, were not considered as part of the child protection response. When it was felt that case work with young people and families was not relevant to the risks that were faced in communities and peer groups by young people, observations in all 14 sites featured examples of social workers stating that the referrals made by other services had not 'reached a threshold' for a social care intervention.

In essence the conceptual and practical limitations of England's child protection have been borne out across these studies intended to understand and enhance local responses to peer abuse. As depicted in Figure 4.1, families are recognised as existing within communities/neighbourhoods. However, the services/professions intended to reach into families – such as social care and health visitors – are positioned to engage with the homes, but not the wider environmental dynamics in which those homes are located.

The risks that may manifest in the neighbourhoods in which families, and their homes, are located, however, are the responsibility of community safety, policing, transport, housing and other statutory, as well as private and voluntary/community services. The field of child protection cannot reshape the neighbourhoods which families are navigating (and in which peer abuse may occur) and instead are focused on creating safety in the home environments of which they, and families, have some influence.

Figure 4.1: Relationships between social fields and statutory structures

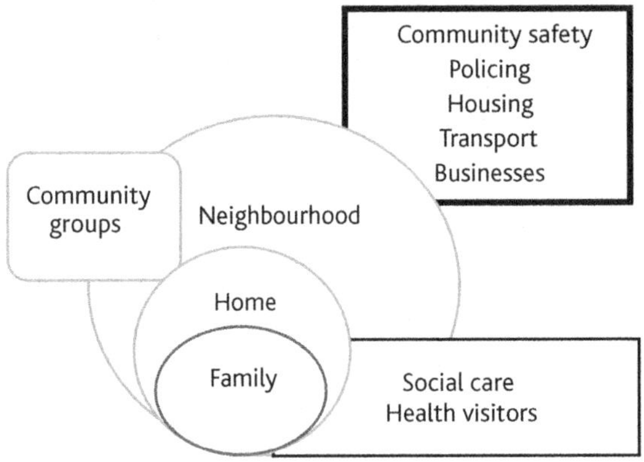

Safeguarding young people in the social field of their peer group

As outlined earlier, adolescence is a time in an individual's development when peer relationships are of increased importance. Within the social field of their peer group young people achieve status – and an ability to engage with the rules at play in any given peer group is important when navigating this social hierarchy. When conducting case reviews, researching responses to harmful sexual behaviours in schools and examining the profiles of young people who had sexually harmed peers in groups, a consistent and cumulative narrative emerged in the dataset about peer group influence, dynamics and impact.

When studying young people's experiencing of relationship abuse, Corr et al described abuse as a 'collective endeavour' among some peer groups (Corr et al 2012); young men supported, encouraged and actively policed the extent to which each other were able to control the behaviour of partners (particularly online). This shared and collective component of abuse, in which the social norms of peer groups bled into young people's intimate relationships and the abusive behaviours they displayed individually and as a group were present across all three studies referenced earlier. Young people who sexually abused peers in groups (n=24), were more likely to share harmful attitudes towards women and girls with peers than those who abused younger children alone. Data within case reviews illustrated processes through which young people who had followed other peers during abusive incidents assumed leadership roles over time and influenced others to sexually and physically harm peers:

> Josh [who had been following the leadership of Micah up until that point] directs Sally, 'Walk up the stairs or I'll beat you up,' and told her, 'Pull them down before I kick you in the head.' (Case 1: Exerpt from witness statement following a multiple perpetrator rape)

Through this process young men were able to demonstrate their loyalty to group norms, perform a hyper-sense of masculinity to their peers, and achieve peer status through this process. In cases where young women were also involved in initiating or facilitating peer sexual assaults, they were provided with an opportunity to align themselves with their male peers, assume an identity of those who had 'control' and thereby avoid peer victimisation.

A fear of social isolation often appeared to drive these behaviours within case reviews and when assessing the profiles of individuals who had sexually abused peers – practitioners believed that young people were motivated by a sense of belonging to a group, particularly one with status; and in community or school contexts where they feared violence this was even more pronounced. In one case reviewed a young man who had physically and sexually assaulted a male peer alongside his peer group stated that he had wanted to be friends with the boy who led the assault as he had been bullied in the past.

He thought that if he aligned himself with this group the bullying would stop and he would get acceptance. But by engaging in the norms of that group he became embroiled in increasingly harmful and abusive behaviours.

Such accounts from case reviews were reinforced by young people who were focus group participants in the study on harmful sexual behaviour in schools. A fear of social isolation was said to not only fuel peer abuse, but also prevented wider peer networks from intervening or seeking help from professionals or trusted adults – 'snitching' as it was referred to also demonstrated a move away from peer norms and would lead to a loss of social status and therefore belonging:

> I think one of the biggest problems is that there's this whole idea that if you tell someone, you're a snake, you're a snitch. That's this really negative view that you can get. (FG YP, Site Z)

> Like, if a Year 7 went to the teacher and told them off, he probably would get a lot of Year 9s going, 'Why are you snitching?' Because people saying you're a snitch and that is a big thing in the school ... Because, like, they don't want to, like, be bullied... If they see something, yeah, that they weren't supposed to see, then, like, they tell of that person that's in their class, then they're going to be called a snitch. (FG YP, Site Y)

Peer group dynamics, associated peer abuse, are evident across the dataset of this research programme and yet sit completely outside of the parameters of traditional child protection systems. The social fields of peer groups are largely ungoverned spaces without a formal institution or system in place intended to respond when they pose a risk to young people – in the way that the child protection system can do for families. Furthermore, young people's peer groups are largely shaped by young people themselves and therefore, in one sense, function independently of any adult oversight – parental, professional or otherwise – at least during adolescence (Gardner and Steinberg 2005; Nickerson and Nagle 2005; Coleman 2011).

There are, however, structures, systems and fields that peer groups navigate which do inform their behaviours, norms and activities – and these are managed by adults. First, 'anti-social' behaviour displayed by young people has been responded to via community safety frameworks in England and Wales – and much of this has been presented as disrupting problematic group behaviour. Through anti-social behaviour orders, policing led policy created civil mechanisms to prevent individuals who are thought to be causing harm from associating with one another or from congregating in public places (CPS, nd). The use of non-association clauses within community behaviour orders or bail conditions imposed on young people were evidenced within the cases reviewed. In fact, where peer relationships were considered a concern in 12 of the 19 cases reviewed, attempts to disrupt these dynamics were firmly framed within policing and community safety frameworks.

Second, many peer relationships form and storm within school environments, and the cultural norms in these spaces have been found to inform the nature of the peer relationships within them (Messerschmidt 1994; Frosh et al 2002; Ringrose et al 2011; Lloyd 2018). As noted earlier, young people reported the influence that the social rules within school had on their decision-making in terms of challenging or normalising incidents of peer abuse. Professionals who participated in the same study however indicated that schools, and partnerships, responded to these dynamics of peer influence via school sanctions if at all. Therefore, the challenges of peer influence and peer pressure was conceptualised as a behaviour problem, and the policies for addressing harmful sexual behaviour, for example, where available, were largely framed within approaches to behaviour management, as opposed to safeguarding, in schools.

In this regard, therefore, social fields of peer groups appeared inextricably connected to young people's experiences of peer abuse across multiple studies, and yet compared to families they appear either largely unregulated and outside of child protection systems, or informed through a behaviour management/enforcement lens as opposed to one concerned with safeguarding. When peer relationships are brought to the fore, the ability of child protection structures to engage with, and reduce risk in, the fields that inform peer abuse are evidently insufficient.

Contextual Safeguarding: protection across fields

If peer abuse is largely informed by the social field of peer groups, and the child protection system has been designed to inform the field of families – how do we bridge the gap? Through action research initiatives between the research team and local authority children's services departments it has been possible to gradually build and test a Contextual Safeguarding system. The detailed workings of such a system remain in the development, but the studies upon which this chapter is built provide an indication of the conceptual components of a child protection system that is equipped to reach into all fields connected with peer abuse.

There are two key elements of existing child protection practice that require reform through a Contextual Safeguarding lens:

1. expanding the test of 'capacity to safeguard' beyond parents;
2. building mechanisms for including peer, as well as family, relationships into assessment processes.

As noted previously, the traditional child protection system is concerned with either abuse that is caused by a parent/carer or occasions where a parent does not have the capacity to protect their child from abuse. Peer abuse sits within the latter category – but in all likelihood, parents will never be able to control the likelihood of their child being sexually abused by their peers at school, in the community or online, as they do not have reach into these spaces. There are services that do, however – such as those who run schools, parks, libraries, retail outlets, transport hubs and other young people themselves. Therefore, a Contextual Safeguarding system would ask questions of the capacity of all those potential partners informed by the location in which the abuse has actually occurred. So, if a young person was sexually abused by peers in school then the capacity of the school leadership, pastoral care and others students to create a safer and protective school environment would be in question (rather than the capacity of the parent of the child who was abused in school). Or if a number of incidents of peer abuse had occurred in a park – those who manage the park such as gardeners, park wardens, community policing, detached youth workers, and those who use the park such as other local residents (adults and young people) would be those engaged in a process of increasing guardianship and safety in the park. Such an approach more formally endows a larger network of individuals and institutions with a role in safeguarding the welfare of young people.

Child protection assessments feature 'genograms' as a matter of course – maps of families drawn up by social workers to identify protective and risk factors in a child's familial relationships and opportunities to increase safety through secure attachments. With a Contextual Safeguarding system a similar approach could be taken to mapping a young person's peer relationships – considering risks and protective factors within them and identifying opportunities to increase a young person's safety through the support of their friends.

From 2013 to 2016 the practical realities of building the two earlier components into responses to peer abuse were tested in 11 local authority areas. Through 18 specific actions professionals tweaked safeguarding practices to include consideration of peer groups (and the school and community settings in which those peer groups functioned), including:

- amending a referral form for schools who wanted to move young people to different schools following incidents of peer abuse (Site X);
- collecting information on peer relationships when receiving sexual exploitation referrals into children's social care (Site B);
- profiling risks of peer abuse with reference to the schools, peer groups and public locations where it was known to occur (as opposed to simply recording the demographics of those involved). (Sites A and X).

Through this process significant practical, procedural and legislative questions emerged about the grounds upon which school leaders, those who worked in public spaces, residents and peers could be compelled to act in response to contextual concerns. Furthermore, once attempts were made to formally include reference to peer relationships into social care referrals and assessments, questions emerged about the ethics and legality of doing so – did such an approach contravene data protection? And if a child was named as a peer of a young person already open to social care did they also have to be opened to the service and their parents informed?

The fact that such questions came to light demonstrated the fact that the system, as it stood, was ill-equipped to engage with and change the extra-familial dynamics of peer abuse. As a result, in addition to the questions posed, the action research process surfaced answers about what a child protection system would need to be capable of in order to address contextual dynamics of peer abuse.

Such a system would be made up of four domains (Figure 4.2) that ensured that: the child protection system targeted the social conditions of abuse (and sought to change the rules within contexts that created those conditions) be they in parks, schools, peer groups or high streets; cases of abuse within communities and schools were framed, and therefore perceived, as child protection as opposed to community safety issues; partnerships between social workers and schools, business leaders, transport providers and others who had reach into the contexts of concern and could therefore deliver contextual intervention plans;

Figure 4.2: Four domains of Contextual Safeguarding

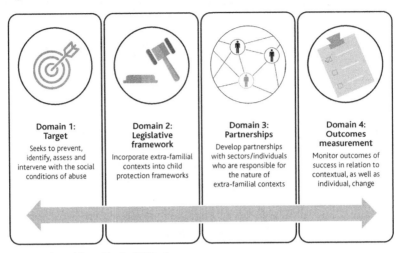

Domain 1: Target	Domain 2: Legislative framework	Domain 3: Partnerships	Domain 4: Outcomes measurement
Seeks to prevent, identify, assess and intervene with the social conditions of abuse	Incorporate extra-familial contexts into child protection frameworks	Develop partnerships with sectors/individuals who are responsible for the nature of extra-familial contexts	Monitor outcomes of success in relation to contextual, as well as individual, change

Source: Adapted from Firmin 2017c: 6

and that the success of interventions could be measured by a change in the rules at play within the contexts in which abuse had occurred, as opposed to a change in the behaviour of individual children who still had to navigate harmful, and unchanging, social fields.

Practically applying these four domains required a whole-systems change process within children's services and in 2017 one local authority in England began that process. Building upon action research activity to introduce elements of contextual practice into an otherwise child and family focused child protection model, this systems-change exercise has sought to create a child protection system that bridges the fields of families and peers. In the first year a pilot to respond to a school referral through a Contextual Safeguarding model was initiated. The participating school was an opportune selection – one which was keen to participate and learn from the process. Using, but expanding, traditional child protection functions, a lead social worker worked through the four domains of the Contextual Safeguarding model (Table 4.1) to assess the relationship between the school and peer group affected by CSE.

This pilot illustrated a significant shift in the approach of social work in this site. Historically, individuals within this peer group may have been referred separately into the local child and family service, and with their parents, been subject to assessment and intervention to reduce their risk of sexual abuse – without affecting change, or even considering the relevance of – the social conditions of the school in which this peer group spent their time. The Contextual Safeguarding

Table 4.1: Pilot outcomes by Contextual Safeguarding domains

Domain 1	Target the social conditions	Conducted an assessment of the social conditions of the school and particular year group in which one peer group was being affected by sexual exploitation.
Domain 2	Use child protection frameworks and structures	A social worker led the assessment, and sought to identify risks and strengths within the school environment as they would a family. A context conference, in place of a child protection conference, was held, chaired by an independent reviewing officer. A plan was built on the findings of the assessment and from the conference overseen by the social worker.
Domain 3	Partnerships	Key partners in delivery of the plan were the school, community safety partnership, the youth service and young people themselves, through the delivery of bystander intervention to address harmful attitudes towards women and girls displayed by the year group.
Domain 4	Outcomes	The school will use their behaviour incident logs and a student survey to measure whether the intervention plan reduces young people's reported experiences of peer-sexual abuse and harmful attitudes within school and whether safety in school and confidence in staff increases.

model that was utilised ensured that the subject of the assessment and intervention could be the school and peer group where the concerns were developing and, through this process, areas in the community where young people also felt unsafe were identified (and mechanisms put in place to begin to respond to these issues). This is the closest an area has come to offering a system-wide response that bridges the gap between the field of child protection and the social fields of peer groups affected by peer abuse.

Discussion and conclusion

Conceptualising peer abuse and child protection systems in the way presented in this chapter signifies a paradigm shift in how safeguarding is conceived and practised. Cultural, structural and practical reforms are required (Figure 4.3) for such an approach to be embedded into any regional or national responses to child sexual abuse.

Culturally, one has to consider the widely held belief in many western contexts that safeguarding is primarily a parenting function, and that parental responsibility and capacity can be assessed abstracted from the social contexts in which a family lives or the additional environments in which children spend their time. While a narrative

Figure 4.3: Culture, structure and practice of existing child protection system

of 'you need to look at the parents' to understand why a child's behaviour persists, we will remain unable to develop and implement child protection systems that view parenting with reference to peer, community and other social influences.

Aligned to this are the child protection structures which translate these cultural narratives into systems. Structural reform of child protection frameworks is required to ensure that those who manage, or have reach into, spaces where young people experience abuse are also held responsible for the nature of those contexts. And finally, assessment frameworks, intervention models and the partnerships that are used to reduce risk all require practical reform. If social workers remain focused on the assessment of, and intervention with, families as the means to addressing all forms of abuse, then the interventions required to reduce risk within peer groups, schools and community settings will continue to be absent from child protection responses. Instead interventions with peer groups, schools and public places, need to be delivered in partnership with educationalists, youth workers, those who manage housing, licensing and lighting and who become guardians of intervention practices (Figure 4.4).

While substantial evidence has been generated on the contextual dynamics of peer abuse, far more studies are required to operationalise, test and practically realise the opportunities and challenges of Contextual Safeguarding systems. The data presented

Figure 4.4: Culture, structure and practice in a Contextual Safeguarding system

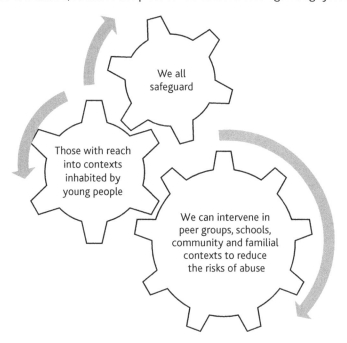

in this chapter provides the theoretical foundations, and initial results, for contextualising child protection responses to peer abuse. Through evidencing this model more extensively in the UK and in other geographical settings practical reforms can be realised – and provide an evidence base upon which to build alternative policy structures. Such structural and practical reform also has the potential to inform the necessary debates about parental responsibility, statutory interventions and sexual abuse prevention that are required to enable a culturally favourable climate for Contextual Safeguarding models. While the relationship between practice, structure and culture is unlikely to be as linear as presented here, the three are interwoven and interdependent cogs in the wheel of contextualising child protection and preventing peer abuse.

References

Barter, C. (2009) 'In the name of love: Partner abuse and violence in teenage relationships', *British Journal of Social Work*, 39: 211–233

Barter, C. and Berridge, D. (2011) *Children Behaving Badly? Peer Violence Between Children and Young People*, Chichester: John Wiley and Sons

BBC (2015) *School Sex Crime Reports in UK top 5,500 in Three Years*, www.bbc.co.uk/news/education-34138287

Bourdieu, P. (1992) *An Invitation to Reflexive Sociology*, Chicago, IL: University of Chicago Press

Casey, B., Getz, S. and Galvan, A. (2008) 'The adolescent brain', *Developmental Review*, (28(1): 62–77

Coleman, J. (2011) *The Nature of Adolescence* (4th edn), Abingdon: Routledge

Corby, B., Shemmings, D. and Wilkins, D. (2012) *Child Abuse: An Evidence Based of Confident Practice* (4th edn), London: Open University Press

Corr, M.L., Gadd, D., Butler, I. and Fox, C.L. (2012) *From Boys to Men: Phase Two Findings,* Manchester: University of Manchester School of Law

CPS (Crown Prosecution Service) (nd) *Anti-social Behaviour Orders Legal Guidance*, www.cps.gov.uk/legal-guidance/anti-social-behaviour-orders-conviction-asbos

DfE (Department for Education) (2018a) *Keeping Children Safe in Education, Consultation Response*, London: DfE

DfE (Department for Education) (2018b) *Working Together to Safeguard Children*, London: DfE

Firmin, C. (2017a) *Abuse Between Young People: A Contextual Account*, Oxon: Routledge

Firmin, C. (2017b) 'Contextualizing case reviews: a methodology for developing systematic safeguarding practices', *Child and Family Social Work*, 23(1): 45–52

Firmin, C. (2017c) *Contextual Safeguarding; An Overview of the Operational, Strategic and Conceptual Framework*, Luton: University of Bedfordshire

Firmin, C., Curtis, G., Fritz, D., Olatain, P., Latchford, L., Lloyd, J. and Larasi, I. (2016) *Towards a Contextual Response to Peer-on- Peer Abuse*, Luton: University of Bedfordshire

Frosh, S., Phoenix, A. and Pattman, R. (2002) *Young Masculinities: Understanding Boys in Contemporary Society*, Basingstoke: Palgrave

Gardner, M. and Steinberg, L. (2005) 'Peer influence on risk taking, risk preference and risky decision making in adolescence and adulthood: An experimental study', *Developmental Psychology*, 41(4): 625–635

Gorin, S. and Jobe, A. (2013) 'Young People who have been maltreated: Different needs – different responses?', *British Journal of Social Work*, 43(7): 1330–1346

Hackett, S. (2014) *Children and Young People with Harmful Sexual Behaviours*, Totnes: Research in Practice

Hanson, E. and Holmes, D. (2015) *That Difficult Age: Developing a More Effective Response to Risks in Adolescence*, Totnes: Research in Practice

Lloyd, J. (2018) *Beyond Referrals Webinar 4: Responding to HSB in Schools,* www.contextualsafeguarding.org.uk/en/publications/beyond-referrals-levers-for-addressing-harmful-sexual-behaviour-in-schools

Lloyd, J. and Firmin, C. (in press) 'No further action: Contextualising social care decisions for children victimised in extra-familial settings', *Youth Justice*

Lloyd, J., Firmin, C. and Fritz, D. (2017) *Contextual Safeguarding audit toolkit*, https://contextualsafeguarding.org.uk/audit toolkit

Losel, F. and Bender, D. (2006) 'Risk factors for serious and violence antisocial behaviour in children and youth', in A. Hagell and R. Jeyarajah-Dent (eds) *Children Who Commit Acts of Serious Interpersonal Violence: Messages for Best Practice*, London: Jessica Kingsley, pp 42–73

Messerschmidt, J.W. (1994) 'Schooling, masculinities and youth crime by white boys', in T. Newburn and E. Stanko (eds) *Just Boys Doing Business?*, London: Routledge, pp 81–99

MOPAC (Mayor's Office for Policing and Crime) (2018) *A Safer City for Women and Girls: The London Tackling Violence Against Women and Girls Strategy 2018–2021*, London: MOPAC

Nickerson, A.B. and Nagle, R.J. (2005) 'Parent and peer relations in middle childhood and early adolescence', *Journal of Adolescence*, 25(2): 223–249

Ofsted (2018) *Growing Up Neglected: A Multi-Agency Response to Older Children*, London: Ofsted

Parton, N. (2014) *The Politics of Child Protection*, Basingstoke: Palgrave

Pitts, J. (2013) 'Drifting into trouble: Sexual exploitation and gang affiliation', in M. Melrose and J. Pearce (eds) *Critical Perspectives on Child Sexual Exploitation and Trafficking*, Basingstoke: Palgrave Macmillan, pp 23–37

Powell, A. (2010) *Sex, Power and Consent: Youth Culture and the Unwritten Rules*, Cambridge: Cambridge University Press

Ringrose, J., Gill, R., Livingstone, S. and Harvey, L. (2011) *A Qualitative Study of Children, Young People and 'Sexting'*, London: National Society for the Prevention of Cruelty to Children (NSPCC)

Sidebotham, P., Brandon, M., Bailey, S., Belderson, P., Dodsworth, J., Garstang, J., Harrison, E., Retzer, A. and Sorensen, P. (2016) *Pathways to Harm, Pathways to Protection: A Triennial Analysis of Serious Case Reviews 2011 to 2014: Final Report*, London: DfE (Department for Education)

Smallbone, S., Rayment-Mchuhgh, S. and Smith, D. (2013) 'Youth sexual offending: Context, good enough lives, and engaging with a wider prevention agenda', *International Journal of Behavioral Consultation and Therapy*, 8(3–4): 49–54

Turner, H. and Ormrod, R. (2008) 'Just kids stuff? Peer and sibling violence', in D Finkelhor (ed) *Childhood Victimization: Violence, Crime and Abuse in the Lives of Young Poeple*, New York: Oxford University Press, pp 92–101

UN (United Nations) (1989) *United Nations Convention on the Rights of the Child*, New York: UN

When Kids Abuse Kids (2017) [Film] Directed by J. Gray, London: BBC

5

'Losing track of morality': understanding online forces and dynamics conducive to child sexual exploitation

Elly Hanson

Introduction

It is commonly understood that the internet and digital technologies confer both positive opportunities and risks to children and young people. This chapter is concerned with the latter, specifically exploring how the evolution, design and control of the internet and digital technology have been conducive to child sexual exploitation (CSE) – both CSE involving online elements and that which does not directly.[1] Theorising and understanding this opens up avenues for more effective prevention and intervention.

Because CSE closely entwines and overlaps with other harms, such as familial sexual abuse, sexist sexual objectification and sexual harassment, this chapter is also relevant to understanding the influence of technology on these problems. Indeed, one argument made here is that online factors have amplified CSE in part via their influence on 'lesser' issues such as harassment and objectification. These may contribute to CSE by implicitly reinforcing harmful gender norms and signalling permission (Thomae and Pina 2015), while also being pernicious in and of themselves, their impact akin to a dripping tap.

Numerous utopian and dystopian visions have been projected onto the continuing evolution of digital technology (Naughton 2012). What these visions often have in common is a sense of inevitability, and this sense is also shared by those claiming the digital future is impossible to predict. This chapter is built on, and evidences, a contrasting position: currently technology (tech) contributes to significant harm to children (notwithstanding its positives), but there is no reason that this has to continue. Technology has been developed by humans, and so humans can further shape it, our understanding of it, and our interactions with it, to now prioritise the rights of children and young people. More specifically, we have agency to make the online space hostile to sexual exploitation.

The rising awareness of the range and severity of problems amplified or brought into motion online (including disinformation and online hatred) is currently provoking calls for fundamental change and a greater determination by governments to more effectively regulate the online space (see for example the UK government's recent Online Harms white paper, and the development of an Age Appropriate Design Code by the Information Commissioner's Office). All of these may lead to increased self-reflection within the tech industry (Zunger 2018). This has created a ripe moment in which to understand and more confidently challenge online practices and dynamics conducive to CSE and to chart new pathways (Davidson and Bifulco 2019).

The central theory presented in this chapter is as follows: the ideology of cyberlibertarianism, combined with organisational social processes and the impact of power, have contributed to tech corporations acting in ways that facilitate CSE (both directly and indirectly), and relatedly, have contributed to online spaces and processes being understood and approached as freer from social and moral concerns than others. Four key (interrelated) online routes to increased CSE are highlighted involving: a) online sex offending psychology, b) the online porn industry, c) online 'escort' agencies, and d) the interaction of social media and gaming platforms with adolescent developmental proclivities. Practice and policy implications of this 'big picture' perspective of online contributors to CSE are explored in the final section.

Some definitions, principles and prevalence data

Child sexual exploitation

As has been discussed elsewhere (Coy in this volume; Beckett and Phoenix; Melrose 2013; Kelly and Karsna 2017), there are fundamental difficulties in defining CSE, in part related to its history within the UK as a replacement for the term 'child prostitution'. Recent guidance from the Department of Education (DfE 2017) states that CSE is a form of child sexual abuse that is distinguishable from other forms by the centrality of exchange dynamics, and the status or financial advantage the abuse affords the perpetrator. However forms of CSA thought not to be CSE also often have exchange or status as part of their dynamics (for example, many cases of intrafamilial sexual abuse), and even if this were not the case, exchange or status dimensions to abuse are often hard to identify, limiting the definition's practical utility and increasing the potential for confusion and 'error'.

When it comes to online abuse, typically 'exploitation' and 'abuse' are used synonymously. For example, research articles variously discussing 'child sexual exploitation material', 'child sexual abuse images', and 'child pornography' are generally discussing the same thing. In the United States, child abuse involving finances is termed 'commercial sexual exploitation of children' (CSEC), a useful term which clearly defines the 'gain' involved in this form of CSE.

For the purpose of this chapter, these definitional issues are not too problematic, because the factors and dynamics discussed here are generally relevant to all forms of child sexual abuse, including what might be thought of as CSE. At the same time particular focus is placed on sexual abuse involving financial exchange; this appears to have been relatively neglected in discussions of online sexual abuse, which is often seen as predominantly the viewing and exchange of child abuse images, and online grooming and blackmail.

Types of online child sexual abuse

Table 5.1 offers a typology of (digital) technology-assisted child sexual abuse.[2] This typology does not include child sexual abuse or exploitation that is only distally influenced by online factors (such as via the influence of online pornography). However, such influence is considered in discussions later in the chapter.

Table 5.1: Ten types of technology-assisted child sexual abuse

Type of online child sexual abuse	Further description and/or example	References for further information
1. Offline abuse shared with and viewed by unknown others via technology	This is often the abuse depicted in child abuse images, also termed 'child pornography' and 'child sexual exploitation material'. *Example*: Sexual abuse perpetrated by a victim's father shared via images and video with others online.	Martin and Alaggia (2013); Mitchell, Finkelhor and Wolak (2005)
2. Abuse (committed via technology or offline) shared with others in the victim's peer group	*Example*: A young person (or persons) filming their abuse of a peer and sharing this with their friends for approval or status, or to shame.	Beckett et al (2013)

(continued)

Table 5.1: Ten types of technology-assisted child sexual abuse (continued)

Type of online child sexual abuse	Further description and/or example	References for further information
3. Sexual images created consensually shared nonconsensually	*Example*: A young person shares images with a romantic partner, the relationship ends and those images are shared by their ex-partner with peers.	Wolak and Finkelhor (2011); Ringrose et al (2012)
4. Live streaming: contact abuse being ordered or directed by those watching online	Perpetrators online direct other perpetrators who are physically with the child to commit abusive acts. *Example*: Individuals in the UK watching and directing live streamed sexual abuse of children by individuals in another country.	NCA (National Crime Agency) (2014)
5. Offline sexual blackmail (imagery as leverage)	Child or young person is abused offline, images are taken and used as leverage in the continuation of the (offline) abuse. *Example*: 'If you tell, I will share this image with your friends and family.'	Gohir (2013)
6. Online sexual blackmail (imagery as leverage)	Sexual imagery of a child or young person is obtained online and then used as leverage in sexual abuse, which may be online, offline or both. *Example*: A child shares a sexual image with a person online; this person (the abuser) then threatens to share this image if the child does not produce further sexual images.	Peachey (2013)
7. Online grooming	This term can include online sexual blackmail, but is more commonly used to describe perpetrators forging a close relationship with a victim online in order to gain the child's compliance in and secrecy around subsequent sexual abuse. *Example*: Perpetrator shows care and interest in young person online who subsequently 'falls in love' and consents to online and/or offline sexual activity despite perpetrator being an adult and/or coercive and/or the young person feeling uncomfortable.	Whittle et al (2015)

(continued)

Table 5.1: Ten types of technology-assisted child sexual abuse (continued)

Type of online child sexual abuse	Further description and/or example	References for further information
8. Offlline or online sexual activity with a child or young person bought online from 'pimps'	People controlling a young person sell sexual activity with her or him using digital technology, for example by advertising them on 'escort' platforms. Both seller and buyer are abusing the young person. When the sexual activity is through technology (eg via webcam) this abuse is similar to the live streaming described as the fourth type of abuse in this table, although will typically involve the buying abuser and victim in direct interaction.	Mazzio (2017); Mitchell et al (2011)
9. Internet-assisted 'child sex tourism'	Offenders using 'sex tour operators' online to organise travel trips to abuse children – these trips are often to countries where protections against child sexual abuse are weaker.	O'Leary and D'Ovidio (2007)
10. Sexual activity bought from a young person online	A person buying and undertaking sexual acts with a young person who has, on their own 'volition', advertised these sexual services online. Typically, the young person has pre-existing vulnerabilities, low self-esteem and constrained choices.	Svensson et al (2013)

Notes:

• Many of these forms of online CSA overlap and frequently co-occur. Distinctions have been made being mindful of victims' experiences – in other words, some forms that might have otherwise been grouped together are separated because the victim experiences are likely to have important differences.

• Exposure of children to online pornography and sexual harassment or solicitations (for example, a person starting up a conversation about sex online) have not been included in this typology, as it was felt that the definition of online sexual abuse would become too wide (while recognising that exposure to such material and comments can be abusive and harmful).

Source: Hanson 2017a: 97–122

'Online', 'internet' and 'digital technology'

For pragmatic purposes, these terms are used interchangeably in this chapter. If a person is online they are using the internet (whether via the world wide web, an app or some other service) and to do so, they are using digital technology. Via smartphones, this technology has brought together communication via online and telephone networks. It is continuing to evolve, creating ever more uses of the internet.

'Both, and'

A dialectic can be thought of as the insights or 'truths' that emerge from keeping together two positions that might otherwise be placed in binary opposition. Dialetics critical to the theories advanced in this chapter are a) *both* individual responsibility on the part of offenders and enablers *and* systemic factors have a part to play in CSE – and they closely entwine; b) *both* children and young people's rights to participate *and* their rights to protection are paramount; and c) *both* adolescent agency *and* adolescent blameless victimisation co-exist, and are most usefully understood together (Hanson and Holmes 2014). The overlap between on- and offline abuse is also emphasised – categories that although merged have often been seen as separate.

Prevalence of technology-assisted CSE

The rise of the internet has enabled a profileration in child abuse image offending, as well as other forms of sexual abuse, such as grooming and sexual blackmail. However, methodologically robust prevalence studies are lacking. The Interpol database of online abuse images contains data relating to approximately 15,000 identified victims and between 60,000 and 70,000 unidentified victims, the majority of whom are pre-pubescent in the images (Moran 2017). Between 100,000 and 590,000 adults in the UK are estimated to have viewed child abuse imagery (Jütte 2016).

Turning to online grooming, a US household telephone survey in 2010 of children aged between 10 and 17 years old found that 9 per cent had received one or more online sexual solicitations that were either from an adult, or, if not, were unwanted (Mitchell et al 2013).

Even less is known about the prevalence of internet-facilitated *commercial* CSE. Jonsson et al (2015) found that 0.9 per cent of boys and 0.6 per cent of girls in a representative sample of Swedish 16- to 22-year-olds reported selling sex online. Mitchell et al (2011) estimated that 8 per cent of arrests in the US for internet child sex offending in 2006 involved financial exchange, with 36 per cent of these involving 'direct offences against victims', that is, the purchase of or profit from either sexual activity with a child or child sexual abuse material (CSAM) produced by an offender. The demographics of the *profiteers* captured in this study, such as high levels of non-sexual offending, differ from those of other sex offender groups and 'suggest more seasoned offenders who are leading or involved with larger, more organized networks of criminals' (p 63). It seems likely that these are pimps involved in wider sexual exploitation of children and adults who are making the most of the internet's affordances for their business.

The perfect storm: cyber-libertarianism, rapid innovation, power and ethical drift

> Civilisation is the process of setting man free from men. (Ayn Rand 1943)

> Technology is not neutral but serves as an overwhelming positive force in human culture…we have a moral obligation to increase technology because it increases opportunities. (Kelly 2010)

People's experiences online are largely mediated by tech corporations. Many of these have not given sufficient priority to the rights of children and young people (Kidron et al, 2018), and one consequence of this has been increased child sexual exploitation. Before providing evidence and examples of this impact, this chapter discusses theories that help us understand *why* this deprioritisation of children's rights and best interests has occurred.

Some might argue that tech-assisted harms can simply be explained by the profit motive: attending to children's rights and best interests may lower financial profits in the short-term, and so in a self-serving fashion, these interests are downplayed, ignored and denied by those who serve to gain the most. This is likely a major part of the picture, but is not satisfactory as a full explanation. In other contexts, people would baulk at increasing their wealth at the expense of increased abuse, and it does not account for governments' comparatively weak regulation of the tech sector (at least up until recently). Alternatively, it might be argued that many of these harms (such as those from pornography) have only recently been substantiated via research, and so they could not be factored into decision-making. Again, this does not satisfy, given that they are all plausible and therefore could have prompted a precautionary, research-first approach along the lines of 'first do no harm'.

I argue here that the libertarian philosophy that has powerfully shaped the internet and perceptions of it, combined with the disruptive innovation enabled by the fundamental architecture of the web, the accruing power of tech corporations, and the processes within organisations that lead to ethical drift within them, have coalesced to produce a perfect storm.[3]

Cyber-libertarianism and disruptive innovation

Libertarianism is a distinct political stance and moral psychology whose guiding principle is the freedom of individuals, in particular from interference by the state. The concern for this 'right' trumps all others: moral values based on altruism, and connection to others, are rejected or downplayed (Iyer et al 2012). Individuals attracted to these beliefs, compared to both conservatives and liberals, tend to have a more cerebral cognitive style and feel less empathy, social connection and interdependence – as Iyer et al (2012) summarise in their large-scale comparison study, 'libertarians have a lower degree of the broad social connection that typifies liberals as well as a lower degree of the tight social connections that typify conservatives' (p 19).

Despite libertarianism being a minority stance across society, it has played an inordinately major part in shaping both economics (championing the 'free market') and cyberspace. To understand its role in the latter we must first appreciate the unique features of the internet, in contrast to other systems and networks.

The internet is a network ideally suited to disruptive innovation, a phenomenon perhaps best captured by Mark Zuckerberg's (2012) exhortation to 'move fast and break things; if you are not breaking stuff, you are not moving fast enough'. This is because, unlike most systems, there is no central control, and it does not aspire to optimise any particular application (Naughton 2012). These features have allowed innovation to progress as fast as inventors can create new uses of the internet, rather than at the speed decided upon by 'controllers', whether governmental or corporate.[4]

The individual 'freedom' therefore afforded by the internet, bound up with absent or ineffectual control by the state, was understandably particularly attractive to those with libertarian leanings from the early days of the internet onwards, disproportionately attracting them to both its development and narration – how it grew and how it was understood. In the 1990s a lot was written about the freeing potential of the internet, and it was constructed as a place that could and should not be bound by the same rules and restrictions governing the rest of life. This 'cyberlibertarianism' (also dubbed the 'Californian Ideology'; Barbrook and Cameron 1996) persists, albeit expressed with more pragmatism and less idealism (Dahlberg 2010) – narrating a dominant discourse for every new iteration of the internet as it stays true to its pattern of disruptive innovation.

The broad idea that 'computerization will set you free' (Golumbia 2013) has now spread extensively into media, government and lay thinking, via its promotion by many who narrate the digital technology sphere, and many with considerable power because of it (see Dahlberg 2010, for example). Assisting this process is the co-option of seductive words and phrases such as 'open', 'opportunity', 'creativity', 'connection' and 'freedom of speech' to champion what is in fact a narrow version of liberty that does not include the 'positive liberty' afforded to people and communities through greater equality and material conditions, and through protection from harm. The 'negative liberty' (Berlin 1958) aspired to by libertarians enables those with some financial power to accrue more and more, enabling corporate oppression and exploitation. By promoting consumerism and 'pacifying modes of existence', and by increasing economic inequality, this results in most people having far less freedom (Golumbia 2013; Dahlberg 2010). Grand abstractions are used to hide these contradictions and, what to most would be, unpalatable aspects.

As a result of this dissemination, many across society at least loosely adhere to a libertarian view of the online world, despite not applying these principles elsewhere and the contradictions that inevitably ensue. For example, in many countries pornography (porn) (whose influence on CSE is discussed later in the chapter) is illegal to sell offline to those under 18 years old, yet online it is freely available to children of all ages – the UK has only recently moved to limit access and is the only country to do so. Similarly, offline in the UK it is illegal to sell pornography containing either adults role-playing as children, real or apparent lack of consent, infliction of pain or lasting physical harm, or threats, humiliation or abuse (BBFC 2014). Online there is a copious amount of such material and there has been no move to restrict access.

Some would argue that the online space is too huge, complex and fast-moving to effectively direct towards prosocial goals and regulate where necessary. Again, there is a contradiction: technological innovation continues apace when it comes to extending highly complex forms of automation and the 'freedom' discussed earlier, but innovation in the service of protecting the rights and welfare of the more vulnerable is deemed impossible to develop or apply, and labelled as naïve wishful thinking.

In short, the moral principles that it is generally wrong to harm others, and right to both protect the vulnerable and move towards greater equality, are relatively absent from libertarian philosophy (Iyer at al 2012; Haidt 2012). As a result, the relative dominance of cyberlibertarian narratives have given permission and encouragement to individuals and corporations to design and evolve online sites, applications and tools without due regard to the protection, welfare and rights of children, and indeed adults. They have also weakened the impetus of governments to regulate in line with these principles, reducing their involvement to pleas to industry to self-regulate. As John Naughton (2018) argues, this represents 'the outsourcing to private corporations of public-interest and free-speech decisions that we would normally expect to be made by democratically accountable institutions'. Such a situation has resulted in various pressing social issues such as the proliferation of fake news, hate speech and online abuse; surreptitious mass data collection; easy online access to child abuse images; easy connections between young people and exploitative persons; and tech corporations' exploitation of young people's developmental proclivities including the 'soft entrapment' of children and young people into social media and gaming (Kidron et al 2018). Sexual exploitation is one of various harms that children and young people are more at risk of as a result.

Beyond cyberlibertarianism and the profit motive, there are other major, interacting contributors to this state of affairs. The fast pace of innovation enabled by the core qualities of the internet[5] contrasts markedly with the slower pace of societal thinking and debate. This means that things can be done that society has not had time to form a collective judgement on or response to. Within this time gap, if enough people take up the new behaviour, system justification psychological processes can take hold, which then influence the societal view. System justification is the tendency to justify something simply because it is part of the status quo: what is perceived as normal is judged to be *acceptable* simply because it is *normal* (Jost et al 2004). Furthermore, there are processes (psychological, social and organisational) that can often operate *within organisations* to pull people away from their moral compasses, and to these this chapter now turns.

Ethical drift within and at the helm of organisations

When people enter into an organisation, they are invited to identify with it, and take on its values and norms. In technology corporations these often emphasise the good of 'freedom', 'connection', 'creativity' (defined in a cyberlibertarian fashion), as well as, of course, company profit. As a consequence, other values such as equality, and protection from exploitation and manipulation are demoted. Value systems are typically conveyed in a variety of explicit and implicit means (for example, what colleagues focus their conversations on), and over time, people can come to internalise them, limiting their exposure and awareness of alternative ways of thinking (Moore and Gino 2013).

Roles and goals can be powerful tools in narrowing people's moral fields of vision, emphasising certain foci of attention at the expense of others (for example, Ordóñez et al 2009). Layering onto this is the diffusion of responsibility people frequently feel when part of an organisation – we can act less ethically when we feel less responsible, as the avoidance of guilt becomes a less salient motivator. Related to this are the natural human proclivities to socially conform and to submit to those higher in (organisational or societal) status and power. Classic psychology studies by Zimbardo and Milgram in the early 1970s (see Bandura 2016), as well as many that have followed, highlight how people can quickly sacrifice moral concerns to social conformity and obedience when these are pitted against one another (see Bandura 2016). Smoothing the way, euphemistic language can help enable unethical behaviour by blurring the harms being wrought (Moore and Gino 2013). An example of this in the tech industry is the use of vague, ambiguous terms such as 'dwell features' to describe tricks and incentives used to manipulate children into greater and more dependent use of various apps and games (Kidron et al 2018).

Much of the psychology outlined earlier would not lead to less ethical behaviour within organisations with strong moral leadership. However, research finds that the power and money often associated with leadership can skew judgement and action away from ethics and towards selfishness, confirming and adding nuance to the old adage 'power corrupts'. Various experimental and naturalistic studies have found that a sense of power can lead people to be less empathic and sensitive, more hypocritical (promoting a self-serving rule for oneself and a different rule for others), and more egocentric (for example, Van Kleef et al 2008; Lammers et al 2010). Power also biases people to see others more in terms of their instrumental value, rather than as fully human (Gruenfeld et al 2008). Similarly, a focus on money can lead people to behave more selfishly and less altruistically (Vohs 2015). These effects may be relevant both to leaders with significant money and power, and to those otherwise working within organisations with high status and worth. All of this means that, in societies that allow for relatively unchecked power and wealth, individuals and organisations with influence are vulnerable to less ethical decision-making than the average person.

The big picture of narratives and dynamics discussed here helps us to understand why many tech companies have acted in ways which have either directly or indirectly facilitated CSE – examples of which are discussed later in this chapter. It also helps to explain why, in interaction, the internet is perceived by many online sex offenders to be a place where their usual morals do not apply, a phenomenon described in brief next.

Online sex offending and perceived freedom

Research suggests that many online sex offenders adopt a libertarian view of the internet which increases the permission they give themselves to offend.[6] Offenders have described the internet seemingly being governed by different rules and norms, clearly boundaried from the offline, and this perspective enables them to develop a new persona that, freed from the ethical codes and social surveillance of the 'real world', can without compunction explore 'taboos'. An offender in Rimer's (2017) anthropological study summarises the perceptions of many in his comments:

> This frontier [the internet] that's just wild and lawless. It's like being, you know, in the Wild West…when you're in that bubble it's like a very strange virtual world that you're in, and, and it becomes, you lose track of time, you lose track of place, but most importantly I think you lose track of morality. (p 41)

Online, offenders may easily find or come across others who, holding similar views of online freedom, celebrate child sexual abuse, argue that it is acceptable, and share CSAM (Prichard et al 2011). These views will likely influence and amplify the individuals' own permission-giving thoughts, and reduce their awareness of the positive values, identity and aspirations that they might hold in other moments. The internet also provides the distance and narratives many offenders may need to escape the empathy for victims that might otherwise inhibit their offending, for example by helping them falsely construct abused children online as 'actors' (Kettleborough and Merdian 2017).

It is important to note the offender's active role in perceiving the online space in this way, and finding many of its offence-facilitating qualities. For example, the demarcation between a 'free' online sphere and a restricted offline one appears to be strengthened by some offenders choosing to view abuse online only using specific computers and only during the night, when the perspective of others may be more easily evaded psychologically (Rimer 2017).

Cyberlibertarianism is also posited to increase CSE offending via its influence on the nature of online content and spaces, most saliently, online pornography and 'escort' services. The role of this online sex industry is now examined, with due attention paid to state responses and omissions.

Online porn and online 'escort' services

People's experiences online are largely mediated by tech corporations, many of which have deprioritised the best interests and rights of children and young people (Kidron et al 2018). This section argues that within this context, online pornography and 'escort' services operate in ways which directly amplify CSE, increasing both the motivation for it and the easy means.

Big Porn and child sexual exploitation

The nature of online pornography[7] is critical to understanding its impact. Klaassen and Peter (2014) analysed the content of 400 of the most popular online pornography films and found that 41 per cent of professional videos[8] depicted violence[9] towards women. Women's responses to this violence were for the most part neutral or positive. Men dominating women were also common, as were women being instrumentalised (that is, used as a sexual object whose own sexual pleasure is not important). A concerning minority of films depicted non-consensual or manipulative sex. 'Teen' is one of the most common search terms on porn sites (Pornhub Insights 2017), and common themes within this genre are cheerleaders and 'girls' in school uniform. Depictions of sex as an expression of love or emotional intimacy are rare. Women and girls are routinely depicted enjoying acts that in reality most would find distressing (for example, one women being penetrated by numerous men sequentially). Pejorative terms for females are frequent (such as 'slut' and 'whore'), as is the labelling of them by their ethnicity (Paasonen 2010). Videos from a range of genres are presented alongside one another, so that users, while sexually aroused, are easily exposed to more taboo-breaking sex than they had first sought (for example, involving family members, aggression or child-like actors). This feature appears central to the porn industry's business model (D'Orlando 2011) and to its negative impact on users.

These features and content help to explain the influence that pornography has on sexual harassment and aggression. Longitudinal studies find that male adolescent pornography usage significantly predicts sexual harassment perpetration over time (Brown and L'Engle 2009; Ybarra et al 2011), and longitudinal, experimental and meta-analytic studies indicate that pornography also increases the risk of adult sexual aggression (Wright et al 2015). It is most likely to contribute to sexual aggression in males who already equate masculinity with dominance (Kingston et al 2008; Malamuth et al 2012).

Pornography seems to contribute to sexual hostility, at least in part, because it develops, strengthens and entrenches certain sexual scripts and conceptions of people, at the expense of others (Wright 2014). It narrates sex as a quest for sexual pleasure via the viewing and use of other people's bodies. Sex is impersonal and other people (generally women) are tools for one's own gratification. In the process of promoting this version of sex (both to be held internally, and perceived in others), other versions of sex are side-lined, such as those that place relational connection (for example, 'chemistry') or intimacy as central. These porn-inspired scripts increase both motivation and perceived permission for sexual coercion; in relation to the former, arousal may become centred on the use of others, and become untethered from reciprocity, mutuality, equality and open communication. Consistent with sexual script theory, research finds that pornography[10] use is linked to sexism, objectified notions of women, and impersonal sexual scripts which demote communication – these in turn are associated with an increased proclivity for sexual coercion (for example, Forbes et al 2004; Peter and Valkenburg 2009; Hald et al 2013; Tomaszewska and Krahé 2016; Wright and Tokunaga 2016).[11]

All of this suggests that pornography is likely to be a potent contributor to the frequent sexual harassment of girls in many adolescent and young adult social groups where sexism and pornography use are common features (Ringrose et al 2012); indeed the links are readily made by young people (Coy et al 2013). And, as noted, 'lower level' sexual hostility, such as the use of words such as 'slut', rating girls on their body parts and sexist sexual jokes, can give implicit permission for abuses such as CSE.

There are also grounds to suspect a major role for pornography in adults' sexual exploitation of children (indeed many CSAM offenders have described it as influential in their pathway to offending, for example, Rimer 2017). Once a person has been inculcated into viewing people on screen as categorised (such as teen or Asian) masturbatory aids, children may be relatively easily integrated as simply another categorised object. Some pornography users describe developing sexual interests that they did not have previously (Wood 2013); this seems to follow from frequent viewing leading users to become desensitised to previously arousing material (D'Orlando 2011), and new 'taboo-breaking' (read: ethical boundary breaking) material being shown during arousal. In short, pornography may both elicit a sexual interest in children, and normalise its enactment.

There is far less research on the content and impact of pornography aimed at gay users; however porn aimed at gay men also appears to promote sex that is impersonal and often involves dominance and submission (Kendall 2011), and so may have similar effects contributing to the sexual exploitation of boys. However, such a hypothesis is more tentative.

The porn industry does not tend to acknowledge its risks and seek to limit these, even though this would normally be expected of an industry whose products can harm (for example, the tobacco or alcohol industries).

Backpage, online 'escort' services, and child sexual exploitation

The online sex industry is a context ripe for child sexual exploitation. In the United States, online classified websites such as Craigslist and Backpage.com have been primary vehicles for the buying and selling of sex, and implicated in facilitating CSE. Backpage appears to have been the most major direct online abettor of CSE, and to have received the most attention. Its story is highlighted here to illustrate how this online sector has contributed to CSE, and also to raise questions about the actions and omissions of governments and justice systems, all arguably influenced by cyberlibertarian ideology.

Up until April 2018, Backpage.com operated as an online advertisement website, with a lucrative business model constructed around sex advertising.[12] In recent years, over 70 per cent of child sex trafficking reports submitted by the public to the central sexual abuse tip-off line in the US concerned Backpage (Souras 2015). Between 2010 and 2018 many survivors of Backpage-facilitated CSE, and/ or their families, came forward to disclose their abuse in the hope of challenging the continued exploitation of children through the site. A common reported modus operandi comprised adolescent girls being identified by pimps, then groomed, plied with drugs and/or terrorised (for example through rape), in turn leading to their entrapment in abuse which comprised rape by consecutive men who had bought them from pimps via Backpage ads – the perpetrators of this CSE therefore being both pimps and buyers.

For many years, lawsuits against Backpage repeatedly failed, mainly due to Section 230 of the US 1996 Communications Decency Act (CDA) which states that providers of interactive computer services will not be liable for content posted through their services by someone else: they will not be treated as its publisher or speaker (Halverson 2018).[13] However survivors and their advocates argued that Backpage was not only tolerating CSE, it was actively facilitating it. It selectively removed from its 'escorts' section postings by victim support organisations and law enforcement sting adverts; it allowed people to post adverts without verified contact details; and it removed meta-data from images, making the identification of victims and perpetrators difficult. Perhaps most disturbingly, if, when reviewing adverts, moderators came across those including terms indicative of child abuse (such as 'Lolita' and 'schoolgirl'), company policy was not to report, but instead, retain the adverts, remove the key indicative terms, and allow their replacement with more subtle, code terms (Kelly 2017).

Events finally took a turn when a Senate investigation in early 2017 concluded that Backpage deliberately facilitated child trafficking for profit. And then, in 2018, the relevant parts of US government approved and endorsed a bill which created an exception to Section 230 of the CDA, removing websites' protection from liability if they knowingly facilitate sex trafficking. This bill was passed despite months of lobbying against it by Big Tech, including by the Internet Association, a trade group representing companies such as Amazon, Google and Facebook. In April 2018 Backpage.com (including its international operations) was finally shut down by US law enforcement.

In the UK, similar legislation has come into force which criminalises websites knowingly facilitating human trafficking. However, not only does there appear to be more debate and reticence about its enforcement, this also looks to be more difficult. Whereas in the US Backpage.com appeared to account for approximately 80 per cent of online sex trafficking, in the UK the industry is thought to be much more diverse (Guilbert 2018).

The journey so far around the role of the online sex industry in CSE gives cause for both optimism and ongoing concern. Acknowledging the role this industry has played and still does is an important and continuing process. As observed by a survivor of British sexual exploitation: 'Technology has created a new age of pimping; it's easy for pimps, profits are lucrative, and the likelihood of being caught is minimal' (Guilbert 2018). As we have seen, this is no less true when it is children who are the exploited. Recent moves to increase the responsibility of tech corporations and demand their moral action around CSE are welcome: an example being the UK government's Online Harms white paper (Gov.uk 2019a). Further steps will likely be assisted by an understanding of the financial gain, ideologies and psychology behind Big Tech's resistance, and the confident articulation of different narratives that emphasise moral values online.

Cyberlibertarianism holding sway combined with the power held by the technology sector, and the ethical drift within it, have arguably led to a situation in which some tech corporations have developed and profited from practices which directly fuel children's sexual exploitation. However, these forces may have amplified CSE just as powerfully in less direct ways; I have already highlighted in the previous section how cyberlibertarian thinking enables sex offenders, and the next section argues that many social media and gaming platforms have exploited adolescent developmental proclivities in ways which too can increase risk of CSE. The common thread that weaves throughout is the departure from a moral stance in which children's rights and best interests are prioritised.

Online features and adolescent psychology

> Young girls generally, of a certain age, who don't have anyone to listen to them, who are alone, who see that their Mums and Dads are disinterested, minding their own business...will naturally think it's good to look for people who seem to be interested and care on the internet. (Victim of online grooming, quoted in Quayle et al 2012:34)

> You feel the need to use social media all the time in order to be social or popular. (14-year-old quoted in Kidron et al 2018:21)

As explored by Coleman in this volume, adolescence is a transformational life stage in which autonomy, identity and self-esteem, intimacy with peers (through friendships and romance), and sexuality all undergo substantial development (Steinberg 2016). To assist in this, adolescents have specific developmental proclivities compared to those younger or older than them – for example, they are more attuned to emotional cues, more likely to take risks, and attach more importance to how they are viewed by their peers (Brown et al 2008; Steinberg 2010). Our focus here is on the ways in which these adolescent tasks and tendencies may interact with features of the internet to increase risk of CSE (often also in combination with cultural norms and sometimes the impact of earlier abusive experiences).[14] One example of this is internet platforms which seamlessly ease young people, acting in line with their desire for social connection and their differential weighting of risk, into connecting with deceptive individuals. In a recent survey of UK 14–24-year-olds (72 per cent of whom were 14–17), 6 per cent of 2008 participants reported meeting an online contact offline and discovering that they were not who they had said they were (McGeeney and Hanson 2017).

A second example concerns adolescent young women's search for others' approval and validation in order to build a positive sense of self (as noted, a key focus for both sexes at this life stage). Social norms (conveyed through various media, and the actions and words of others) teach girls that their status is inextricably bound to perceptions of their physical attractiveness. While social media can help to boost self-esteem (Best et al 2014), when it leads to greater comparisons between one's own and one's peers' perceived attractiveness, it can worsen it (Ferguson et al 2014; Vandenbosch and Eggermont 2016). The combination of feeling unattractive while being (implicitly) told that attractiveness equals significance, can propel girls towards people online who praise their appearance as part of a strategy to exploit them. And it can also push girls to seek this praise through 'initiating' sexually explicit conversation or images. When a girl's self-esteem has already been undermined by earlier childhood experiences, such as neglect or abuse, her need for affirmation is likely to be further heightened, which may lead to more serious or risky attempts to meet it, such as offering sex for money, which is made much easier online (Svensson et al 2013; Jonsson et al 2014; Hanson 2016). More generally, a variety of mainstream social media platforms make it straightforward for children and adolescents to have sexual communication with people whom they have met or become familiar with online, placing no or only minor obstacles in the way of vulnerability meeting exploitation. Young people's consent in these circumstances is constrained and abused (Pearce 2013).

Young people have often been seen as to blame for their exploitation, making 'lifestyle choices' and unthinkingly putting themselves at risk. This victim-blaming may be particularly common in cases of online CSE (Hamilton-Giachritsis et al 2017), where the victim's actions are often more visible than those of the perpetrator, the company hosting the relevant platform, or indeed those who promote conducive social norms. The argument here, that adaptive developmental proclivities and needs interact with societal norms, internet affordances, and, at times, responses to earlier life experiences, to increase vulnerability, offers a challenge to victim-blaming, while also rejecting the alternative narrative often offered, that of a passive victim (Hanson and Holmes 2014). It places attention on the factors that lead to young people's needs being left unmet, and the factors that constrain their actions, encouraging them to strive to meet their needs in the short-term in ways that undermine them in the long-term.

Conclusions and implications for practice

> This is not simply a war of ideas; it is a real struggle over real
> issues with direct impact on real human lives, and unless we
> develop more critical attitudes towards digital technologies
> and in particular toward cyberlibertarianism, we will find
> much more than our 'digital freedom' – whatever exactly
> that is supposed to mean – put at risk. (Golumbia 2013:23)

The central thesis of this chapter is that online features, dynamics and
narratives interact with the psychology of various groups to increase
and change the nature of CSE both off- and online. Cyberlibertarian
ideology has shaped the internet, and our perceptions, use and (under-)
regulation of it, so that it has become a space in social life where unethical
behaviour, including sexual exploitation, has far greater licence and
freedom than offline. Within at least some tech corporations, libertarian
understandings are likely to have blended with organisational social
processes and the blinkering effects of power, money and status to cause
significant ethical drift. This drift coupled with relative inaction by others
such as governments and society (influenced by cyberlibertarianism
and system-justification) has led to the development of online content,
narratives and processes that facilitate child sexual exploitation – the
clearest examples of this being the online pornography industry and
online 'escort' services; other examples include peer-to-peer file sharing
which allow for child abuse terms, the online accessibility of CSAM, the
general sense of the online as a 'bubble', and social media that allow for
anonymous posting and/or seamless connection between young people
and those looking to exploit them. Human agency plays a part in all of
this, and the moral responsibility of those whose actions and omissions
harm others and violate their rights.

At a fundamental level what is required is a paradigm shift in
which a new understanding of the internet is narrated, in which the
aspiration that it will increase freedom is retained, but the version
of freedom aspired to is very different. Notions of 'good freedoms'
should be demonstrably tied to other rights and ethics (such as fairness,
protection, equality and welfare); young people should be able to
enjoy the online, and draw on it in their development, free from
abuse, harassment, prejudice and exploitation. And in the words of
Gail Dines (2017:8), they should 'have the right to author a sexuality
that is authentic and rooted in respect, intimacy and connection'.
These rightful freedoms are contrasted with individuals using their
freedom and power to act in ways which hurt or oppress others.

Aspiring to these freedoms that intersect with other rights and ethics leads to different emphases and actions: concentrations of power are prevented and challenged, rather than encouraged and seen as the de facto result of freedom; regulation and public health initiatives are seen as a duty rather than an embarrassment or last resort; and the myth of online fantasies and actions operating in a vacuum is cast away, in the recognition that we are all interdependent.

In short it is hoped that reflection and understanding of cyberlibertarianism and its influence will enable the increased growth of confident and effective counter-arguments and action. Everyday conversations, campaigns, public pressure on tech corporations through selective use of sites, informed government regulation and its support, can all play a part in this process.

Online industries that significantly harm others should not escape the scrutiny, regulation and public health strategies that would otherwise be expected offline. The advent of age verification to access major online pornography sites should make it more difficult for young people to access it, in turn reducing (while not eliminating) usage and exposure. Next, there should be enforced rules against online content that is already effectively banned offline, such as sexual films with adults role-playing as children, or involving physical harm, humiliation or apparent lack of consent (BBFC 2014). Alongside this, users should be educated on online porn's risks to self and others before using it (analogous to health warnings on cigarette packets) and have mandated 'spaces' to reflect on this. Similar public health strategies, alongside more robust law enforcement, could be applied to online prostitution and escort services. It may be that much of this could be achieved through the new regulation system proposed by the UK government in the aforementioned Online Harm White Paper (Gov.uk 2019a) and an enforced age appropriate design code which prioritises protection from harm as well as children's privacy rights (Gov.uk 2019b).

This accords with what I suggest is a further fundamental principle for practice: positive change will generally follow from people having greater awareness of a) themselves (in particular their values, aspirations, rights and positive identities), b) others (their thoughts, feelings, rights), and c) the invitations of various powers (such as certain corporations and mainstream media) to act against these aspects of ourselves and others. This awareness principle can be applied creatively in many different areas of practice to reduce sexual exploitation and other harms – examples and suggestions of such an approach with the general population, young people and tech corporations are summarised in Table 5.2.

Table 5.2: Examples of self- and other-awareness raising

Group	Example	References or further information
Young people	Personal, social, health education (PSHE) that, through a variety of methods including role-play, discussion and guided self-reflection, supports young people in becoming more aware of their values, aspirations and positive identities. These can act to counter invitations in various parts of society to ignore their values and to buy into identities and narratives (such as traditional gender norms) that can hurt them in the long term. A bedrock of awareness, knowledge and skills teaching can replace the approach of bombarding young people with various risks and harms.	Such an approach fits with the principles of good PSHE promoted by the PSHE Association (2016)
General population	Campaigns that invite people to consider the influence of the online on their behaviour, and encourage them to match their online actions to their 'best selves', inviting moral equivalence between on- and offline. Such campaigns should be informed by the developing literature on effective social norm campaigns.	Such campaigns would usefully follow a recent campaign led by the Home Office and partners aimed at educating young adults about the law regarding viewing sexual images of those aged under 18. Cislaghi and Heise (2018) discuss pitfalls to avoid in social norm interventions.
Tech corporations	Close user involvement, for example panels of young people advising and sharing their experiences with social media companies. Mandatory training that teaches more holistic versions of freedom (that connect to other rights and social goods), and develops ethical decision-making skills.	Wider approaches to combat organisational ethical drift are discussed in Moore and Gino (2013).

Turning to direct work with young people who have experienced CSE or are at risk, practitioners should recognise and harness young people's agency and work collaboratively with them and those around them to help meet their unmet needs, build their positive sense of self, and identify and work towards their deep aspirations.[15] This approach avoids both victim-blaming and victim-passivity narratives, which can often be conveyed implicitly. As an example of implicit blame, in recent research interviewing young people who had experienced sexual abuse (much of it technology-assisted) good PSHE was highly valued and sought after by participants. However, online safety (a part of PSHE) offered as a stand-alone to a victim of online CSE was experienced as blaming and compounded the impact of the abuse (Hamilton-Giachritsis et al 2017).

There is currently more thinking about the online world and its role in our lives than ever before. The time is ripe for new iterations of technology and new relationships with it, which place children and young people's rights, including freedom from exploitation, centre-stage.

Notes

[1]   For theories regarding how online factors affect the *impact* (versus the prevalence and dynamics) of CSE see Hanson (2017a).

[2]   This is a revised version of those that appear in Hamilton-Giachritsis et al (2017) and Hanson (2017a).

[3]   As with any broad social phenomenon, involving numerous groups, organisations and subcultures, there are likely to be a large number of contributory factors. Therefore, this does not aim to be an exhaustive explanation, but a distillation of those factors thought to be particularly germane to this space and sector.

[4]   However, this feature may be in decline with the increasing dominance of a small number of large tech corporations (Naughton, 2012).

[5]   None of this discussion should be taken as arguing that innovation powered by the internet is inherently negative – it has shaped human life in numerous positive ways. The challenge is finding ways to ensure that ongoing innovation is human- versus technology-centred (Carr, 2016).

[6]   This is one of a number of ways in which online dynamics and affordances facilitate sex offending; others (which overlap and interact) include the affordability, anonymity and accessibility of the online world – the Triple A engine of online offending articulated by Cooper (1998) in the internet's early days.

[7]   In this chapter the terms *pornography* and *porn* are used to denote online sexually explicit material involving adults and with some form of commercial element. *Big Porn* refers to the online pornography industry.

[8]   This percentage dropped to 37 per cent when films labelled 'amateur' were also included in the analysis.

[9]   The two most common forms depicted were spanking and gagging (inserting a penis very far into the mouth).

[10] Some of these studies have explored the impact of online pornography specifically, others have considered offline and online porn together.

[11] Some of these studies are cross-sectional; further longitudinal mediation studies are now required to tease out causality.

[12] The California Attorney General's office, based on internal Backpage documents, reported that 99 per cent of Backpage's internal revenue between January 2013 and March 2015 was directly attributable to its 'adult' section (cited in Halverson, 2018). Its founders and CEO each reportedly received bonuses of $10 million in 2014 (Kelly, 2017).

[13] Similar laws exist in other jurisdictions including the UK.

[14] See Hanson and Holmes (2014:20) for a schematic of interacting contributors to CSE, including to risk behaviours, albeit without the role of the internet delineated.

[15] Further discussion of adolescent-centred practice, that understands and works with their agency, can be found in Hanson and Holmes (2014). Also, for discussion of therapeutic work with victims of CSE where there is an online element, see Hanson (2017b), and where there might be risk of further revictimisation see Hanson (2016).

References

Bandura, A. (2016) *Moral Disengagement: How People Do Harm and Live With Themselves*. New York: Worth Publishers

Barbrook, R. and Cameron, A. (1996) 'The Californian ideology', *Science as Culture*, 6(1): 44–72

BBFC (British Board of Film Classification) (2014) *BBFC Guidelines: Age Ratings You Trust*, www.bbfc.co.uk

Beckett, H., Brodie, I., Factor, F., Melrose, M., Pearce, J., Pitts, J., Shuker, L. and Warrington, C. (2013) *'It's wrong ... but you get used to it': A qualitative study of gang-associated sexual violence towards, and exploitation of, young people in England*, Bedfordshire: University of Bedfordshire

Berlin, I. (1958) 'Two concepts of liberty', An inaugural lecture delivered before the University of Oxford, 31 October

Best, P., Manktelow, R. and Taylor, B. (2014) 'Online communication, social media and adolescent wellbeing: A systematic narrative review', *Children and Youth Services Review*, 41: 27–36

Brown, B.B., Bakken, J.P., Ameringer, S.W. and Mahon, S.D. (2008) 'A comprehensive conceptualization of the peer influence process in adolescence', in M.J. Prinstein and K. Dodge (eds) *Understanding Peer Influence in Children and Adolescents*, New York: Guilford Press, pp 17–44

Brown, J.D. and L'Engle, K.L. (2009) 'X-rated: Sexual attitudes and behaviors associated with US early adolescents' exposure to sexually explicit media', *Communication Research*, 36(1): 129–151

Carr, N. (2016) *The Glass Cage: Who Needs Humans Anyway?*, London: Vintage

Coy, M. (this volume) 'What's gender got to do with it? Sexual exploitation of children as a form of patriarchal violence'

Coy, M., Kelly, L., Elvines, F., Garner, M. and Kanyeredzi, A. (2013) *'Sex without consent, I suppose that is rape': how young people in England understand sexual consent*, London: Office of the Children's Commissioner

Cooper, A. (1998) 'Sexuality and the internet: Surfing into the new millennium', *CyberPsychology and Behavior*, 1(2): 187–193

Davidson, J. and Bifulco, A. (2019) *Child Abuse and Protection: Contemporary Issues in Research, Policy and Practice*, London: Routledge

Dahlberg, L. (2010) 'Cyber-libertarianism 2.0: A discourse theory/critical political economy examination', *Cultural Politics*, 6(3): 331–356

DfE (Department for Education) (2017) *Child Sexual Exploitation: Definition and Guide for Practitioners*, www.gov.uk/government/publications/child-sexual-exploitation-definition-and-guide-for-practitioners

Dines, G. (2017) 'Growing up with porn: The developmental and societal impact of pornography on children', *Dignity: A Journal on Sexual Exploitation and Violence*, 2(3): Article 3, https://digitalcommons.uri.edu/dignity/vol2/iss3/3

D'Orlando, F. (2011) 'The demand for pornography', *Journal of Happiness Studies*, 12(1): 51–75

Ferguson, C.J., Muñoz, M.E., Garza, A. and Galindo, M. (2014) 'Concurrent and prospective analyses of peer, television and social media influences on body dissatisfaction, eating disorder symptoms and life satisfaction in adolescent girls', *Journal of Youth and Adolescence*, 43(1): 1–14

Forbes, G.B., Adams-Curtis, L.E. and White, K.B. (2004) 'First-and second-generation measures of sexism, rape myths and related beliefs, and hostility toward women: Their interrelationships and association with college students' experiences with dating aggression and sexual coercion', *Violence Against Women*, 10(3): 236–261

Gohir, S. (2013) *Unheard Voices: The Sexual Exploitation of Asian Girls and Young Women*, Birmingham: Muslim Women's Network UK

Golumbia, D. (2013) *Cyberlibertarianism: The Extremist Foundations of 'Digital Freedom'*, Clemson, SC: Clemson University Department of English (September), www.uncomputing.org

Gov.uk (2019a) Online Harms White Paper, www.gov.uk/government/consultations/online-harms-white-paper

Gov.uk (2019b) 'Age-verification for online pornography to begin in July', www.gov.uk/government/news/age-verification-for-online-pornography-to-begin-in-july

Gruenfeld, D.H., Inesi, M.E., Magee, J.C. and Galinsky, A.D. (2008) 'Power and the objectification of social targets', *Journal of Personality and Social Psychology*, 95(1): 111–127

Guilbert, K. (2018) 'Online sex slavery more complicated in Britain than in the United States with Backpage just the tip of the iceberg', 9 April, London: Thomson Reuters Foundation

Haidt, J. (2012) *The Righteous Mind: Why Good People Are Divided by Politics and Religion*, New York: Vintage

Hald, G.M., Malamuth, N.N. and Lange, T. (2013) 'Pornography and sexist attitudes among heterosexuals', *Journal of Communication*, 63(4): 638–660

Halverson, H.C. (2018) 'The Communications Decency Act: Immunity for internet-facilitated commercial sexual exploitation', *Dignity: A Journal on Sexual Exploitation and Violence*, 3(1): Article 12, https://digitalcommons.uri.edu/dignity/vol3/iss1/12

Hamilton-Giachritsis, C., Hanson, E., Whittle, H.C. and Beech, A.R. (2017) *'Everyone Deserves to be Happy and Safe': A mixed Methods Study Exploring How Online and Offline Child Sexual Abuse Impact Young people and How Professionals Respond To It*, London: National Society for the Prevention of Cruelty to Children (NSPCC)

Hanson, E. (2016) *Exploring the Relationship Between Neglect and Child Sexual Exploitation: Evidence Scope 1*, Totnes: Research in Practice, National Society for the Prevention of Cruelty to Children (NSPCC) and Action for Children

Hanson, E. (2017a) 'The impact of online sexual abuse on children and young people', in J. Brown (ed), *Online Risk to Children: Impact, Protection and Prevention*, London: Wiley, pp 97–122

Hanson, E. (2017b) 'Promising therapeutic approaches for children, young people and their families following online sexual abuse', in J. Brown (ed), *Online Risk to Children: Impact, Protection and Prevention*, London: Wiley, pp 123–142

Hanson, E. and Holmes, D. (2014) *That Difficult Age: Developing a More Effective Response to Risks in Adolescence*, Totnes: Research in Practice, www.rip.org.uk/news-and-views/latest-news/evidence-scope-risks-in-adolescence/

Iyer, R., Koleva, S., Graham, J., Ditto, P. and Haidt, J. (2012) 'Understanding libertarian morality: The psychological dispositions of self-identified libertarians', *PloS one*, 7(8): e42366

Jonsson, L.S., Svedin, C.G. and Hydén, M. (2014) '"Without the internet, I never would have sold sex": Young women selling sex online', *Cyberpsychology: Journal of Psychosocial Research on Cyberspace*, 8(1): Article 4, http://dx.doi.org/10.5817/CP2014-1-4

Jonsson, L.S., Bladh, M., Priebe, G. and Svedin, C.G. (2015) 'Online sexual behaviours among Swedish youth: associations to background factors, behaviours and abuse', *European Child & Adolescent Psychiatry*, 24(10): 1245–1260

Jost, J.T., Banaji, M.R. and Nosek, B.A. (2004) 'A decade of system justification theory: Accumulated evidence of conscious and unconscious bolstering of the status quo', *Political Psychology*, 25(6): 881–919

Jütte, S. (2016) *Online Child Abuse Images: Doing More to Tackle Demand and Supply*, London: National Society for the Prevention of Cruelty to Children (NSPCC)

Kelly, A. (2017) 'Small ads sex trafficking: The battle against backpage', *Guardian*, 2 July

Kelly, K. (2010) 'What technology wants', *Cool Tools*, 18 October, kk.org/cooltools/archives/4749

Kelly, L. and Karsna, K. (2017) *Measuring the Scale and Changing Nature of Child Sexual Abuse and Child Sexual Exploitation*, London: Centre of Expertise on Child Sexual Abuse

Kendall, C.N. (2011) 'The harms of gay male pornography', in M.T. Reist and A. Bray (eds) *Big Porn Inc: Exposing the Harms of the Global Pornography Industry*, North Melbourne: Spinifex

Kettleborough, D.G. and Merdian, H.L. (2017) 'Gateway to offending behaviour: Permission-giving thoughts of online users of child sexual exploitation material', *Journal of Sexual Aggression*, 23(1): 19–32

Kidron, B., Evans, A. and Afia, J. (2018) *Disrupted Childhood: The Cost of Persuasive Design*, London: 5Rights Foundation, https://5rightsframework.com/resources.html

Kingston, D.A., Fedoroff, P., Firestone, P., Curry, S. and Bradford, J.M. (2008) 'Pornography use and sexual aggression: The impact of frequency and type of pornography use on recidivism among sexual offenders', *Aggressive Behavior: Official Journal of the International Society for Research on Aggression*, 34(4): 341–351

Klaassen, M.J. and Peter, J. (2015) 'Gender (in) equality in Internet pornography: A content analysis of popular pornographic Internet videos', *The Journal of Sex Research*, 52(7): 721–735

Lammers, J., Stapel, D.A. and Galinsky, A.D. (2010) 'Power increases hypocrisy: Moralizing in reasoning, immorality in behavior', *Psychological Science*, 21(5): 737–744

Malamuth, N.M., Hald, G.M. and Koss, M. (2012) 'Pornography, individual differences in risk and men's acceptance of violence against women in a representative sample', Sex Roles, 66(7–8): 427–439

Martin, J. and Alaggia, R. (2013) 'Sexual abuse images in cyberspace: Expanding the ecology of the child', *Journal of Child Sexual Abuse*, 22: 398–415

Mazzio, M. (2017) *I am Jane Doe*, Documentary film, 50 Eggs Films

McGeeney, E. and Hanson, E. (2017) *Digital Romance: A Research Project Exploring Young People's Use of technology in Their Romantic Relationships and Love Lives*, London: CEOP and Brook

Melrose, M. (2013) 'Young people and sexual exploitation: A critical discourse analysis', in M. Melrose and J. Pearce (eds) *Critical Perspectives on Child Sexual Exploitation and Related Trafficking*, Basingstoke: Palgrave Macmillan, pp 9–22

Mitchell K.J., Finkelhor, D. and Wolak, J. (2005) 'The internet and family and acquaintance sexual abuse', *Child Maltreatment*, 10: 49–60

Mitchell, K.J., Jones, L.M., Finkelhor, D. and Wolak, J. (2011) 'Internet-facilitated commercial sexual exploitation of children: Findings from a nationally representative sample of law enforcement agencies in the United States', *Sexual Abuse*, 23(1): 43–71

Mitchell, K.J., Jones, L.M., Finkelhor, D. and Wolak, J. (2013) 'Understanding the decline in unwanted online sexual solicitations for US youth 2000–2010: Findings from three Youth Internet Safety Surveys', *Child Abuse and Neglect*, 37(12): 1225–1236

Moore, C. and Gino, F. (2013) 'Ethically adrift: How others pull our moral compass from true North, and how we can fix it', *Research in Organizational Behavior*, 33: 53–77

Moran, M. (2017) 'Online child sexual exploitation: A global problem with a local solution', Talk given at the European Society for Trauma and Dissociation (ESTD) conference, Bern, Switzerland, 11 November

Naughton, J. (2012) *What You Really Need to Know About the Internet: From Gutenberg to Zuckerberg*, London: Quercus

Naughton, J. (2018) 'Theresa May thinks Facebook will police itself? Some hope', *Guardian*, 11 February

NCA (National Crime Agency) (2014) *National Strategic Assessment of Serious and Organised Crime 2014*, London: National Crime Agency

O'Leary, R. and D'Ovidio, R. (2007) *Online Sexual Exploitation of Children*, Leesburg, VA: The International Association of Computer Investigative Specialists

Ordóñez, L.D., Schweitzer, M.E., Galinsky, A.D. and Bazerman, M.H. (2009) 'Goals gone wild: The systematic side effects of overprescribing goal setting', *Academy of Management Perspectives*, 23(1): 6–16

Paasonen, S. (2010) 'Repetition and hyperbole: The gendered choreographies of heteroporn', in K. Boyle (ed) *Everyday Pornography*, Abingdon: Routledge, pp 75–88

Peachey, P. (2013) 'Paedophiles blackmail thousands of UK teens into online sex acts', *The Independent*, 20 September

Pearce, J. (2013) 'A social model of "abused consent"', in M. Melrose and J. Pearce (eds) *Critical Perspectives on Child Sexual Exploitation and Related Trafficking*, Basingstoke: Palgrave Macmillan, pp 52–68

Peter, J. and Valkenburg, P.M. (2009) 'Adolescents' exposure to sexually explicit internet material and notions of women as sex objects: Assessing causality and underlying processes', *Journal of Communication*, 59: 407–433

Peter, J. and Valkenburg, P.M. (2014) 'Does exposure to sexually explicit internet material increase body dissatisfaction? A longitudinal study', *Computers in Human Behavior*, 36: 297–307

Pornhub Insights (2017) *2017: Year in Review*, www.pornhub.com/insights/2017-year-in-review

Prichard, J., Watters, P.A. and Spiranovic, C. (2011) 'Internet subcultures and pathways to the use of child pornography', *Computer Law and Security Review*, 27(6): 585–600

PSHE (Personal, Social, Health and Economic) Association (2016) *Key Principles of Effective Prevention Education*, London: PSHE Association

Quayle, E., Allegro, S., Hutton, L., Sheath, M., Lööf, L. (2012) *Online Behaviour Related to Child Sexual Abuse: Creating a Private Space in Which to Offend. Interviews with Online Child Sex Offenders*, Stockholm: Council of the Baltic Sea States, ROBERT (Risktaking online behaviour, empowerment through research and training) project

Rand, A. (1943) *The Fountainhead*, Indianapolis, IN: Bobbs Merrill

Rimer, J.R. (2017) 'Internet sexual offending from an anthropological perspective: Analysing offender perceptions of online spaces', *Journal of Sexual Aggression*, 23(1): 33–45

Ringrose, J., Gill, R., Livingstone, S. and Harvey, L. (2012) *A Qualitative Study of Children, Young People and 'Sexting': A Report Prepared for the NSPCC*, London: National Society for the Prevention of Cruelty to Children (NSPCC)

Souras, Y.G., Senior Vice President and General Counsel for the NCMEC (National Center for Missing and Exploited Children) (2015) 'Human trafficking Investigation', Hearing before the permanent subcommittee on Investigations of the Senate Committee on Homeland Security and Governmental Affairs. Senate Hearing no 114–179, 114th Congress, 39

Steinberg, L. (2010) 'A dual systems model of adolescent risk-taking', *Developmental Psychobiology*, 52(3): 216–224.

Steinberg, L. (2016) *Adolescence* (11th edn), Maidenhead: McGraw-Hill Education

Svensson, F., Fredlund, C., Svedin, C.G., Priebe, G. and Wadsby, M. (2013) 'Adolescents selling sex: Exposure to abuse, mental health, self-harm behaviour and the need for help and support. A study of a Swedish national sample', *Nordic Journal of Psychiatry*, 67(2): 81–88

Thomae, M. and Pina, A. (2015) 'Sexist humor and social identity: The role of sexist humor in men's in-group cohesion, sexual harassment, rape proclivity, and victim blame', *Humor*, 28(2): 187–204

Tomaszewska, P. and Krahé, B. (2016) 'Attitudes towards sexual coercion by Polish high school students: Links with risky sexual scripts, pornography use, and religiosity', *Journal of Sexual Aggression*, 22(3): 291–307

Van Kleef, G.A., Oveis, C., Van Der Löwe, I., LuoKogan, A., Goetz, J. and Keltner, D. (2008) 'Power, distress, and compassion: Turning a blind eye to the suffering of others', *Psychological Science*, 19(12): 1315–1322

Vandenbosch, L. and Eggermont, S. (2016) 'The interrelated roles of mass media and social media in adolescents' development of an objectified self-concept: a longitudinal study', *Communication Research*, 43(8): 1116–1140

Vohs, K.D. (2015) 'Money priming can change people's thoughts, feelings, motivations, and behaviors: An update on 10 years of experiments', *Journal of Experimental Psychology: General*, 144(4): e86–e93. http://dx.doi.org/10.1037/xge0000091

Whittle, H.C., Hamilton-Giachritsis, C.E. and Beech, A.R. (2015) 'A comparison of victim and offender perspectives of grooming and sexual abuse', *Deviant Behavior*, 36(7): 539–564

Wolak, J. and Finkelhor, D. (2011) *Sexting: A typology*, Durham, NH: Crimes Against Children Research Centre

Wood, H. (2013) 'Internet pornography and paedophilia', *Psychoanalytic Psychotherapy*, 27(4): 319–338

Wright, P.J. (2014) 'Pornography and the sexual socialization of children: Current knowledge and a theoretical future', *Journal of Children and Media*, 8(3): 305–312

Wright, P.J. and Tokunaga, R.S. (2016) 'Men's objectifying media consumption, objectification of women, and attitudes supportive of violence against women', *Archives of Sexual Behavior*, 45(4): 955–964

Wright, P.J., Tokunaga, R.S. and Kraus, A. (2015) 'A meta-analysis of pornography consumption and actual acts of sexual aggression in general population studies', *Journal of Communication*, 66(1): 183–205

Ybarra, M. L., Mitchell, K.J., Hamburger, M., Diener-West, M. and Leaf, P.J. (2011) 'X-rated material and perpetration of sexually aggressive behavior among children and adolescents: Is there a link?', *Aggressive Behavior*, 37(1): 1–18.

Zuckerberg, M. (2012) Letter to investors, www.sec.gov/Archives/edgar/data/1326801/000119312512034517/d287954ds1.htm#toc287954_10; discussed here: https://mashable.com/2014/03/13/facebook-move-fast-break-things/?europe=true

Zunger, Y. (2018) 'Computer science faces an ethics crisis: The Cambridge Analytica scandal proves it', *Boston Globe*, 22 March, www.bostonglobe.com/ideas/2018/03/22/computer-science-faces-ethics-crisis-the-cambridge-analytica-scandal-proves/IzaXxl2BsYBtwM4nxezgcP/story.html

6

Understanding adolescent development in the context of child sexual exploitation

John Coleman

There are many ways of conceptualising the circumstances of those affected by child sexual exploitation. In this chapter consideration will be given to a theoretical framework – lifespan developmental theory – which will assist in shedding light on the processes underlying human development. In the context of this theory there will be a particular focus on adolescence as a developmental stage within the lifespan. The notion of transition will be explored, and this will include reference to puberty, brain development and the variety of social and emotional changes that impact on the young person during this period. The chapter will conclude by examining possible reasons why certain young people might be vulnerable in their early sexual relationships.

Lifespan development theory

Lifespan development theory is an approach that explores particular challenges associated with different life stages, and identifies factors affecting adjustment across the lifespan (see Coleman 2011; Hendry 2015). In this case I will concentrate on those factors associated with the adolescent life stage. Lifespan developmental theory emphasises four elements which affect human development. I will deal with each of these concepts in turn, showing how they assist us in grasping the nature of adolescent development while also contributing to a better understanding of both strengths and vulnerabilities (Coleman and Hagell 2007).

Continuity

The concept of continuity underlines the fact that human development can only be understood if we look at each stage in relation to previous stages. In the case of adolescence this is especially important since so much changes following puberty. As a result, there is sometimes the experience of the adolescent as a 'new' person arriving in the family. This means we cannot make sense of the behaviour and experiences of a young person without taking into account what has happened in childhood.

This is not necessarily a deterministic point of view. Much can change during the adolescent period. Nonetheless the young person does not arrive at the age of 13 without a history. If we are able to understand that history we will be better able to understand the young person as an adolescent. In recent years there has been much discussion (for example, Ogden and Hagen 2018) of what are known as ACEs (adverse childhood experiences). It is precisely through the lens of continuity that such a notion has been investigated. How do early experiences, especially if they involve trauma or disruption, affect later development?

This is obviously pertinent in the case of CSE. Here some key elements of an earlier history will have to do with the relationship and attachment experiences during the early years. The development of trust with key carers, and the role models provided by these carers, will have an impact on the internal world of the young person. There seems little doubt that these aspects of early experience will play their part in the sexual relationships established in early adolescence.

Context

The second concept inherent in the lifespan development model has to do with context. This is sometimes referred to as historical time and place. The argument here is that all human development occurs in a particular context, and that we need to take this into account if we wish to understand a particular individual's path through life. With respect to adolescence, the premise is that, at least to a certain extent, the experience of this life stage is fundamentally altered by the environment in which it occurs. Growing up today is not the same as growing up 20 years ago. Growing up today in a culturally diverse inner-city setting cannot be the same as growing up in a much less diverse rural environment. This may sound simplistic. However, it is an argument that hitherto has been overlooked, and may have a lot to do with our understanding of behaviours and experiences associated with CSE. Recent developments in Contextual Safeguarding are addressing this question of 'context' and abuse in more detail.

Timing

Third lifespan developmental theory emphasises the importance of understanding the timing of events affecting development. This is especially significant for adolescents, since the number of life events occurring at the same time influences the degree of stress experienced by the young person. The more life events there are that occur simultaneously, the more stress there will be. When we consider the possibility of a move of school, the arrival of puberty, and the changes in relationships both at home and in the peer group, it is easy to see how this might, for some, be a challenging period.

Agency

Finally, this theoretical approach highlights the importance of agency. This idea is linked to the search for autonomy and independence that is so central to the adolescent life stage. The notion of agency refers to the fact that the adolescent will be playing an active role in shaping the context in which he or she develops. I appreciate that this concept has implications for the debate over how young people might become involved in CSE: if we think of this experience as one of victimhood, then the idea that there has been any choice in the situation is hard to accept. Furthermore, it will certainly be the case that there is very large variation in the degree to which young people are able to exercise their agency. The elements already mentioned, such as context and timing, may serve to restrict or limit the extent of the agency of any one individual. This is an issue to which I will return at the end of the chapter.

Adolescent development

While it is essential for the practitioner to understand the individual experiences of the young person with whom they are working, it is also necessary for the professional adult to know something about development during the years of adolescence and young adulthood. These years represent a particular life stage. The behaviours associated with it are frequently experienced by adults as both puzzling and challenging. There are a number of features of this stage that will help adults make sense of these behaviours.

Transition

The first feature of this developmental stage is that it can be considered as a major transition. Good descriptions of the adolescent transition can be found in Coleman (2013) and in Steinberg (2015). At this time there are educational transitions, social and relationship transitions and physical transitions. The key element of a transition is an uncertainty about whether you are one or the other, or to put it another way, whether you are a child or an adult. It can be useful to think that inside every teenager is *both* a child and an adult. This may help to explain some of the inconsistent behaviour. Transitions have a number of common characteristics, and these are especially pertinent in the case of the adolescent. The characteristics of transitions include:

- an eager anticipation of the future (wanting to be grown up);
- a sense of loss or regret for the stage that has been left behind (still showing childish behaviour or expressing childish needs);
- a sense of anxiety about what is unknown (worrying about the future);
- a major psychological readjustment (changes in all domains);
- a degree of ambiguity of status during the transition (no one knowing quite what status should be accorded to the young person during this stage).

Every adult who knows teenagers will be familiar with the 'flip-flop' of emotions that is such a common feature of this stage. As one parent put it: 'You never know where you stand. One moment they're up, the next they're down.' It is important to recognise that being 'neither one thing nor the other' poses especial difficulties for all concerned. Everyone wants to know where they stand and what is expected of them. Yet during the process of transition this is not always possible. Parents, carers and professionals are never quite sure how to treat the young person during these years. It is difficult for the adult to determine quite how much to expect of the teenager and how much autonomy to allow.

Transition is tricky for the young person too. What is reasonable to expect from the adults around you? One the one hand the young person wants to be treated as a responsible person, but sometimes that can be scary. Being looked after and having things done for you can feel safe and comforting. Add to that the swings of emotion that the young person experiences almost daily, and we can see that transitions can be challenging for all concerned. The development of sexuality may pose particular challenges during this stage, and I will return to this topic later in the chapter.

Transitions can be especially problematic when other factors come into play. Thus, for example, where a young person has experienced disruption in relationships or personal difficulties during childhood it is likely that transitions during the teenage years will be additionally problematic. There are a number of reasons for this. These may include the lack of a stable attachment base, low self-esteem, inconsistency in school experiences, poor peer relationships and so on.

Puberty

The second point to recognise at this stage is the impact of puberty. When most people talk about puberty, they think of a girl starting her periods or a boy whose voice has just broken. These are only some of the signs of a major process of change within the body that takes place any time between the ages of 9 and 14. Puberty is the time of the second biggest change in human development. The only time when there is a larger scale of change is in infancy. Puberty involves a lot more than the outward signs of sexual maturation. Puberty involves changes in all organs of the body, including the lungs, the heart and the brain. The composition of the blood alters at this time, as does the hormone balance, a topic I will return to in the next section. A good description of puberty can be found in Temple-Smith et al (2016). Here are some basic facts about this phenomenon:

- the beginning of puberty is triggered primarily by the release of sex hormones – testosterone in the case of boys and oestrogen in the case of girls;
- all the different changes associated with puberty will last about two years;
- puberty starts between one year and 18 months earlier for girls than it does for boys;
- there is wide individual variation in the age at the onset of puberty and in the sequence of changes; this is perfectly normal;
- the average age for a girl to start her periods in Britain today is 11 years 10 months;
- however, one in five girls will have started their periods while still in primary school;
- the age of the commencement of puberty dropped between 1900 and 1960, but since that time there has been little further reduction in the age of puberty;

- although the physical changes will be the obvious ones that can be seen by the outside world, there are emotional changes that can have a significant impact too.

I should emphasise that there are wide individual differences in the age at which young people experience puberty. Some can start as early as 9 or 10, while others will commence at 13 or even 14. All this is perfectly normal, and has no implications for later sexual or other development. However, very few of us want to stand out as being different. Being in step, and not standing out from the crowd matters hugely to many young people, and for some this can be a painful process. Many young people get worried about the pace of change. Some worry that nothing is happening, while others worry whether the changes that are happening to them are normal or not.

There are a few individuals who start puberty either very early or very late. This can cause great anxiety for the young people who are affected and of course for the adults who care for them. It is important for parents and carers to know that none of these experiences need have lasting effects. What is critical is that adults know about the possible risks and are able to provide the necessary information and support for the adolescents who experience puberty outside the normally expected age range.

Research has shown that boys who mature very early usually do well, as they are stronger, taller and more developed than their peers. This often means that they are good at sport, something that is associated with popularity. On the other hand boys who mature very much later than others are not necessarily popular, and do not do so well in their school work. As far as girls are concerned, both early and late development can be problematic. Early puberty may lead girls into early sexual activity, often with older boys or young men. This is clearly of great importance where CSE is concerned. Practitioners should be aware of the pubertal status of any girl or young woman they are concerned about, since very early puberty is an important risk factor. Very late pubertal development in young women has much the same impact as it does in boys, often leading to poor social relationships and lower school attainment. The impact of early and late development is summarised in Temple-Smith et al (2016, Chapter 3).

Puberty can be very straightforward for some, and complicated for others. For some it is a time of anxiety and stress, while others pass through it without a second thought. One key feature is that it leads to emotional changes as well as physical maturation. Puberty can have an impact on a young person's self-image and on their sense of self-worth.

We know from research that the self-concept of girls suffers around puberty, with nearly half of all girls feeling dissatisfied with their bodies. Puberty is closely tied up with early sexual feelings and behaviour. For those who feel vulnerable at this time sexuality can become a very complicated aspect of life. This may lead to inappropriate relationships or risky behaviour. I will consider this aspect of development later in the chapter.

Brain development

The third aspect of adolescent development to be considered here is brain development. In recent years there has been a remarkable increase in knowledge of what happens in the brain during adolescence. Until the year 2000 it was believed that the brain stopped developing at the end of childhood. We now know that the brain continues to develop until early adulthood. More importantly, the period of adolescence is the time of the greatest change in the brain apart from the period of early infancy. The development of the technology of scanning has enabled us to take pictures of the brain without causing distress or pain to the individual. Good descriptions of the developing teenage brain can be found in Jensen (2015) and in Blakemore (2018). We now know that there are many changes occurring at this time. Here I will concentrate on some of the most important of these.

The first change to mention has to do with pruning. This may seem an odd thing to be happening, but in essence the brain produces far more neural connections than are necessary at the end of childhood. During adolescence pruning takes place to ensure that effective connections are created and useless connections are allowed to die away. The result of this is that a lot of reorganisation and restructuring takes place, inevitably leading to a period of readjustment. This may have the effect of causing uncertainty, confusion or difficulty in making decisions.

As part of the pruning process new connections are being formed that will enable new skills to develop. More complicated and sophisticated neural networks are being created. A good example of this is that the bridge connecting the two halves of the brain develops rapidly at this time. In childhood this bridge is active, but it grows and becomes more important during the teenage years. The development of the bridge between the two hemispheres allows the brain to use its different capacities in a more organised fashion.

In addition to all this we now know that there are parts of the brain which show especially rapid change and development at this time. Two sites in particular may be mentioned. These are known as the prefrontal cortex and the amygdala. Evidence shows that these two sites may not necessarily develop at the same pace. The amygdala, associated with emotion, sensation and arousal, may develop faster than the prefrontal cortex which is associated with thinking, reasoning and problem-solving. It may be the case, therefore, that for some young people there will be a time when planning and thinking about consequences will come second to exploration and experimentation. This is also a useful explanation for the fact that some individuals may prefer 'living in the moment' to thinking about the future (Coleman, 2019).

Part of the new knowledge about the brain has included information about the way in which the changing hormone balance influences adolescent development. It has always been known that teenagers are affected by their hormones. This upset in the hormone balance has been seen as an explanation for moody or irritable behaviour. What is new in our knowledge is that the balance of hormones affects brain development. The alterations and fluctuations of hormones act on various parts of the brain that have already been mentioned, such as the prefrontal cortex and the amygdala.

High levels of sex hormones, such as testosterone and progesterone, have an impact not only on the development of the sex organs and on sexual behaviour, but they also lead to changes in behaviour more generally. Surges of these hormones may encourage young people to seek out emotionally charged experiences, or to look for novelty and excitement.

It is worth noting that levels of hormones such as cortisol and serotonin fluctuate considerably during this stage. The release of cortisol is linked to experiences of anxiety, while serotonin helps to moderate anxiety. If these hormones are in flux it will be apparent that emotions may be difficult to manage. It is also important to mention dopamine. This is the hormone which is released when we get pleasure of enjoyment from an activity. The brain is particularly sensitive to dopamine during the teenage years, and some risky or thrill-seeking behaviours can be explained by increased dopamine activity at this time.

Last, there is one other hormone which plays its part in adolescent development, and this is melatonin. Melatonin is the hormone which is released at night to inform us that it is time to go to sleep. In the last few years we have learnt that melatonin is released later among adolescents than in other age groups. This has significant implications since it means that young people may have more difficulty getting to sleep than the adults in the family.

Sleep is very important for teenagers (see Walker 2017). We know that teenagers need more sleep than younger children. If young people have to get up early for school, they may be missing hours of much-needed sleep. Research shows that sleep deficit (less than seven hours a night) has an impact on both learning and on behaviour. There is a further reason why good sleep can make a difference. This is because recent research shows that sleep is the time of memory consolidation. In other words, the information that has been learnt during the day is stored and cemented during certain phases of sleep. Adults can help young people get into good sleep routines. The melatonin effect can be overcome, but this will only happen if teenagers have the support of caring adults.

To conclude this section, it is important to state that the more adults understand adolescent brain development, the more they can work effectively with this age group. It is very easy to be critical of some of the emotional, changeable, inconsistent or puzzling teenage behaviour. However, almost all of this behaviour has its roots in the change and readjustment that is occurring in the brain and in the environment around the young person. Of course, early experiences, especially adverse experiences, will also play their part. These experiences may well lead to more troubled or troubling behaviours. Nonetheless the knowledge that has been gained in recent years about brain development has provided new insights which should help professional adults take a more sympathetic and informed stance in their work with young people. Other useful information about this topic can be found in Crone (2017).

Vulnerability

Much of what has been said already can be seen to contribute to a better understanding of vulnerability. In the first place, lifespan developmental theory throws a spotlight on aspects of the lifecourse which may cause increased distress or dysfunction. A good example here concerns the timing of life events. As noted earlier, when the individual experiences a range of events and stresses that all occur at the same time it is much harder to adjust than if such events are spaced out over time. Agency is another element of the theory that has relevance to vulnerability and CSE. As I have mentioned, most young people are able to develop agency during the teenage years so that they can gradually become more independent and self-governing. However, there are factors which may inhibit or restrict the development of agency. These may cause the young person to lose control over events or to engage in unsafe or self-harming behaviours. Many adverse childhood experiences would fall into this category. Further information may be found in Campbell et al (2016) and in Ogden and Hagen (2018).

The nature of transitions, as well as elements of brain development, may also contribute to vulnerability. For example, delayed transitions, or very rapid transitions, might leave the individual being vulnerable to experiences that severely test the resources available. As far as brain development is concerned, there are many ways in which what happens in the brain can contribute to increased vulnerability. These may include extreme fluctuations in hormone levels, slower than normal development of the prefrontal cortex, or a more difficult period of readjustment due to pruning and other changes in the major sites of the brain. It is important to recognise that the brain and the environment interact, each influencing the other. Thus, adverse aspects of the environment can have an impact on the way the brain develops, while at the same time problems in brain development will influence behaviour and thus have an impact on the context in which the young person is growing up.

Another factor to be considered is chronological age. Although the teenage transition takes place over a number of years, it would appear that some periods during the transition are more vulnerable than others. There is good evidence to show that problem behaviours do not occur equally across the age span. A glance at the statistics concerning offending behaviour, self-harm or eating disorders shows that these troubling episodes are more likely to occur at specific ages. For example, eating disorders and self-harm among girls peak around the age of 15, while offending behaviour in males peaks at 18. This finding highlights the fact that vulnerability is influenced by the developmental process, with some problem behaviours being more likely to occur at particular ages (Hagell et al 2017).

Risk-taking

One of the most common ideas about teenagers, as described in Coleman (2013; 2019), is that they are risk-takers. One explanation for this is that the part of the brain to do with thinking and problem-solving develops at a slower rate than the area to do with sensation and arousal. However not everyone agrees with this view. Some have argued that there are wide individual differences in the pace of brain development, so that only a small number experience the delayed maturation of the prefrontal cortex. Others have suggested that experimentation and novelty-seeking is a positive aspect of growing up. Thus, it may be lack of experience, combined with the desire to explore the world and look for novelty and new experiences that are better explanations for these behaviours.

Another possible reason for risky behaviour has to do with the role of the hormone dopamine (see Jensen 2015). Research shows that heightened levels of dopamine, and the effect this has on the certain centres in the brain, may have the effect of leading some teenagers to seek thrills and pleasure, without taking into account what may happen as a result of these activities.

There are, of course, additional explanations for risky behaviour during this stage. Low self-esteem may lead young people into social groups which are more likely to engage in anti-social behaviour or to disregard issues of personal safety. We know that during these years young people are especially likely to be influenced by the peer group, so that pressures to conform to the norms of the social group may play a part in encouraging risky behaviour.

Last, it is important to consider the role of adverse childhood experiences (Hagell 2012). As has been noted these may have an effect on brain development, but they may also affect many other aspects of the personality. The role of adults is crucial in providing role models and supporting the development of resilience. If such features of childhood are missing it is likely that the individual will struggle when faced with challenges during the teenage years.

It is all too easy to stereotype teenagers as risk-takers. This notion is linked to a more generally negative view of this age group. Young people themselves describe situations when adults cross the road rather than walk past a group of teenagers. As one young person put it: 'They judge you by your age, they don't judge you by the person you are.' It is important to be cautious and to think carefully when we assess a teenager's behaviour. However as has been described here, there are factors that may make it more likely that a young person will engage in risky or harmful behaviour. The role of professionals is key in being able to provide appropriate support in order to reduce the likelihood of risk-taking behaviour.

Sexuality and sexual health

Sexual development is a critical feature of the teenage years for all young people, and nowhere more so than for those who have lived through adverse childhood experiences. This is partly to do with the possibility that such young people may have experienced abuse of various types, exploitation or other forms of inappropriate sexual experience. In addition, the lack of suitable role models and/ or disrupted family relationships all contribute to possible difficulties in sexual development. It is important to recognise that sexual development can be derailed as a result of trauma, dysfunctional attachments or developmental delay (Temple-Smith et al 2016).

This creates a major task for professionals working with young people. Young people experiencing problems with 'healthy' sexual development will be in need of good education about sex and relationships which addresses feelings that are experienced in relationships. Topics should include consent in sexual relationships, bullying and peer pressure and should cover information about the legal framework of applying to sexual relationships. This may not have been provided in the school setting, and so extra responsibilities fall on the social worker, foster carer or other professional. Even if information has been provided in school, vulnerable young people will need to be supported by professionals to make sense of the sex education they have received. They will need to be able to ask about issues that are worrying them in a safe and supported environment. Furthermore, safe and accessible sexual health services are likely to be necessary, and policymakers and professionals have a responsibility to make sure these are available.

Many young people who have experienced adverse childhood events will be uncertain or confused about what constitutes healthy sexual development. Many young people worry about their gender identity, and this may cause some individuals anxiety or distress. It is important for professionals to hold fast to a non-judgemental stance. A key role for adults here is to support the individual young person to talk, to avoid further risk, to seek help and to make informed decisions.

It has to be acknowledged that some teenagers will have had experiences that make it more difficult for them to develop healthy sexual relationships. If a young person engages in, or is forced or manipulated into inappropriate or unsafe sexual activity, this poses a significant challenge for any professional working in this field. Safe and trusting relationships with professionals can be a powerful tool for safeguarding teenagers and building their resilience so that they can avoid further harm to themselves. For this reason, good training for professionals on the topic of sexual health is absolutely essential for work in this field.

When young people engage with services following sexual exploitation or sexual abuse, it is all too easy to label them as 'victims' or as 'being at risk'. This is not always helpful, since it can ignore the differences between young people's reactions to these experiences, and their capacity to manage the effects. It is essential to recognise the different perspectives that young people bring to this issue, as well as each person's age and maturity. Young people should be seen as individuals who have resources and capabilities. Building on the strengths of the individual will be the most helpful way of mitigating risk (see Rutter 2013; Frydenberg 2019).

A framework for effective work with young people affected by CSE

I am going to conclude this chapter by outlining a framework that may be helpful in considering how best to work with vulnerable young people, especially those affected by CSE. I have called this framework the STAGE framework (Coleman 2019). There are a number of reasons for naming the framework in this way. In the first place I believe that it is very important to recognise that adolescence is a stage in human development with certain characteristics that make it unique in the lifespan. It is only possible to understand the trajectories taken by young people during this period if we acknowledge the particular processes that operate at this time. Behaviours that may seem puzzling or contradictory become understandable once it is recognised that they are part of the transition occurring during adolescence (Coleman 2011).

The second reason for using the term STAGE is in order for both professionals and carers to recognise that the behaviours are not going to last for ever. All too often adults believe that challenging teenage behaviour is something that will be with them for the foreseeable future. Of course, this is not the case. This period of life represents a process, a move from childhood to maturity, and there will continue to be change and readjustment as the young person progresses towards adulthood.

No matter how volatile and difficult the relationship between adult and teenager is, the role of the adult is to build a sustainable and caring relationship. The STAGE framework can be helpful in these circumstances. Each of the letters in the word represents a key element of the relationship between adult and young person, no matter whether that relationship is a professional one or embedded in a family context. I will start with the first letter of STAGE, the letter S.

This letter stands for *significance* – the significance of adults. When a teenager is refusing to cooperate, staying silent, or being rude and disrespectful it is hard to imagine that the adult has an important role to play. However, we know that adults are just as important during the teenage years as they are during childhood. They are just important in a different way. Adults often feel that they have very little influence, as the young person appears to reject what they have to say, and prefers listening to friends and the peer group. Yet this is misleading. Without a relationship with a caring and trusted adult it is so much harder for a young person to manage the challenges of this period. Parents and carers are of course critical here, but research evidence shows that professionals do also play a key role (see Misca and Smith 2014).

The second letter is T, standing for *two-way communication*. Young people often say that communication with adults involves either being asked things or being told things. This is one-way communication. It is a message that goes from the adult to the young person. Yet we know that good communication involves a two-way process. All young people want to feel that they are being listened to, and that their voice is heard. Good communication between adult and young person involves as much listening as talking (Smetana 2011).

The third letter is A – standing for *authority*. This raises the question of how adults exercise authority during the teenage years. The point here is to emphasise that the authority of an adult during adolescence cannot be based on the same principles as the use of authority during childhood (Manzi et al 2012; Misca and Smith 2014). Adult authority at this stage cannot be based on power, on force or on punishment. The adult has a responsibility to keep the young person safe, but authority at this stage has to be based on respect and on good communication. Rules will be more acceptable if they are negotiated rather than imposed. A structure has to be in place, but it has to be reasonable and to take into account the age and circumstances of the young person.

The fourth letter is G – standing for the *generation gap*. Adults are sometimes too quick to judge adolescent behaviour. Such judgements can all too easily be based on the experiences of the previous generation, rather than on the experiences of today's generation of young people (Ponappa et al 2014). Growing up today is so very different and is ever-changing, with the advent of social media, different attitudes to sex and gender, and changing social circumstances in education and the job market. Adults must be careful not to make judgements based on their own experiences.

The last letter in STAGE is the E – standing for *emotion*. It is important to keep in mind that the management of emotion can be very difficult during the teenage years (Smetana 2011; Assor and Tal 2012; Barber et al 2012). The hormone balance is unsettled, and the brain itself takes time to mature and allow good emotion regulation. In addition, research has shown that earlier distress or trauma will leave the young person with powerful emotions that may be unhelpful or even destructive. Of course, teenagers have the capacity to arouse strong emotions in the adults around them. Adults will certainly experience anger and frustration, but their feelings may include elements of sadness, distress and even shame when things go wrong. It is essential for professionals to receive support in learning to recognise and manage their emotions. It is only in this way that adults can help young people develop a better means of managing their own feelings.

References

Assor, A. and Tal, K. (2012) 'When parents' affection depends on the child's achievement', *Journal of Adolescence*, 35: 249–260

Barber, K., Xia, M. and Bose, K. (2012) 'Feeling disrespected by parents: understanding psychological control', *Journal of Adolescence*, 35: 273–289

Blakemore, S.-J. (2018) *Inventing Ourselves: The Secret Life of the Teenage Brain*, London: Penguin Random House

Campbell, S., Morley, D. and Catchpole, R. (2016) *Critical Issues in Child and Adolescent Mental Health*, London: Palgrave Macmillan

Coleman, J. (2011) *The Nature of Adolescence* (4th edn), London: Routledge

Coleman, J. (2013) 'Adolescence', in M. Davies (ed) *The Blackwell Companion to Social Work*, Oxford: Wiley-Blackwell

Coleman, J. (2019) *Why Won't My Teenager Talk To Me?* (2nd edn), London: Routledge

Coleman, J. and Hagell, A. (eds) (2007) *Adolescence: Risk and Resilience*, Chichester: John Wiley

Crone, E. (2017) *The Adolescent Brain*, London: Psychology Press

Frydenberg, E. (2019) *Adolescent Coping: Promoting Resilience and Well-being*, London: Routledge

Hagell, A. (ed) (2012) *Changing Adolescence: Social Trends and Mental Health*, Policy Press. Bristol.

Hagell, A., Shah, R. and Coleman, J. (2017) 'Key data on young people: 2017', *The Association for Young People's Health*, www.youngpeopleshealth.org.uk

Hendry, L. (2015) *Developmental Transitions Across the Lifespan*, Hove: Psychology Press

Jensen, F. (2015) *The Teenage Brain: A Neuroscientist's Survival Guide to Raising Adolescents and Young Adults*, New York: Harper

Manzi, C., Regalia, C. and Fincham, F. (2012) 'Documenting different domains of the promotion of autonomy in families', *Journal of Adolescence*, 35: 289–298

Misca, G. and Smith, J. (2014) 'Mothers, fathers, families and child development', in A. Abela and J. Walker (eds) *Contemporary Issues in Family Studies*, Chichester: Wiley-Blackwell

Ogden, T. and Hagen, K. (2018) *Adolescent Mental Health: Prevention and Intervention,* Abingdon: Routledge

Ponappa, S., Bartle-Haring, S. and Day, R. (2014) 'Connection to parents and healthy separation during adolescence', Journal of Adolescence, 37: 555–566

Rutter, M. (2013) 'Annual research review: Resilience and its clinical applications', *Journal of Child Psychology and Psychiatry*, 54: 474–487

Smetana, J. (2011) *Adolescents, Families and Social Development*, Oxford: Wiley-Blackwell

Steinberg, L. (2015) 'The age of opportunity: Lessons from the new science of adolescence', New York: Houghton Mifflin Harcourt

Temple-Smith, M., Moore, S. and Rosenthal, D. (2016) *Sexuality in Adolescence: The Digital Generation*, Abingdon: Routledge

Walker, M. (2017) *Why We Sleep*, London: Penguin Random House

7

Some psychodynamic understandings of child sexual exploitation

Nick Luxmoore

This chapter tries to understand child sexual exploitation (CSE) through the lens of psychodynamic theory. As babies and as children growing up, how do we develop a sense of who and how we're supposed to be? How do the potentially loving, creative, assertive parts of ourselves get distorted and damaged? How do our earliest relationships affect the anxieties driving our subsequent behaviours? How do we defend ourselves against powerlessness and shame? Why do perpetrators and victims often find themselves stuck in certain roles? How might we understand hatred and guilt, aggression and sexuality in relation to CSE? In short, how does CSE become the focus of intra-psychic and inter-personal dynamics?

Trying to understand these things doesn't excuse the perpetrators, nor does it suggest that the victims are culpable. It doesn't assume that victims can't also be perpetrators or perpetrators victims. It's just that, until we understand, it's hard to know how to respond to CSE and how to prevent further exploitation. Can children and young people (CYP) be active *and* passive participants in their own exploitation? Are they pressed into lives of misery or do they undertake these lives with some degree of choice? Pearce (2009) describes the complexity of these questions for legislators as well as for those trying to intervene and help. The answers aren't simple because CYP aren't simple. Developmentally, they're forever exploring their own sense of agency, the extent to which they control the world or are controlled by it. And their sense of sexual agency is no less important than any other kind of agency.

Few of us change our behaviours until the causes of our behaviours have been understood. Of course, it's easy to distance ourselves from CSE by simply blaming other people. We might try to blame CYP for their misfortune, men for the many cruelties they inflict and mothers for absolutely everything! But blaming other people tries to simplify what isn't simple and suggests that the rest of us are somehow off the hook.

CSE is everyone's concern, everyone's responsibility.

A developing sense of self

There are environmental factors that might predispose someone to becoming vulnerable to CSE either as a perpetrator or victim (poverty, lack of educational opportunity, unemployment, family circumstances), but what of the *psychodynamic* factors? What goes on in someone's head and how is that 'head', that sense of self created in the first place?

According to the theorists (Winnicott 1971; 1975; Stern 1985; Fonagy et al 2004), we're not born with a sense of self. We certainly have a DNA self; we're born with some biological predispositions and theologians might argue that we each have a soul. But our sense of who we are is socially constructed, born out of relationships with other people. Winnicott (1975) jokes that 'there is no such thing as a baby' because, to begin with, the infant and its mother (or, as argued by later theorists, its 'primary carer') are inseparable, their identities mutually dependent. The infant is physically and psychologically merged with the other person and only begins to separate, to develop a sense of itself as individual by looking in the mirror. But of course, a baby can't climb out of its cot and crawl across to the bathroom mirror. Instead, the mirror that the baby looks into is the mirror of the face looking down at it, reflecting the baby back to itself, imitating its sounds and facial expressions. Only by seeing itself in this mirror does the baby know that it exists. Otherwise it resorts to panic-stricken howling, desperate for the mirroring face to appear, to recognise and respond to it, confirming the baby's existence. How much of CSE, we might therefore wonder, stems from a CYP's most primitive need to be recognised at all costs by someone – anyone, and in any way – in order to exist and to be worth something? How much do children need to interest other people, to be sexually interesting if nothing else, in order to be deserving of recognition?

We know from neuroscience (Gerhardt 2004) that a depressed, unmoving parental face will contribute to the creation of a depressed, unmoving baby because, in simple terms, what we initially see in the parental face is what we become. If the face only reflects back, is only interested in our anger, then we become merely the angry baby. If the face is only interested in our smiling, then we become the perpetually smiling baby, desperately turning all experiences into an anxious smile. By extension, if a CYP is only recognised, only gets attention as a flirtatious, potentially sexual person, then that's who the CYP becomes.

But if the face reflects back a *range* of emotions, then babies develop an emotional repertoire, evolving into CYP capable of playing a variety of roles, assertive as well as passive, combative as well as submissive. The theory goes (Fonagy et al 2004; Hill 2015) that if a child gets enough of this attuned, mirroring attention, reflecting it back to itself, then it gradually internalises a capacity to reflect *on itself*, no longer needing another person to be physically present to provide the reflecting face. This is crucial because, while some CYP have learned to think about themselves and reflect on their situations, others haven't: they lurch from one relationship to the next, always in search of recognition, never able to relax or take their own existence, their own worth for granted. To be visible, to feel that they exist, they need the attention of other people and, for some, any kind of attention will do.

Freud (1923) suggests that we begin life as 'body' egos with our sense of self concentrated entirely in our physical bodies: feeding, excreting, screaming, writhing, lashing out. A reflective mind, able to be simultaneously *in* our bodies while also *thinking about* our bodies, develops out of the mirroring experience that I've described. Without that experience, without the development of a 'mind' able to think about itself, a child remains a body capable only of action, never of thought. When afraid, it has no way of thinking about its situation and making rational choices. Instead, it enacts, it externalises its fears, its anxieties, its uncertainties. Self-harming, for example, becomes an objectification of the body, a way of locating and controlling fears, anxieties and uncertainties through controlling the body when there's no mind available to contain or make sense of things (Lemma 2015). In some cases, CSE might be thought of as a kind of self-harming whereby anxieties that can't be thought about get enacted, turned into behaviours. What this means is that – through no fault of our own it's hard to take charge of our lives if we can't think about our lives.

Attachment and privacy

We exist, therefore, in relation to other people, and like many crimes, CSE emerges out of relationships. Questions like 'Didn't you realise what was happening? Couldn't you have said no?' are meaningless for a CYP who's been desperate for any kind of recognition. 'Yes, I realised what was happening,' the CYP might reply, 'and yes, I might have been capable of saying no, but my need for affection, for attention and recognition was too powerful.'

Bowlby (1969; 1973; 1980) demonstrates through experiments like the 'Strange Situation Test' the delicacy of a child's gradual separation from its mother or primary caregiver. Separate too abruptly and a child is left with anxieties that can stretch into adult life, never able to rely on other people, always expecting to be abandoned and sometimes unwittingly provoking abandonment because that's what's familiar. Winnicott (1965) argues that the 'good enough' mother (the good enough caregiver, we might say) provides an environment that protects the child from unplanned occurrences, from sudden threats, until the child has internalised a fundamental sense of safety and is better able to bear the unexpected. After that, Winnicott argues, the 'mother' needs to expose the child appropriately to 'impingements' so that the child can develop the resilience to withstand setbacks in the future. Too many impingements too soon and the child will be traumatised, but with gentle, gradual exposure to impingements, the child will learn to cope.

The delicacy of this also applies to a CYP's ability to manage privacy. It's as if there's a membrane between Winnicott's mother and child with the mother gradually teaching the child how much to let the world in and how much to keep it out. I've written elsewhere (Luxmoore 2000) about a CYP's developmental progression from a simple sense of things either being completely open or completely secret to a sense that there are degrees of privacy and such a thing as 'appropriateness'. We learn that it's appropriate to tell each other some things but not others, to make conscious decisions about how much or how little of ourselves to share autobiographically or sexually. Subjected to grooming and to other kinds of manipulative abuse, CYP unable to manage privacy might end up sending naked pictures of themselves to abusers and then struggling with the consequences. They might end up agreeing to have sex with people, somehow believing that these people can be trusted.

Winnicott (1965) argues that our ability to be alone (something many CYP struggle with) depends on the extent to which we've internalised a mother or caregiver's presence. If we've grown up safe in the knowledge that this person's absences are only ever temporary and that we're never forgotten, then we can gradually tolerate longer and longer absences because it feels as if we're still thought about, even when the other person is physically absent. Glasser (1979) describes the quality of this separation as the 'core complex' underpinning our most primitive anxieties and therefore powering our most extreme behaviours.

CSE might feed off CYP's inability to be alone for fear of being forgotten. If no one in the world appears to be thinking about us, it might feel as if we don't actually exist which is terrifying. Better, in that case, to cling to an abuser or to hang out with a group of manipulative people, however malevolent they may be, if – at the very least – they notice us and affirm our existence.

Love, hate and guilt

In these ways, attachment anxieties potentially allow CSE to flourish. Freud's (1923) assertion is that anxiety drives all our behaviours. We always do things for a reason: our behaviours are always ways of assuaging or trying to deal with underlying anxieties. And 'anxiety' might usefully be thought about as a conflict of some sort: between the part of us that wants to grow up and the part that wants to remain a child, between the part that wants to take control and the part that wants to be controlled, between the brave and the fearful parts of ourselves.

CYP's anxiety is especially powered by a conflict between loving and hating that results in feelings of tremendous guilt. Developing Freud's thinking, Klein's (1957) idea – put simply – is that we're born experiencing our mother (our caregiver) as wholly good. We're umbilically attached to her; she feeds us automatically and appears to love us unconditionally. She's a 'good mother' whom we love. But no sooner are we born than there are times when this good mother appears to go off shift, replaced by a mother who's distracted and irritable, who isn't always there and doesn't always understand. This mother seems completely different from the good mother and we *hate* this second mother for being such a let-down. We conclude that we must have two mothers – the one we love and the one we hate – and we grow up trying to come to terms with the fact that these two mothers are one and the same person about whom we might feel (in Freud's terms) 'ambivalent'.

But the task of accepting our caregivers as they are, as necessarily flawed, might take a lifetime. In the meantime, with these two original 'mothers' as our template, we tend to see the whole world in these terms, splitting everything into things that are either good or bad, loveable or hateful. 'He's either with me or against me...She's either a friend or an enemy.'

Following Klein, Winnicott (1965) argues that there comes a time when we start to feel guilty for having hated the very person we also love, and without opportunities to make it up to that person, to make reparation, we're left ashamed, with a sense of our own personal badness. A CYP might conclude, 'I've done all these bad things, hated so many people, so I deserve whatever bad things happen to me!'

How much do the perpetrators of CSE take advantage of this vulnerability in CYP, exploiting a CYP's sense that 'I'm bad already so what difference does it make?' When CYP themselves are sometimes the perpetrators of CSE, how much are they able to take advantage of each other because they can see their own vulnerability in their peers and know how to exploit it? Freud (1916) suggests that we commit crimes because of guilt. The guilt precedes the crime, he argues, with crime becoming a way of unconsciously focusing the guilt. So loving *and* hating the important people in our lives and feeling guilty as a consequence, CYP might end up committing offences in order to concretise their guilt, to prove their essential badness to themselves and to others because 'What the hell! What does it matter? I've already ruined my life!'

Getting stuck in a role

CYP will tend *not* to get stuck in a rut of this kind, however ('I'm bad, I'm worthless, I'm a liar and that's all there is to know!'), if – with the help of an attentive, reflecting mirror – they've already developed a wider role repertoire (Moreno 1972), a sense of themselves as able to play many roles, 'Yes, I can be bad, but I can also be good! Yes, I can be a liar but I can also tell the truth!' As the attentive, mirroring face draws out and brings to life the baby's many potential roles, these roles are expanded, consolidated or constrained by family life. In families we might get stuck forever playing the bad, unreliable daughter, or the dishonest, good-for-nothing son unless roles in the family are more fluid and we're freed to play a whole variety of roles necessary to survive and thrive in adult life.

What causes us to get stuck in a role is either our own predisposition ('I've always been bad so I'll automatically take on the role of the bad person wherever I am') or our family's unconscious need to project certain qualities onto us in order for the rest of the family not to have to acknowledge these qualities in themselves. If sex is associated with badness in the family, then the 'bad' child might well incorporate sex into his or her sense of badness, 'I'm already the bad child, so – threatened by other people – I have no choice but to have sex with strangers and with people I thought were my friends.' Of course, some CYP might leave home having had positive childhood experiences, with the blessing of parents who believe them to be escaping from war or from poverty to better lives, rather than to lives of abuse. Perpetrators might therefore be forcing some CYP into wholly unfamiliar roles. But for many of us as CYP, the roles we learn in the early years of our lives and in our families are the roles we tend to play long after we've grown up and long after we've left our families. Some perpetrators and some victims of CSE might well be continuing to act out roles they learned and got stuck with when they were much younger. The roles of sexual bully or sexual slave, for example, might well have had their origins in childhood or adolescence when, once upon a time, a CYP tried things out, learning what got approval and what didn't, what felt powerful and what didn't.

Adolescence is often described as a recapitulation of infancy (Blos 1962) where, as Jones (1922) argues, 'the precise way in which a given person will pass through the necessary stages of development in adolescence is to a very great extent determined by the form of his infantile development' (pp 39–40). Spurred on in adolescence by hormonal and neurological changes, the turbulence of infancy is re-stimulated. Like infants, adolescents are beset by questions of how much power, how much control, how much agency they can have in their lives, trying things out (including sexual things), testing, confronting, fighting, surrendering. Phillips (2012) argues that the main task of adolescence is learning to bear frustration, learning to live with boundaries. Elsewhere (Luxmoore 2012), I've tried to describe what causes adolescents to choose (if choice is possible) *un*protected sex when they know all the reasons why protected sex makes absolute sense. What causes them to take so many risks, to put themselves in so many dangerous situations? To what extent are they desperately trying out roles, testing boundaries, challenging fate to do its worst, sometimes believing that they're invincible ('It could never happen to me!') and sometimes believing that they deserve any punishment or misfortune coming their way? All CYP are inevitably exploring an experience of power and powerlessness. It's just that, without adult support, some get stuck along the way through no fault of their own, trapped in destructive lifestyles and belief-systems.

Behaviour as an expression of anxiety

While all this might describe the developmental context in which CYP find themselves (a collage of unconscious, psychodynamic processes), I want to turn more specifically to some of the behaviours involved in CSE.

Driven by the unconscious anxieties I've been describing, our behaviour is always an attempted solution to a problem. 'I don't know why I did it but it made sense at the time,' a CYP might say. 'At the time, it seemed to be the only thing to do.' CYP's behaviour *does* always make sense to CYP at the time. So, appealing to their rational brains ('You need to stop making bad choices!') is often futile because, in the heat of the moment, their behaviour is driven, not by rationality, but by irrational, overwhelming anxiety. Writing about the psychopathology of sexual offending, Cox (1979: 312) describes 'the offence as a defence', as a way of keeping anxiety at bay. At its most extreme, that anxiety might cause a perpetrator to feel as if his or her whole sense of self is at stake, at risk of shame, humiliation, annihilation even (Kohut 1971). Winnicott (1965) describes panic attacks, for example, as 'unthinkable anxiety', anxiety that can no longer be thought about. So when a CYP's carefully constructed sense of self is under threat from bullying, from scorn, from extreme peer pressure or from simple physical violence, he or she is likely to regress. When a CYP's fledgling repertoire of roles (kind as well as cruel, generous as well as selfish) can no longer be sustained, a CYP is – again – likely to regress, desperately attaching to something to stay safe. That 'something' might be a person, however dangerous or disagreeable; it might be a particular behaviour such as flirtatiousness or a need to please; it might be a single personal characteristic such as stubbornness, silence or hostility; it might be a part of the body – a fist, a vagina, a penis. Reduced to something so simple, life becomes easier to bear because it no longer needs to be thought about, 'I'm just a vagina to be penetrated, a penis to be touched. I'm just an addict in search of a fix, a bully in search of a victim.' Attachment-seeking behaviour is really safety-seeking behaviour, recognition-seeking behaviour.

Trauma

In this context it's worth thinking of trauma as experience that destroys our habitual ways of coping, our defence mechanisms. Elsewhere in this book, Chapter 8 explores the meaning and impact of trauma on CYP and on the perpetrators of CSE, as well as their responses to it. For the purposes of this chapter, it's enough to note that when a CYP has been traumatised by rape, by violence, by unending fear, then his or her whole sense of self – all those previously recognised personal characteristics, all that role-playing potential, all those familiar ways of dealing with anxiety – is broken down and barbarised, reduced to something that can easily be controlled by the perpetrators of CSE, with CYP sometimes seeming to go along with the cruelties inflicted on them.

Freud (1914a) is interested in this apparently collusive behaviour. Why do some people repeat and keep repeating the bad things that have already happened to them? By extension, why do some CYP keep going back to their abusers? What Freud calls 'repetition compulsion' is when 'the patient does not remember anything of what he has forgotten and repressed, but acts it out. He reproduces it not as a memory but as an action; he *repeats* it, without, of course, knowing that he is repeating it' (p 150). Freud's suggestion is that we keep going back to traumatic situations in an unconscious attempt eventually to master them.

Projection and projective identification

This behaviour makes absolute sense. If our whole sense of self is threatened by traumatic experience, then we'll do whatever it takes to hold ourselves together and survive. If necessary, we'll put ourselves in physical danger in order to survive psychologically. If necessary, we'll project all our badness, fear and vulnerability onto other people in order not to feel those feelings ourselves.

One of the important understandings of psychodynamic theory is the idea that we project the uncomfortable parts of ourselves onto other people. So, rather than acknowledge our own childishness or greed or weakness, we ascribe those characteristics to other people – we say that *another* person is like that, not me – and we disparage and attack those characteristics in that other person in the unconscious belief that this will make those characteristics go away, that somehow we'll be purged of them ourselves. One way of understanding CSE, therefore, is that the perpetrator corrupts or terrorises the CYP believing that 'If I can control the CYP, then I can control whatever the CYP represents to me, those parts of myself that I can't acknowledge or can't bear to be reminded of.' If the perpetrator is emotionally carrying around an abused or frightened child inside him or herself, a child screaming for attention or longing for love, a child whose real needs have never been acknowledged, then that internal, unconscious child potentially upsets the perpetrator's conscious belief in him or herself as autonomous and in control of everything. To maintain this belief, the perpetrator's vulnerable-child self must be unconsciously 'split off' or disavowed, treated and attacked as something entirely alien about whom the perpetrator can (try to) feel indifferent.

The opposite also happens. Some perpetrators might be drawn to CYP, might want to befriend and love CYP, because unconsciously this resolves something for the perpetrators, re-uniting them with a part of themselves that was previously lost or abused. *This* time around (the unconscious belief might suggest) that previously vulnerable part of the perpetrator can be experienced from a position of strength not weakness, with perpetrators able to control and manipulate their vulnerable selves where in earlier life they were themselves controlled and manipulated.

How might CYP act into this? Most projection bounces off the recipient ('I *know* I'm not like that! I know those things aren't true about me!'), but if the recipient of the projection is *already* feeling vulnerable, unlovable or in need of recognition, then he or she might receive the projection and identify with it, internalising it as his or her *own* vulnerability, *own* unlovableness or *own* need for recognition. In this way, we unconsciously project our feelings into other people, getting them to feel things on our behalves so that we don't have to, getting other people to believe what we tell them, in effect. It may be that the perpetrators of CSE have an unconscious sense of who's most vulnerable to exploitation because they themselves have been there: they know what powerless feels like; they know what it's like to long for affection, affirmation, recognition.

Narcissism

These processes of projective identification are subtle. Less subtle are the narcissistic processes that simply aim to control other people as brutally as necessary. Freud (1914b) describes a phase of 'primary narcissism' whereby, as babies, we believe that the world is simply an extension of ourselves to be controlled in the same way that we control our own arms and legs. Freud jokingly refers to 'His majesty the baby', presiding over such a world. But eventually, out of our relationship with the attentive, reflecting, mirroring face I described earlier in this chapter, we learn that we're actually separate, no longer merged with the other person; we learn that he or she *can't* always be controlled by us, that things happen to us despite ourselves and that we can tolerate these experiences. Frustrating though it may be, we learn to bear this experience and move out of our narcissistic phase, able to negotiate with the external world as autonomous individuals negotiating with other autonomous individuals.

Pathological or 'malignant' narcissism (Kernberg 1970), however, doesn't allow us to move out of this phase. Either because the mirroring face disappears before any separation has been established, or because the face forbids any separation to happen, remaining merged with the baby and allowing itself always to be controlled by the baby, the malignantly narcissistic baby grows into a person still convinced that everything is within his or her majesty's control – all physical objects and all people. Then when an object or a person refuses to do as he or she's told, it feels as dangerous as when part of the narcissist's own body refuses to function properly (Wolf 1988). That part has to be broken, crushed or killed off in order to re-establish the narcissist's belief in his or her own omnipotence. A CYP who protests, therefore, who refuses to do as she's told, risks terrible punishment from someone with a narcissistic personality disorder. Narcissists are dangerous because their lives depend on staying in control of everyone and everything. Forever.

Identifying with the aggressor

CYP might, therefore, find themselves dealing with perpetrators whose lives depend on controlling other people in as brutal a way as necessary.

One way of dealing with a perpetrator's overwhelming power is to identify with it. Anna Freud (2015) notes that, feeling anxious and afraid of the other person's aggression, children sometimes defend themselves by imitating the aggressor, thereby becoming aggressive and powerful themselves rather than anxious and afraid. A child might defend him or herself against feeling powerless by joining the gang and becoming one of the powerful ones, or might defend against feeling exploited by becoming exploitative in the way that someone selling sex might insist, 'I'm not the one being exploited! I'm the one doing the exploiting. For money!' A CYP involved in CSE might *unconsciously* reason that 'If I collude with what the other person wants, if I convince myself that I want it as well, then I won't have to feel helpless or exploited or powerless. I'll be the person who wants rather than the person who's wanted.'

The development of sexuality

In this way, CYP's behaviour might sometimes appear to be enthusiastic or assertive while actually being defensive. While there continues to be debate about whether CYP can ever be the enthusiastic agents of their own sexual experience, the insistence that all CYP are innocents, completely uninterested and uninvolved in sexual activity has arguably contributed to our difficulties in responding adequately to CSE. If we believe that adults are adults and children are children and never the twain shall meet, we deny that the two species might have anything in common. Freud (1905) has much to say on this subject, believing that babies are 'sexual' in the broadest sense from the moment of their birth, responding to touch and wanting to touch. Their relationship with the breast is sensual, soothing, affirming and reassuring, exciting a primitive kind of recognition. Thereafter children are intensely interested in the potential of their own bodies, including their genitals and other people's.

The idea that children are somehow asexual until they reach the age of consent (which varies considerably across the world) has long been discredited. This is *not* to suggest that CYP are therefore complicit in CSE or that our laws and punishments shouldn't apply. We believe that adults are responsible for their behaviours in ways that CYP can't be. But in trying to understand CSE, we have to acknowledge that CYP – babies even – are sexually curious, just as they're curious about every other kind of knowledge. Klein (1928) calls this the 'epistemophilic instinct'. We have to acknowledge that 'sexuality' is much more than just an expression of libido, of genital desire. Sexuality is to do with how we see ourselves, how we value or don't value ourselves, how we relate or don't relate to other people. We have to understand sexuality as active, alive and vital without ever implying that CSE is therefore the fault of CYP.

Aggression

And yet sex and sexuality have traditionally been taboo subjects that respectable people don't talk about. In the aftermath of the First World War, Freud (1920) comes to associate sex and sexuality (Eros) with an aggressive instinct he eventually describes as a 'death instinct' (Thanatos). (In French, 'orgasm' translates as 'le petit mort'.) While Freud proposes that aggression is essentially self-destructive, Winnicott (1958) changes the focus, arguing that aggression (and by implication, sexuality) isn't self-destructive but self-preservative, a kind of assertiveness without which we perish: 'aggressiveness is almost synonymous with activity,' he writes (p 204). For Winnicott, aggression is a necessary life force. The baby must scream aggressively, asserting itself, or it'll remain unnoticed and die. We need our aggression, therefore, as we need our everyday assertiveness, including our sexual assertiveness.

The way in which we respond to a baby's aggression is what makes the vital difference, argues Winnicott. If a baby's aggression scares its caregiver, reducing the carer to tears or panic, then the baby learns over time that its aggression is dangerous and potentially destructive, to be repressed or displaced into some other activity. Equally, if the baby's aggression is met with the carer's own overwhelming aggression, then again, the baby learns that its aggression needs to be hidden away for fear of reprisals. These responses are potentially damaging for the baby, whereas a 'good enough' experience involves the carer understanding the baby's aggression as necessary and vital, involves the carer neither capitulating nor retaliating, but simply putting appropriate, supportive, containing boundaries around the aggression.

From an early age, CYP internalise messages about their aggression, about their ability to assert themselves and about their sexual expressiveness. When their inevitable sexual curiosity is met with extremes of either disdain or delight, they might become unduly shy or excessively grandiose. They learn quickly what makes adults happy when their early attempts to practise sexual roles (trying on new clothes and make-up, enjoying innuendo and flirtation) are met either with withering scorn or exaggerated praise. In these situations, it's easy enough for perpetrators to take advantage of CYP, manipulating and compromising what began as a CYP's natural curiosity and harmless, tentative sexual expressiveness.

Sexuality within professional relationships

If CYP are lucky, their sexual expressiveness will be affirmed as *part* of their role repertoire without adults becoming overly dismayed or excited. What Freud infers is that all relationships are sexual. Young or old, we respond sensually to each other, attracted to each other to a greater or lesser extent. We *mean* things to each other.

This is challenging for professionals working with CYP. It would be much easier if sexuality could be put in a box to be opened on a CYP's 16th birthday, after which date concerned professionals would feel free to question CYP where before that date all questioning was forbidden. But if sexuality in the broadest sense begins at birth, and if the mirroring faces of parents and professionals are always giving CYP feedback, feedback CYP need, then professionals can't afford to be squeamish, however fearful they may be of 'underage' sexuality somehow expressing itself in their own relationships with CYP (Luxmoore 2016). The quality of Sex and Relationships Education in schools has always been determined by the confidence of the professionals involved. When those professionals are squeamish about addressing important issues, CYP are obliged to get their information from elsewhere: from friends or from pornography. And in porn, everyone appears to be having a great time. In porn, there are no such things as love or consent. People are merely bodies, doing their thing. Small wonder that so many adolescent relationships flounder when real life doesn't imitate porn. Small wonder that CYP look into the mirroring face of pornography and inevitably draw conclusions about how they're supposed to be.

The need for parents and professionals proactively to contextualise porn for CYP has never been greater: oral sex is not obligatory; anal sex is not obligatory; orgies are not obligatory; physical pain and humiliation are not obligatory; underage sex is not obligatory. In fact, sex itself is not obligatory. But if the parental or professional face is absent, CYP will simply look into the stylised face of porn and be inclined to imitate whatever they see.

The meaning of child protection and safeguarding

Passing on our responsibilities for protecting CYP isn't an option. Yet Pearce (2018) describes how tempting it is to assume that 'other' people are the ones involved in CSE, not us, and that there are 'other' people whose job it is to sort these things out, to protect CYP and to punish the perpetrators of CSE.

Faced with the horrors of CSE it's tempting to regress, absolving ourselves of responsibility and relying on safeguarding agencies to play the parental role for us, a role which (like children) we can idealise, believing that these parent-figures will make everything all right. Then, as soon as the parent-figures turn out to be fallible, neither omniscient nor omnipotent but capable of making mistakes, we can demonise them, blaming and attacking them for their failures. We can try to make up for their fallibility by re-equipping them with 'rules', with apparent certainties, by inventing new and more elaborate protocols to help them keep our CYP safe. But understandably, the professionals involved might then complain that it's never that simple, that more paperwork will mean less time for human beings, that guidelines are helpful but that, unfortunately, human judgement *will* sometimes be fallible.

Psychodynamically, we bring a range of autobiographical experiences to bear on the idea of CSE and on the agencies charged with ensuring the safety of CYP. We might criticise girls who wear short skirts because we were never allowed to wear short skirts; we might complain that children are too soft nowadays because we ourselves were left to our own devices as children and never enjoyed any parental support; we might call for tougher sentences for perpetrators in order to disavow the times when we've felt cruel or done cruel things to children ourselves; we might want to lynch paedophiles in order to deny the parts of ourselves that might sometimes find younger people sexually attractive.

Last thoughts

Our vehement certainties attempt to defend us against uncertainties because uncertainties make us anxious. As this chapter has described, we're inclined to simplify, reducing life to love or hate, young or old, right or wrong in order to make the anxieties go away. But the terrible fact is that our anxieties never go away, however far-reaching our protocols, however well-trained our professionals. We do get better at bearing those anxieties, however, the more we're able to acknowledge them and the more we're able to acknowledge our own responsibilities as ordinary adults.

Our ability to bear our own anxieties and acknowledge our own responsibilities begins with an understanding not only of the objective, practical circumstances of CSE but also of the subjective, unconscious processes by which people become perpetrators, victims or both. As I said at the beginning of this chapter, few of us change our behaviours until the causes of those behaviours have been understood. Whether as legislators, practitioners, therapists or carers, our interventions – however well-intentioned – are likely to flounder without adequate understanding. Given this, there's never a substitute for the painstaking and sometimes painful task of listening to CYP.

References

Blos, P. (1962) *On Adolescence: A Psychoanalytic Interpretation*, New York: The Free Press

Bowlby, J. (1969, 1973, 1980) *Attachment and Loss: Volumes 1, 2 and 3*, London: Hogarth Press

Cox, M. (1979) 'Dynamic psychotherapy with sex offenders', in L. Rosen (ed) *Sexual Deviation*, Oxford, New York and Toronto: Oxford University Press

Fonagy, P., Gergely, G., Jurist, E.J. and Target, M. (2004) *Affect Regulation, Mentalisation and the Development of the Self*, London: Karnac Books

Freud, A. (2015) 'Identification with the aggressor', in *Selected Writings*, London: Penguin Books

Freud, S. (1905) 'Three essays on the theory of sexuality', in *The Standard Edition of the Complete Psychological Works of Sigmund Freud (Vol. 7)*, London: Hogarth Press

Freud, S. (1914a) 'Remembering, repeating and working-through', in *The Standard Edition of the Complete Psychological Works of Sigmund Freud (Vol. 12)*, London: Hogarth Press

Freud, S. (1914b) 'On narcissism: An introduction', in *The Standard Edition of the Complete Psychological Works of Sigmund Freud (Vol. 12)*, London: Hogarth Press

Freud, S. (1916) 'Criminals from a sense of guilt', in *The Standard Edition of the Complete Psychological Works of Sigmund Freud (Vol. 14)*, London: Hogarth Press

Freud, S. (1920) 'Beyond the pleasure principle', in *The Standard Edition of the Complete Psychological Works of Sigmund Freud (Vol. 18)*, London: Hogarth Press

Freud, S. (1923) 'The Ego and the Id', in *The Standard Edition of the Complete Psychological Works of Sigmund Freud (Vol. 19)*, London: Hogarth Press

Gerhardt, S. (2004) *Why Love Matters: How Affection Shapes a Baby's Brain*, Hove: Brunner-Routledge

Glasser, M. (1979) 'Some aspects of the role of aggression in the perversions', in L. Rosen (ed) *Sexual Deviation*, Oxford, New York and Toronto: Oxford University Press

Hill, D. (2015) *Affect Regulation Theory: A Clinical Model*, New York and London: W.W. Norton and Company

Jones, E. (1922) 'Some problems of adolescence', in *British Journal of Psychoanalysis* 13: 31–47.

Kernberg, O.F. (1970) 'A psychoanalytic classification of character pathology', *Journal of the American Psychoanalytical Association*, 18: 800–822

Klein, M. (1928) 'Early stages of the Oedipus conflict', in J. Mitchell (ed) *The Selected Melanie Klein*, London: Penguin Books (1986)

Klein, M. (1957) *Envy and Gratitude: A Study of Unconscious Sources*, London: Tavistock Publications

Kohut, H. (1971) *The Analysis of the Self: A Systematic Approach to the Psychoanalytic Treatment of Narcissistic Personality Disorders*, New York: International universities Press

Lemma, A. (2015) *Minding the Body: The Body in Psychoanalysis and Beyond*, London: Routledge

Luxmoore, N. (2000) *Listening to Young People in School, Youth Work and Counselling*, London: Jessica Kingsley Publishers

Luxmoore, N. (2012) *Young People, Death and the Unfairness of Everything*, London: Jessica Kingsley Publishers.

Luxmoore, N. (2016) *Horny and Hormonal: Young People, Sex and the Anxieties of Sexuality*, London: Jessica Kingsley Publishers.

Moreno, J.L. (1972) 'The role concept, a bridge between psychiatry and sociology', in J. Fox (ed) *The Essential Moreno*, New York: Springer

Pearce, J.J. (2009) *Young People and Sexual Exploitation*, London and New York: Routledge

Pearce, J.J. (2018) 'Private/public bodies: "Normalised prevention" of sexual violence against children', in H. Beckett and J.J. Pearce (eds) *Understanding and Responding to Child Sexual Exploitation*, Abingdon and New York: Routledge

Phillips, A. (2012) *Missing Out: In Praise of the Unlived Life*, London: Hamish Hamilton

Stern, D.N. (1985) *The Interpersonal World of the Infant*, New York: Basic Books

Winnicott, D.W. (1965) *The Maturational Processes and the Facilitating Environment*, London: Hogarth Press

Winnicott, D.W. (1971) *Playing and Reality*, London: Routledge

Winnicott, D.W. (1975) *Through Paediatrics to Psychoanalysis: Collected Papers*, London: Hogarth Press

Wolf, E.S. (1988) *Treating the Self: Elements of Clinical Self Psychology*, New York: The Guilford Press

8

Understanding trauma and its relevance to child sexual exploitation

Kristine Hickle

Introduction

Child sexual exploitation (CSE) is a form of child sexual abuse which may expose children and young people to a range of traumatic physical, sexual and relational experiences. For some of these children and young people, early life exposure to abuse and neglect and/or time in public care (Scott and Skidmore 2006) represent additional traumatic experiences that have helped shape how they view themselves and interact with others (Herman 1992). Research on child sexual abuse and other forms of child maltreatment indicates that survivors need access to services that recognise trauma and seek to mitigate the impact of traumatic experiences on their lives (Finkelhor and Browne 1985).

Trauma can be defined as 'any exposure to an extraordinary experience that presents a physical or psychological threat to oneself or others and generates a reaction of helplessness and fear' (American Psychiatric Association 2013). More simply, a traumatic event overwhelms typical adaptations to human life (Herman 1992). Traumatic experiences can take many forms, and may include natural disaster, car accidents, war, childhood maltreatment or community violence. Research on adverse child experiences (ACEs) indicates that exposure to prejudice, poverty, bereavement, being forced to take on adult responsibilities, or difficult adjustments (for example, migration, asylum) are also traumatic (Bush 2018), and the effects of being exposed to traumatic experiences are varied, often lasting into adulthood (Felitti et al 1998).

Understanding CSE through the lenses of contemporary trauma theory and research can provide insight into the experiences of children and young people affected by CSE. This chapter will provide a brief overview of the research on trauma, specifically in relation to the impact of developmental and complex trauma and sexual abuse, and the growing body of research on trauma-informed approaches to practice. It will consider how trauma responses are developed while enduring extreme stress, and how these responses may be evident among children and young people with CSE experiences. This chapter will also consider how systems designed to protect and support traumatised children and young people often contribute to their re-traumatisation (Harris and Fallot 2001). It will explore principles of trauma-informed practice that are useful in meeting the needs of young people victimised by CSE (Hampton and Leiggi 2017), discuss how trauma-informed approaches align with strengths-based and relationship-based approaches to CSE practice (Lefevre et al 2017), and how such approaches can help practitioners understand and promote resilience (Harvey 2007).

Trauma: a historical perspective

Trauma theory is best understood as an approach to working with trauma (Gibson and Gibson 2015). Our modern understanding of trauma can be traced to the work of Jean Martin Charcot in the late nineteenth century (Ringell 2012), whose work with women diagnosed with hysteria led him to believe that the symptoms he observed in women may be the result of prior traumatic experiences. Others, including Freud, later built upon Charcot's work by considering the ways in which hysteria could be rooted in early life traumas, such as sexual abuse (Herman 1992). Freud's views changed over time, but the link between traumatic experiences and a person's mental health and behaviours remained. A few decades later, the term 'shell shock' was used during the First World War and 'combat stress reaction' during the Second World War to describe trauma symptoms among soldiers who seemed overcome with periods of crying, memory loss, a lack of responsiveness and physical paralysis (Herman 1992). Following the Second World War, research and treatment of trauma developed further, particularly in relation to the effects of prolonged traumatic experiences among Holocaust survivors. Practitioners who treated these survivors observed the way in which they struggled to make sense of their own emotional reactions and gain a sense of control over their emotions (Ringell 2011).

Trauma theory and practice developed further in the mid-twentieth century following other large-scale events such as the Vietnam War and the women's movement of the 1970s that raised awareness regarding the prevalence of sexual violence and child abuse and the impact of such abuse on those affected (Ringell 2011). This included a growing awareness of the ways in which experiencing trauma could leave people feeling physically unwell, disorganised, overwhelmed and coping with these feelings in unhealthy ways (for example, drug and alcohol misuse, aggressive behaviour and violence). People began to understand that the psychological distress resulting from trauma was not necessarily due to individual predisposition or family history. It was recognised that the distress could be a response to the traumatic event itself (Jones and Wessely 2006). In 1980, the diagnosis of post-traumatic stress disorder (PTSD) was named and introduced into the *Diagnostic and Statistical Manual of Mental Disorders* (third edition) (American Psychiatric Association 1980).

Over the past several decades, the way in which we understand trauma and posttraumatic stress responses have been further refined to account more specifically for traumatic abuse and neglect in childhood, termed 'developmental trauma' (van der Kolk 1994), and 'complex trauma' experienced by people who undergo repeated/multiple traumatic stressors over time (Courtois 2008). In the late 1990s a landmark epidemiological study on the impact of childhood trauma, the 'Adverse Childhood Experiences' (ACEs) study, provided new and compelling evidence that children who experience multiple adversities are at an increased risk for a range of physical and mental health difficulties throughout their lives (Felitti et al 1998). More recent conceptualisations of trauma also better account for historical, social and cultural contexts that influence how an individual experiences trauma. This is particularly true regarding our understanding of the impact that racial discrimination and prejudice can have on children and young people. Experiencing racism can be a form of trauma, and racial discrimination within society contributes to the overrepresentation of Black, Asia, Arab and other ethnic minority (BAME) young people in school exclusions and/or youth justice systems, which can themselves contribute to additional trauma and adversity (Adebowale et al 2017).

Our understanding of gender differences in trauma has advanced as well. For example, research indicates that girls and boys differ regarding the type of traumatic experiences they are more likely to experience; research suggesting that boys are more likely to experience physical assaults, injuries and witness death while girls are more likely to experience traumatic sexual abuse, exploitation and sexual assault (Tolin and Foa 2006; Sack-Jones 2017). There are gender differences in responses to trauma as well, with girls more likely to be identified as meeting posttraumatic stress disorder criteria (Abram et al 2004; Tolin and Foa 2006). Girls are also more likely to have similar responses to trauma, exhibiting internalising behaviours such as anxiety, depression and other mental health issues (Christie 2018) whether they personally experienced it or witnessed something traumatic happening to another person (Foster et al 2004).

While gender differences in trauma responses should be understood, it is also important to recognise that responses to trauma vary and are unique to each individual (Knight 2015). Some people may experience trauma that does not lead to long-term difficulty or dysfunction, and not everyone who has experienced a traumatic event will be significantly affected, or in need of trauma-specific interventions (Bonanno 2004). Even among those who have been negatively affected, their capacity for self-efficacy, growth and enhanced ability to cope with future challenges is increasingly recognised in the literature on resilience and post-traumatic growth (Calhoun and Tedeschi 2014).

Trauma responses

While individual responses may vary, there is broad consensus regarding the ways in which trauma symptoms, or responses, can manifest in people who have experienced ongoing or single incidences of trauma. These responses can take many forms, but can be categorised as: avoidance and arousal. Also, trauma survivors might re-experience the trauma through intrusive thoughts and memories, flashbacks and nightmares (Brown et al 2014). They may find themselves avoiding thoughts, feelings, conversations, activities, places, or people that elicit memories of the trauma (Gibson and Gibson 2015), and they may also find themselves dissociating when reminded of the trauma. Dissociation involves disconnecting or detaching from an experience; it is thought to be connected with the body's stress response system, and serves a function by automating behaviour when a person feels overwhelmed (Nijenhuis and Van der Hart 2011). Dissociation is an important, adaptive survival instinct that can kick in when someone is psychologically overwhelmed. A person who is dissociating may appear avoidant or numb and may 'check out' when being spoken to. As a result, dissociation can be misinterpreted by professionals as sign of being untruthful or unaffected by the traumatic event(s).

Arousal responses may also be misinterpreted by professionals who observe trauma survivors presenting as hyper-aroused, always in a state of high energy, wired and unable to relax (NHS England 2015) or hypervigilant, when they are overly alert to potential danger (Bloom 2005). When experiencing hypervigilance, a person can appear to be tense, fidgeting, 'on edge' and even hostile. Additional trauma responses include depression and/or anxiety, or suicidal thoughts. Some people may also self-harm or experience physical symptoms in response to trauma including nausea, trembling or panic attacks (NHS England 2015). Anger and aggression are also common, and some may have difficulty explaining or rationalising these emotions (Gibson and Gibson 2015). Substance misuse may become a problem among trauma survivors looking for a reprieve from feeling hyper-aroused or distressed by flashbacks or intrusive memories. All of these responses can be easily misunderstood by professionals who do not have a good understanding of trauma, and of how human brains and bodies are 'hardwired' to survive and stay safe during traumatic experiences. For further discussion about this from a psychodynamic perspective see Chapter 7 in this volume.

In the last 15 years, there has been greater consideration of the ways in which experiencing ongoing, complex trauma in childhood and adolescence can disrupt a sense of safety, identity and place in the social world. Research on complex trauma in childhood has repeatedly found that children are likely to struggle with impulse control, regulating their emotions, learning, paying attention, solving problems, attachment and interpersonal relationships, self-esteem and memory (Cook et al 2003; D'Andrea et al 2012; Kisiel et al 2014). According to Shepherd and Wild (2014), more severe trauma responses are also associated with difficulties in cognitive reappraisal (that is, changing the way one interprets and responds to a situation), and emotional regulation such that a traumatised person is less able to reduce emotional intensity and arousal. These complex trauma responses can become part of a destructive cycle for children and young people. Their behaviours are first a result of the interpersonal violence and trauma they have experienced, and then become the problem that leads to placement disruptions (Kisiel et al 2014), difficulty in traditional education settings, criminal justice system involvement and problems forming trusting relationships (Levenson 2017).

Trauma, child sexual abuse and CSE

Sexual abuse comes in many forms. Regardless of how a person is victimised, the experience is traumatic. Sexual abuse in childhood occurs when a child is persuaded or forced to participate in sexual activities that may include physical contact or non-contact activities including grooming a child for abuse, having a child view the sexual activity of others, encouraging them to behave in sexually inappropriate ways, or participate in making child abuse images (DfE 2017). Child sexual abuse often involves feeling physically and psychologically threatened, and survivors are likely to feel overwhelmed and unable to protect themselves. As a result, the trauma responses discussed earlier are commonly experienced by survivors of child sexual abuse (Schneider et al 2013).

CSE is a form of child sexual abuse (Beckett and Walker 2017) and a growing body of research on the impact of CSE indicates that, like many other survivors of child sexual abuse, children and young people victimised by CSE are likely to experience trauma symptoms and respond to trauma in similar ways. For example, Berelowitz et al (2013) identified common experiences among CSE survivors such as drug and alcohol problems, depression, low self-esteem, anger, self-harm, suicide attempts and increased involvement in criminal activity. These findings align with what is known about responses to trauma and indicate how young people victimised by CSE are trying to self-sooth, self-regulate and cope with traumatic experiences, albeit in sometimes negative and harmful ways. Unfortunately, many professionals lack a sufficient understanding of trauma and how it affects CSE survivors (Beckett and Warrington 2015). As a result, victim-blaming and punitive punishments remain common within a system that is generally designed to recognise and respond to the *effects* of trauma (manifesting in emotional and behavioural difficulties) rather than the underlying traumatic experiences themselves (Christie 2018). This lack of awareness and inadequate response is both unproductive and harmful. Professionals who do not understand trauma can, unknowingly, try to strip away the attempts at coping young people have developed to keep themselves safe. This is done at the expense of understanding *why* the child or young person developed these responses in the first place and what purpose they served in helping them to feel safe. For example, when a young person victimised by CSE presents as hyperaroused, full of energy, distracted and aggressive, these presenting behaviours can easily become the focus of any intervention because the behaviours are disruptive, perhaps dangerous and difficult to handle. Reframing these behaviours through the lens of trauma helps us understand that they may be responses to the traumatic experiences she/he has been through and were initially helpful to the young person in enabling them to be aware of their surroundings, alert to danger and ready to protect themselves.

When professionals begin to understand trauma, and how trauma symptoms/responses manifest in young people victimised by CSE, they are better equipped to work with a young person to stay safe. They can develop interventions that prioritise long-term emotional safety and stabilisation (Herman 1992) so that the young person can begin learning new ways of responding to their environment and getting their needs met. This way of working has been described as 'trauma-informed'. Trauma-informed practice is inherently relational and strengths-based, (Sweeney et al 2016) and provides multi-disciplinary professionals with a framework for understanding a child or young person's present difficulties in the context of prior trauma (Knight 2015). We will now consider principles of trauma-informed practice and how professionals might apply this approach to practice with children and young people who have experienced sexual exploitation.

Trauma-informed practice

> 'An abnormal reaction to an abnormal situation is normal
> behaviour.' (Victor Frankl)

A trauma-informed approach can be defined as 'a strengths-based framework that is grounded in an understanding of and responsiveness to the impact of trauma, that emphasises physical, psychological, and emotional safety for both providers and survivors, and that creates opportunities for survivors to rebuild a sense of control and empowerment' (Hopper et al 2010:82). This approach was initially conceptualised in the United States by Harris and Fallot (2001) in response to a growing awareness that traumatised children, young people and adults interact with health and human service systems that are not designed to recognise the impact of trauma in their lives. They envisioned a paradigm shift, which required stakeholders across these systems to prioritise returning autonomy and control to the trauma survivor. This shift also involved recognising that trauma responses, however problematic or disruptive they may seem for an individual and the people around them, are what Victor Frankl (2004) called perfectly *normal* responses to abnormal traumatic experiences. This approach enables professionals across a range of disciplines to:

> conceptualize negative behaviors as coping strategies that
> were once adaptive in the traumagenic environment but
> which have become self-destructive or harmful across
> different domains of human functioning. By viewing the
> collective experiences of the individual in this holistic way,
> client behaviours that seem irrational, self-destructive, or
> even abusive are reconceptualized as survival skills that once
> helped the individual respond to threatening encounters

but which now impede the ability to tolerate distress and set boundaries. (Levenson 2017:107)

This way of thinking developed purchase first throughout the USA and in 2005 the Substance Abuse and Mental Health Services Administration (SAMHSA) created the National Centre for Trauma-Informed Care (SAMHSA 2015). Several evidence-based approaches, such as Sandra Bloom's Sanctuary Model (Bloom 2005; Bloom and Sreedhar 2008) were identified as best practice in adopting a trauma-informed approach (TIA). The Sanctuary Model is innovative in its emphasis on moving beyond a clinical, diagnostic understanding of trauma in order to focus on creating an environment that is safe for both service users and staff; the model prioritises attachment and connection, open communication, a commitment to inquiry and social learning, and building resilience for individuals and the organisation as a whole (Bloom 2005; Bush 2018). While this promising model of practice is supported by research, the evidence base for TIAs remain limited and they are challenging to study because they often involve multiple interventions (thus making it difficult to pinpoint exactly what causes improvement for service users). However, the body of research on TIAs is growing, along with evidence of TIAs implemented in the USA, Canada, New Zealand and Australia (see Sweeney et al 2016).

A trauma-informed approach requires practitioners to promote safety, trust, choice, collaboration and empowerment in their work with service users (Harris and Fallot 2001). This approach contrasts with the medicalisation of human suffering, and the coercive practices that often prioritise organisational needs over staff and service users (Sweeney et al 2016). While TIAs are useful across a range of professional roles, they are particularly important for professionals not engaged in trauma-specific work who are likely to feel less confident to address trauma in service users' lives (Hickle 2018). Being trauma-informed requires practitioners to follow several key principles in practice, summarised from the work of Knight (2015) and Levenson (2017) in the USA and Sweeney et al (2016) in the UK. These are to:

- understand and acknowledge the impact of trauma in people's lives;
- be able to recognise the signs and symptoms/responses common among trauma survivors;
- ensure service provision environments are physically, psychologically, socially and culturally safe;
- prioritise trustworthiness and transparency in building relationships with survivors;

- recognise cultural, historical and gendered contexts that trauma survivors are living within and ensure services are best suited to meet their needs;
- take every opportunity to support survivors in taking control of their own lives, making choices and feeling empowered. This is incredibly important for those who have trauma experiences that were characterised by a lack of autonomy and control;
- ensure services are structured to promote collaboration, mutuality and peer support;
- promote access to trauma-specific care (for example, specialist mental health services) when and if appropriate;
- make an effort to avoid retraumatising someone, particularly when organisational practices and necessary legal and/or safeguarding procedures are likely to do so (Christie 2018);
- integrate this understanding of trauma more widely into organisational policy and practice to ensure practitioners are well-supported in this work.

These principles were evident in recent research on a TIA adopted by a large voluntary sector organisation in Southeast England (Hickle 2018), where young people were able to describe how staff members understood the impact trauma has in their lives, helped to normalise their trauma responses, and communicated with them in a collaborative and empowering way. One young person described how they were able to do this even amid serious safeguarding concerns:

> I recently moved in…and I self-harmed and was suicidal. They had to follow the procedure, they called the paramedic and an ambulance turned up for me and I think the way they relayed that to me and they helped me with my own care was by saying, 'do you want us to come with you?' While I'm getting shoved into the back of an ambulance. And going through the safeguarding form afterwards, they didn't just forget it, they didn't just say, 'we will contact you if you want us to.' It was, 'come downstairs and we'll go through a safeguarding form with you, which is how we can help you to stop this from happening again, because we care about you'. It wasn't just forgotten or left about like other places do. (p 287)

This young person's experience represents several key principles of trauma-informed care. These principles translate across disciplinary boundaries and provide a useful starting point for considering how a TIA is relevant for work with young people victimised by CSE in its many forms. The following section describes how these principles align with the growing body of research on the needs and experiences of young people who have been victimised by CSE.

Trauma-informed practice for CSE

Trauma-informed practice first begins with an understanding of trauma and common trauma responses. In the context of work with CSE, this means that practitioners understand the particular nature of traumatic sexual abuse and how repeated trauma in childhood can influence a young person's view of the world and their response to it. In practice, this will enable them to more fully acknowledge the way in which a young person's choices and actions have been shaped by the need to survive and stay safe. It may also help them consider how services meant to help young people might unintentionally re-traumatise them. For example, a young person who feels controlled by a perpetrator and is unable to make decisions about where they go and whom they contact may feel re-traumatised by restrictive efforts to keep them safe (for example, the use of secure accommodation), or being pressured to speak with professionals they do not know or trust. Professionals who are mindful of avoiding re-traumatisation can then work with the young person to ensure that they feel some control over their situation and advocate for an approach that does not mirror the controlling behaviour of a perpetrator. Instead, they might provide the young person with a choice regarding whom they work with (for example, social worker/other supportive adult); work alongside them to make decisions about living arrangements; speak honestly about professionals' concerns and what may happen if professionals feel the young person is not safe, ensure that the young person is prepared for what might come next (for example, meetings they will be asked to attend, the court process); and seek to normalise trauma responses so that the young person does not feel frightened, confused, or isolated in their experience.

Safety and trust

Safety and trust are foundational to a TIA, and ensuring the physical safety of young people experiencing (or 'at risk of') CSE has been a primary focus for professionals in recent years, particularly in light of widely publicised incidences when professionals failed to do so

(Lefevre et al 2017). While physical safety is a key element of trauma-informed practice, trauma survivors often feel emotionally unsafe while, and long after, they become physically safe (Herman 1992). This can be challenging for both young people and professionals with safeguarding responsibilities, as efforts to 'keep' someone physically safe can be unsuccessful if they do not yet know how to calm their minds and bodies long enough to actually experience feeling safe. This may be particularly true for young people who have been exploited for a long period of time and/or perhaps experienced trauma prior to CSE, as feeling unsafe is something they will be familiar with (Hallett 2017). Young peoples' difficulties in feeling safe can be reinforced by an overemphasis on policing their behaviour in an effort to keep them safe (for example, to prevent missing episodes) and lack of emphasis on creating safety in the places and contexts in which young people are abused (Christie 2018; Firmin 2017).

According to Shuker (2013) safety is three-dimensional, involving physical, emotional and relational safety. This conceptualisation of safety is important for understanding young people who have experienced CSE; in order to feel safe, they need professionals to first recognise that beginning to feel wholly safe (across all three dimensions) takes time. CSE often involves coercion, deception and psychological manipulation by peers, romantic partners or other trusted relationships (Reid 2011), and so it is entirely rational that young people adapt and survive CSE experiences by learning not to trust others. Restoring the ability to trust happens in the context of relationships that are predictable, persevering and authentic (Hickle 2018). Re-learning how to trust and feel safe takes time. Lefevre et al's (2017) study of three local authorities in England found that professionals were able to identify time – and flexibility – as key elements in effective CSE practice and recognised the need for organisational structures to account for the time it may take for a young person to feel safe again. Another recent study exploring trauma-informed practices for responding to CSE found that young people also emphasised the importance of time and flexibility as necessary for building a trusting relationship, particularly when young people and professionals disagree (Christie 2018). Professionals must be willing to listen to what the young person has to say about who and what makes them feel safe, ensure the young person is aware of how this information is incorporated into the professionals' plan for keeping them safe (Warrington and Brodie 2018), and work to prioritise safety in the geographic and social spaces where young people are vulnerable to exploitation. Creating a safe environment might also involve teaching young people how to self sooth by using grounding techniques (that is, breathing exercises or physical movement to help a young person feel mentally and physically present), facilitating connections with people who are important to them, and helping them to understand their own responses to trauma (van der Kolk 1994).

Choice, collaboration and empowerment

The way in which professionals conceptualise agency and choice in relation to CSE has transformed in the last ten years. The pendulum has swung between believing young people 'choose' to engage in relationships with older men (Jay 2014), to believing CSE victims are without agency once they have been groomed for sexual exploitation (Melrose 2012). More recently, research has highlighted the need for a more nuanced approach to understanding the 'interplay between structure and agency to elucidate the relationship between young people's choices and abusive social environments' (Firmin et al 2016:2318). Taking a more nuanced approach requires prioritising collaboration, choice and control in CSE practice, as a report by the Office of the Children's Commissioner's in their inquiry into CSE in groups and gangs in England highlights (Berelowitz et al 2013):

> Children and young people told us repeatedly that 'being done to' by the agencies charged with their care compounded their sense of powerlessness and hopelessness. They want to be partners in their protection and recovery plans and those that had this experience valued it immensely and felt stronger for being involved. (Berelowitz, et al 2013:56)

Using trauma-informed practice as a framework for understanding these children and young people's experiences is useful as it enables us to see why 'being done to' is so problematic. In order to begin feeling safe again, to recover, and move on from CSE, young people must begin feeling some sense of control over their own lives, and have opportunities to make choices. While these principles align with how we understand children's' rights more generally (UNICEF 2015), taking a TIA enables us to see choice and control as *foundational* to trauma recovery. Research has identified a range of ways in which practice systems, and individual practitioners, can engage in trauma-informed practice through supporting choice and control among young people. For example, they could take a strengths-based approach to practice (Dodsworth 2014), emphasising the skills and positive characteristics of young people that have enabled them to survive difficult, dangerous and traumatic experiences. Professionals may also consider principles of harm reduction to help support the young person in taking the lead to keep themselves safe (Hickle and Hallett 2016). This may involve exploring ways a young person can keep safe in dangerous situations and working to build a supportive relationship with them, even amid episodes of going missing. Wherever possible, professionals can also promote voluntary engagement in services (Christie 2018; Warrington and Brodie 2018) and demonstrate to the young person that they are able to listen to and respect them (Gilligan 2016). They can also ensure reciprocity and interdependency in caregiving relationships (Hallett 2015), which indicates to the young person that the connection they have with a (trusted) adult is authentic and human. In research on trauma-informed practice, young people have emphatically stated the need for helping professionals to be 'like normal adults, normal human begins', and they wanted to be treated 'just like a person' (Hickle 2018:9).

Trauma-informed organisational practices

Harris and Fallot (2001) originally described trauma-informed practice as a way of working that required a whole organisation to understand and commit to trauma-informed care. This included care of staff and those engaged in direct work with service users, and an explicit acknowledgement that working with traumatised young people exposes staff to difficult and emotionally challenging work that can change the way they see and interact with the world (Cunningham 2003). While a professional working in a trauma-informed way may be better prepared to hear and respond to the experiences of traumatised young people, they are still exposing themselves to demanding and difficult circumstances through this work. For example, they may be able to recognise that a young person who is shouting at them and threatening them does this because they have difficulty regulating their emotions and feels most able to keep themselves safe by avoiding any engagement with a trustworthy adult; however, this does not negate the fact that being threatened is a stressful experience.

It also does not ensure that they are sufficiently supported by their organisation to take care of themselves and manage feelings of secondary traumatisation (Cunningham 2003). Re-orienting organisational practices around a TIA first requires an acknowledgement that organisations often engage in practices that contraindicate trauma-informed practice. This happens when service delivery is fragmented, communication within and across agencies is poor, decision-making is hierarchical instead of collaborative, and punitive measures are used towards staff (Bloom 2005).

In order to engage in trauma-informed practice, practitioners need to feel that their organisation supports *them* in a trauma-informed way. They need to feel safe, hopeful and have a sense of control over their work; they also need clear expectations and boundaries (Bloom 2005). The small, but growing body of research evidence on TIAs indicates that effective implementation of any trauma-informed strategy involves a clear focus on employees, including procedures for addressing secondary traumatic stress and ensuring collaboration and communication within staff teams (Hanson and Lang 2016). Research on effective professional practice with CSE also indicates that they need to feel confident that their supervisory arrangements are able to address the impact of working with trauma: 'Regular, reflective supervision (group and individual) and informal workplace support were considered vital by interviewees in helping professionals to provide a containing, supportive, therapeutic and child-centred environment which enables children to feel safe and cared for' (Lefevre et al 2017:2469).

Thus, widening the lens through which we apply a TIA to include organisational practice is necessary for ensuring the safety and wellbeing of both staff and service users. We must also look further, beyond organisational practices and into the wider contexts in which young people are victimised to avoid de-contextualising and de-politicising the trauma inflicted upon young people who have experienced CSE. In their research on youth homelessness, McKenzie-Mohr, Coates and McLeod (2012) argue that trauma-informed service provision must incorporate an understanding of the contexts within which young people are victimised, and take into account the impact of living in a classist, racist, patriarchal and heterosexist society. Their work aligns with Ackerley and Latchford (2018) who call for an intersectional approach to addressing CSE that recognises the way in which CSE intersects with other forms of inequality and harm. This requires an acknowledgement that some groups of young people, including Black, Asian and minority ethnic young people and/or young people with disabilities, may have experienced traumatic oppression and discrimination alongside experiences of CSE. They are less likely to receive CSE services and/or have 'their needs supported in ways that work for them' (Ackerley and Latchford 2018:61). Taking a TIA in

CSE work requires a commitment to ensuring that the needs of all young people can be met.

Conclusion

In this chapter I have proposed that considering young people's experiences of CSE through the lens of contemporary trauma theory, particularly in relation to more recent conceptualisations of developmental and complex trauma, can help practitioners better understand young people's experiences, behaviours and needs. I have considered how using the framework of trauma-informed practice can help practitioners promote safety, trust, choice, collaboration and empowerment (Harris and Fallot 2001), and find a way of working with young people that is respectful, authentic and productive.

Effective CSE practice requires a robust multi-agency response (Pearce 2014), and TIA was intended for implementation across a range of disciplines. TIAs can be adapted to fit within diverse agency structures, and can be aligned to support traditional measures of safety and care. While a TIA would be most effective if implemented across a practice system, this can be challenging as it requires (for many) a paradigm shift. It means changing the way that practitioners think about young people and themselves. TIA is also conceptually challenging; it is a complex idea that is often made more complicated when professionals cannot agree on a common definition or approach to implementation (Berliner and Kolko 2016). Furthermore, any real evidence of change across a practice system will take time (Sweeney et al 2016). Additional research is needed to investigate the effectiveness of TIAs in the UK, and to examine how a TIA can be specifically tailored to meet the needs of young people who have experienced CSE in its many forms.

While we should acknowledge the need for a more robust evidence base in relation to TIA, recent research provides a compelling case for applying TIA principles in practice. These principles are ethical, just and align with core professional values (for example, BASW 2015). They also generally align with accepted practice wisdom; for example, most people can agree that safety and collaboration are part of any good service (Sweeney et al 2016). Trauma-informed practices are evident within the CSE research literature discussed throughout this chapter, indicating that a TIA framework can be useful in CSE work, enabling professionals to more helpfully interpret young people's present difficulties in the context of their prior traumas (Knight 2015). Professionals might then be well-positioned to ensure the services they deliver avoid re-traumatisation and coercive practices, engender trust and provide every opportunity for young people to feel safe, resilient and powerful in their lives.

References

Abram, K.M., Teplin, L.A., Charles, D.R., Longworth, S., McClelland, G. and Dulcan, M. (2004) 'Posttraumatic stress disorder and trauma in youth in juvenile detention', *Archives of General Psychiatry*, 61: 403–410

Ackerley, E. and Latchford, L. (2018) 'Applying an intersectional lens to sexual violence research and practice', in H. Beckett and J. Pearce (eds) *Understanding and Responding to Child Sexual Exploitation*, Abingdon: Taylor and Francis, pp 54–66

Adebowale, V., Bush, M., Verghese, S. (2017) 'Responding to the traumatic impact of racial prejudice', in M. Bush (ed) *Addressing Adversity*, London: Young Minds Trust, pp 199–217

American Psychiatric Association (1980) *Diagnostic and Statistical Manual of Mental Disorders* (3rd edn), Washington, DC: American Psychiatric Publishing.

American Psychiatric Association (2013) *Diagnostic and Statistical Manual of Mental Disorders* (5th edn), Arlington, VA: American Psychiatric Publishing.

BASW (British Association of Social Workers) (2015) *BASW Code of Ethics*, www.basw.co.uk/codeofethics/

Beckett, H. and Warrington, C. (2015) 'Making justice work: Experiences of criminal justice for children and young people affected by sexual exploitation as victims and witnesses', www.beds.ac.uk/__data/assets/pdf_file/0006/461868/Beckett-and-Warrington-2015-Making-Justice-Work.pdf

Beckett, H. and Walker, J. (2017) 'Words matter: Reconceptualising the conceptualisation of child sexual exploitation', in H. Beckett, and J. Pearce (eds) *Understanding and Responding to Child Sexual Exploitation*, London: Routledge, pp 9–23

Berelowitz, S., Firmin, C., Edwards, G. and Gulyurtlu, S. (2012) *I thought I was the only one. The only one in the world. The Office of the Children's Commissioner's Inquiry into Child Sexual Exploitation In Gangs and Groups: Interim report*, London: The Office of the Children's Commissioner in England

Berelowitz, S., Clifton, J., Firmin, C., Gulyurtlu, S. and Edwards, G. (2013) *'If Only Someone Had Listened': Office of the Children's Commissioner's Inquiry into Child Sexual Exploitation in Gangs and Groups. Final Report*, London: Office of the Children's Commissioner.

Berliner, L. and Kolko, D.J. (2016) 'Trauma informed care: A commentary and critique', *Child Maltreatment*, 21(2): 168–172

Bloom, S.L. (2005) 'The sanctuary model of organizational change for children's residential treatment', *Therapeutic Community: The International Journal for Therapeutic and Supportive Organizations*, 26(1): 65–81

Bloom, S.L. and Sreedhar, S.Y. (2008) 'The sanctuary model of trauma-informed organizational change', *Reclaiming Children and Youth*, 17(3): 48–53

Bonanno, G.A. (2004) 'Loss, trauma, and human resilience: Have we underestimated the human capacity to thrive after extremely aversive events?', *American Psychologist*, 59(1): 20–28

Brown, A., Bollini, A., Craighead, L., Astin, M., Norrholm, S. and Bradley, B. (2014) 'Self-monitoring of reexperiencing symptoms: A randomized trial', *Journal of Traumatic Stress*, 27(5): 519–525

Bush, M. (2018). 'Child adversity and trauma: an introduction' in M. Bush (ed) *Addressing Adversity: Prioritising adversity and trauma-informed care for children and young people in England*, London: Young Minds Trust, pp 26–56

Calhoun, L.G. and Tedeschi, R.G. (eds) (2014) *Handbook of Posttraumatic Growth: Research and Practice*, Abingdon: Routledge

Christie, C. (2018) *A Trauma-Informed Health and Care Approach for Responding to Child Sexual Abuse and Exploitation Current Knowledge Report*, Department of Health and Social Care, https://assets.publishing.service.gov.uk/government/uploads/system/uploads/attachment_data/file/712725/trauma-informed-health-and-care-approach-report.pdf

Cook, A., Blanustein, M., Spinazzola, J. and van der Kolk, B. (eds) (2003) *Complex Trauma in Children and Adolescents*, Durham, NC: National Child Traumatic Stress Network

Courtois, C.A. (2008) 'Complex trauma, complex reactions: Assessment and treatment', *Psychological Trauma: Theory, Research, Practice, and Policy*, S(1): 86–100

Cunningham, M. (2003) 'Impact of trauma work on social work clinicians: Empirical findings', *Social Work*, 48(4): 451–459

D'Andrea, W., Ford, J., Stolbach, B., Spinazzola, J. and van der Kolk, B.A. (2012) 'Understanding interpersonal trauma in children: Why we need a developmentally appropriate trauma diagnosis', *American Journal of Orthopsychiatry*, 82(2): 187–200.

DfE (Department for Education) (2017) *Child sexual exploitation: Definition and a guide for practitioners, local leaders and decision makers working to protect children from child sexual exploitation*, www.gov.uk/government/uploads/system/uploads/attachment_data/file/591903/CSE_Guidance_Core_Document_13.02.2017.pdf

Dodsworth, J. (2014) 'Sexual exploitation, selling and swapping sex: Victimhood and agency', *Child Abuse Review*, 23(3): 185–199

Felitti, V.J., Anda, R.F., Nordenberg, D., Williamson, D.F., Spitz, A M., Edwards, V., Koss, M.P. and Marks, J.S. (1998) 'Relationship of childhood abuse and household dysfunction to many of the leading causes of death in adults: The Adverse Childhood Experiences (ACE) Study', *American Journal of Preventive Medicine*, 14(4): 245–258

Finkelhor, D. and Browne, A. (1985) 'The traumatic impact of child sexual abuse: A conceptualization', *American Journal of Orthopsychiatry*, 55(4): 530–541

Firmin, C. (2017) *Abuse Between Young People: A Contextual Account*, London: Routledge

Firmin, C., Warrington, C. and Pearce, J. (2016) 'Sexual exploitation and its impact on developing sexualities and sexual relationships: The need for contextual social work interventions', *The British Journal of Social Work*, 46: 2318–2337

Foster, J.D., Kuperminc, G.P. and Price, A.W. (2004) 'Gender differences in posttraumatic stress and related symptoms among inner-city minority youth exposed to community violence', *Journal of Youth and Adolescence*, 33: 59–69

Frankl, V.E. (2004) *Man's Search for Meaning: The Classic Tribute to Hope from the Holocaust*, Random House.

Gibson, A. and Gibson, N. (2015) *Human Growth, Behaviour and Development: Essential Theory and Application in Social Work*, Sage

Gilligan, P. (2016) 'Turning it around: What do young women say helps them to move on from child sexual exploitation?', *Child Abuse Review*, 25(2): 115–127

Hallett, S. (2015) '"An uncomfortable comfortableness": "Care", child protection and child sexual exploitation', *British Journal of Social Work*, 46(7): 2137–2152

Hallett, S. (2017) *Making Sense of Child Sexual Exploitation: Exchange, Abuse, and Young People*, Bristol: Policy Press

Hampton, M.D. and Lieggi, M. (2017) 'Commercial sexual exploitation of youth in the United States: A qualitative systematic review', *Trauma, Violence, and Abuse*, 1524838017742168

Hanson, R.F. and Lang, J. (2016) 'A critical look at trauma-informed care among agencies and systems serving maltreated youth and their families', *Child Maltreatment*, 21(2): 95–100

Harris, M.E. and Fallot, R.D. (2001) *Using Trauma Theory to Design Service Systems*, Chicago, IL: Jossey-Bass

Harvey, M.R. (2007) 'Towards an ecological understanding of resilience in trauma survivors: Implications for theory, research, and practice', *Journal of Aggression, Maltreatment and Trauma*, 14(1–2): 9–32

Herman, J. (1992) *Trauma and Recovery: The Aftermath of Violence – From Domestic Abuse to Political Terror*, New York: Basic Books

Hickle, K. (2018) *Trauma Informed Evaluation Report*, Hove: YMCA Downslink Group

Hickle, K. and Hallett, S. (2016) 'Mitigating harm: considering harm reduction principles in work with sexually exploited young people', *Children and Society*, 30, 302–313

Hickle, K., Lefevre, M., Luckock, B. and Ruch, G. (2017) *Piloting and Evaluating the 'See Me, Hear Me' Framework for Working with Child Sexual Exploitation*. Final report. University of Sussex

Hopper, E.K., Bassuk, E.L. and Olivet, J. (2010) 'Shelter from the storm: Trauma-informed care in homelessness services settings', *The Open Health Services and Policy Journal*, 3(1): 80-100

Jay, A. (2014) *Independent Inquiry Into Child Sexual Exploitation in Rotherham: 1997–2013*, Rotherham Metropolitan Borough Council.

Jones, E. and Wessely, S. (2006) 'Psychological trauma: A historical perspective', *Psychiatry*, 5: 217–220

Kisiel, C.L., Fehrenbach, T., Torgersen, E., Stolbach, B., McClelland, G., Griffin, G. and Burkman, K. (2014) 'Constellations of interpersonal trauma and symptoms in child welfare: Implications for a developmental trauma framework', *Journal of Family Violence*, 29(1): 1014, doi: org.ezproxy.sussex.ac.uk/10.1007/s10896-013-9559-0

Knight, C. (2015) 'Trauma-informed social work practice: Practice considerations and challenges', *Clinical Social Work Journal*, 43(1): 25–37

Lefevre, M., Hickle, K., Luckock, B. and Ruch, G. (2017) 'Building trust with children and young people at risk of child sexual exploitation: The professional challenge', *The British Journal of Social Work*, 47(8): 2456–2473

Levenson, J. (2017) 'Trauma-informed social work practice', *Social work*, 62(2): 105–113

McKenzie-Mohr, S., Coates, J. and McLeod, H. (2012) 'Responding to the needs of youth who are homeless: Calling for politicized trauma-informed intervention', *Children and Youth Services Review*, 34(1): 136–143

Melrose, M. (2012) 'Twenty-first century party people: Young people and sexual exploitation in the new millennium', *Child Abuse Review*, 22(3): 155–168

NHS England (2015) 'Post-traumatic stress disorder (PTSD)', www.nhs.uk/conditions/post-traumatic-stress-disorder-ptsd/symptoms/

Nijenhuis, E.R. and Van der Hart, O. (2011) 'Dissociation in trauma: A new definition and comparison with previous formulations', *Journal of Trauma & Dissociation*, 12(4): 416–445

Pearce, J.J. (2014) '"What's going on" to safeguard children and young people from child sexual exploitation: A review of local safeguarding children boards' work to protect children from sexual exploitation', *Child Abuse Review*, 23(3): 159–170

Reid, J. A. (2011) 'An exploratory model of girl's vulnerability to commercial sexual exploitation in prostitution', *Child Maltreatment*, 16(2): 146–157

Ringel, S. (2011) 'Overview', in S. Ringel and J.R. Brandell (eds) *Trauma: Contemporary Directions in Theory, Practice, and Research*, Sage, pp 1–12.

Sack-Jones, K. (2017) 'Investing in gender and trauma-informed services', in M. Bush (ed) *Addressing Adversity*, London: Young Minds Trust, pp 219–227

SAMHSA (Substance Abuse and Mental Health Services Administration) (2015) *Trauma-Informed Approach and Trauma-specific Interventions*, www.samhsa.gov/nctic/trauma-interventions

Schneider, S., Grilli, S. and Schneider, J. (2013) 'Evidence-based treatments for traumatized children and adolescents', *Current Psychiatry Reports*, 15(1): 1–9.

Scott, S. and Skidmore, P. (2006) *Reducing the Risk: Barnardo's Support for Sexually Exploited Young People: A Two-year Evaluation. Summary Report*, London: Barnardo's

Shepherd, L. and Wild, J. (2014) 'Emotion regulation, physiological arousal and PTSD symptoms in trauma-exposed individuals', *Journal of Behavior Therapy and Experimental Psychiatry*, 45(3): 360–367

Shuker, L. (2013) 'Constructs of safety for children in care affected by sexual exploitation', in M Melrose (ed) *Critical Perspectives on Child Sexual Exploitation and Trafficking*, Basingstoke: Palgrave Macmillan

Sweeney, A., Clement, S., Filson, B. and Kennedy, A. (2016) 'Trauma-informed mental healthcare in the UK: What is it and how can we further its development?', *Mental Health Review Journal*, 21(3): 174–192

Tolin, D.F. and Foa, E.B. (2006) 'Sex differences in trauma and posttraumatic stress disorder: A quantitative review of 25 years of research', *Psychological Bulletin*, 132: 959–992

UNICEF (2015) *Fact Sheet: A Summary of the Rights Under the Convention on the Rights of the Child*, www.unicef.org/crc/files/Rights_overview.pdf

Van der Kolk, B.A. (1994) 'The body keeps the score: Memory and the evolving psychobiology of posttraumatic stress', *Harvard Review of Psychiatry*, 1(5): 253–265

Warrington, C. and Brodie, I. (2018) 'Developing participatory practice and culture in CSE services', in H. Beckett and J. Pearce (eds) *Understanding and Responding to Child Sexual Exploitation*, Abingdon: Taylor and Francis Group, pp 121–133

9

Social support, empathy and ecology: a theoretical underpinning for working with young people who have suffered child sexual abuse or exploitation

Pat Dolan and Caroline McGregor

Introduction

It has been argued that while factors such as respect and compassion are critical to good practices in working in child welfare, they may sometimes be overlooked, assumed to be present or more simply, taken for granted. More specifically, while cultivating the promotion of positive and helpful social interactions among young people, their parents and the services who work with and for them is gaining momentum, it may still be seen as 'soft' and in need of a more declared theoretical justification base. This is particularly the case when one focuses on child protection and maltreatment and the requisite socio-legal response from both judicial and social work systems.

The particular area of child sexual abuse (CSA), which includes child sexual exploitation (CSE) under its definition, is the way this abuse can raise challenges around secrecy, shame and stigma. Often there can be reluctance for families and close relatives to want to talk about the issues because of this. Moreover, workers who support young people who are abused can themselves also struggle with the intensity and emotion of the work. We argue that the functions of empathy, social support and socialisation, and ecological theories can offer a theoretical framework to deal with these challenges and offer improved guidance for practice. In this chapter, these three interrelated approaches are explored in respect of child and youth safety, prevention of exploitation and as intervention in the sexual abuse of children. We argue that there is the need for an increasing paradigm from passive empathy, which is static, (understanding only) to activated empathy (understanding coupled with compassionate acts of support) on the part of professionals working with those who experience abuse. Alongside this, we argue that use of the theories explored enables an approach to CSA that maximises the potential of the informal and formal social network as an intervention and support mechanism.

Our overall argument is that given the delicacy of the topic of child abuse, it rightfully focuses on the cessation, the legal and or preventive elements, but sometimes implies a cooling off of social support or even a lack of willingness to intervene by others during this time. Conversely, it is strongly recommended here that there is a need to open up discourse on understanding how active empathy can act positively in the lives of those children and youth who suffer violent harm or neglect. In this chapter, we present the three proposed theoretical frameworks that can be usefully applied in working in the field of CSA and from this we outline three possible practice examples that could emerge from such an approach. In the discussion, we consider how these three theoretical considerations can come together to offer direction for improving how CSA is understood and responded to with an emphasis on improving outcomes for children who experience sexual abuse. Our discussion also looks at how these theoretical approaches can promote a preventative approach that tackles social and cultural as well as individual factors that result in such harmful abuse of children that it often has life-long negative impacts.

Social support and social networks

Since the early pioneering work of Cassel (1976) and Berkman and Syme (1979) in the 1970s, the importance of social support as a buffer to stress and as a crucial aid to coping with health and social adversity and negative life events has been well proven. In a wide-ranging set of studies over decades, from the field of physical healthcare such as cancer research (Cutrona 2000) to mental healthcare such as depression (Lewinsohn et al 1998), the importance of social networks as key to helping others overcome illness and trauma has been well established. Social support can be neatly defined as 'acts of assistance between human beings' (Cutrona 2000). In terms of sourcing support, social networks are key and have been described by Garbarino (1983:xii) as the bread and butter of relationships. Within our networks, informal supporters such as family and friends (those who are not paid to provide support) are key and are generally preferable to formal supporters (professionals). The reasons for this are threefold, first, they are a natural source of support (normative), second, they generally provide support at all times such as at weekends when professionals are hard to access, and finally, they save the state in terms of funding, albeit at a personal cost to carers. Whereas social support is important in our daily living (maintenance support) and in times of extreme adversity (crisis support) what is even more crucial is the conditions under which our social networks offer us real and useful help.

Social support should not be perceived as utopian, however, not least because not all families get on all the time, family-based relationships can be the cause of stress and strain and the division of labour for caring responsibilities within the family may be gendered. Similarly, it is often assumed that a large network equates with more support, but it may often be the case that a lower density of social network contacts actually provides more help.

Despite the early and very well made case by those who have advocated to ensure that the role of social support is not overlooked in child protection, including CSA and physical maltreatment (see Thompson 1995; and Burnham et al 1999), for many families and professionals the concept of basic support provision during and post disclosure of abuse is often bypassed. The need for specialist therapeutic intervention from the point of disclosure in CSA can inadvertently shut out other important supports at this time. This lack of support provision may also come from a sense of awkwardness and or embarrassment.

Within Family Support more directly, family members may feel a sense of shame, guilt and regret towards the victim. This essentially has the double negative effect of victim isolation post revelation of their experience(s) of being harmed (Feiring et al, 2002). Ironically, in such instances, social support may be most needed even in terms of the provision of emotional reassurance. Sadly, for the reasons listed earlier, this is unlikely to be provided. Also, in some cases of abuse, family members, both nuclear and extended, who are not directly party to or fully informed of the allegations, can become essentially 'uninformed' or 'paralysed' in terms of being able to support.

Whereas literature on the role of social support highlights that professionals should associate their supportive interventions with families in terms of better outcomes resulting in families being capable of solving their own difficulties (Wadsworth et al 2005), it has also been stressed that social support has a 'coping' function as well (Dolan and Pinkerton 2007). One could argue that in the case of CSA, particularly in the early stages post disclosure, support that enables coping from day to day for all parties, is key. The timing of this support is significant to ensure that an abused child or youth who might experience an initial 'honeymoon' period of support from caring family and friends, receives continued input. It is known that over time this 'moon of support' can also wane and that it may be years later that the impact of the harm takes effect on the victim and that by this time there is less support available to him or her. In sum, timing of the provision of help is an essential factor in social support (Tracy and Brown 2011) and for both informal supporters such as family and for professionals as formal helpers. They must know when, where and how to support best.

Empathy

Whereas Barr and Higgins-D'Alessandro (2009) remind us that empathy is a multidimensional concept, for our purposes here empathy can be most simply described as the ability to understand and identify with another person's experience of adversity. There is also a strong consensus that empathy has two core dimensions. First, cognitive empathy – the understanding of another person's mental state; and second, affective empathy – the possession of an emotional response to another person's plight when in need of support (Ferguson 2016). These two aspects mirror neatly with the concept of static empathy: 'I understand what you are experiencing' and active empathy which goes further: 'and here is what I am going to do for you'.

What is important is that from the perspective of supporting a young person who has experience of harm, including sexual abuse or exploitation, or from the perspective of supporting their caregiver(s), typically their parent(s), three core factors on the part of the supporter are crucial. First, the demonstration of empathy is human and relational, so this requires a positive relationship and an emotional response towards the experiences of the other person. Second, it requires ability within the supporter for perspective-taking in relation to the person in need. Third, it requires an ability to regulate one's own emotional response to the experiences of the other person in a way that allows for putting in place compassionate helpful acts of assistance. So, empathy is a complex relational process that involves understanding the feelings and perspectives of another person as well as taking action that is experienced by that other person as being responsive to his or her needs. What is important across a range of disciplines, is that research has conclusively shown that the presence of empathy is related to positive academic, social, psychological and personal developmental outcomes (van Noorden et al 2015). Other evidence suggests that lower social empathy appears to be associated with higher levels of interpersonal and psychological difficulties (Miller and Eisenberg 1988).

Empathy is closely associated with prosocial behaviours and social responsibility (Benita et al 2017). Whereas over the last decade there has been increasing interest in neuroscience on the brain development and its connection to empathy (Kliemann and Adolphs 2018) in what is now being termed the 'social brain', others such as Segal (2011), highlight the sociological aspects of empathy in what she distinctly terms 'social empathy'. This can also be seen as linking to core aspects of resilience theory and Ann Masten's (2015) well-known 'ordinary magic' for resilience-building through daily living supportive acts which enable those who experience adversity to not feel alone, to bounce back and recover, and essentially, to thrive. This concept of social empathy which is a community and relationship-based resilience builder is further supported by a distinct body of research which evidences that social and educational interventions developed to promote empathy among children and young people can be very effective.

While it is known that one's set of moral principles relating to empathy and social responsibility, such as caring, respect, compassion, perspective taking and concern are key to social connectedness and the betterment of society, it may often be assumed as 'always present' among professionals who work with and for those who have been sexually abused or exploited (Howe 2012; Wagaman 2011). However, there may often be cases where the difficulty in continuously doing such difficult work and an accumulated sense of burden for the caregiver might over time impair their capacity to care. It may be the case for some who work with children and young people who have been subjected to sexual abuse or exploitation, that they experience (often unknowingly) their levels of capacity to care wane.

Whereas Thompson (2018) suggests that reflective practice and core caring for the carer through consistent professional supervision is key, he does also state that reflective practice involves the 'phenomenology of phenomenology' (Thompson and Thompson 2018). This requires strong quality assurance particularly for those in helping professions working with the very sensitive issue of CSA. Similarly, for some professionals the 'elephant in the room' aspect to the work lies in the simple fact that he/she may themselves have had past abuse experiences in their own lives which can have a negative impact on their capacity to care. In some cases, this can lead to being over involved or under involved in working with and for those for whom they care (Will 1999).

Working with children who have been harmed is often reliant upon the worker and young person having a strong personal connection and real relationship. We know that for any young person to be resilient it is key that they see at least one of those adults who care for them or work with them as demonstrating 'real caring'. Lynn Jameson neatly disaggregates this as the difference between those (family friends and professionals) who 'care for and not just care about' the young people with whom they engage. For professionals working with young people, particularly those who have been harmed, sexually abused, trafficked or exploited in some way, being empathic and caring for them and not just about them needs to be defended as core relational practice (Howe 2012). The ever-increasing focus on better outcomes working through fidelity to proven evaluated intervention programmes needs to be counterbalanced (Fives et al 2017). The importance of everyday relationship-based working through supportive acts including the provision of active empathy and compassion is core to enabling a young person simply to cope and should be valued as highly as any programme based work (Pinkerton and Dolan 2007; Dolan et al 2017).

Social ecological theory

Ecological theory for human development and the social environment derives from the work of Uri Bronfenbrenner who focused on various aspects of the relationship between the individual and their environment through his theory development and research from the 1970s to the end of the century. The ecological 'framework' is well known and applied across many domains. Richard et al (2011), for example, consider how ecological models have been used in health promotion fields specifically and many authors make a strong connection between the ecological model and public health approaches (for example, Kenny and Wurtule, 2012). Indeed, Chapter 4 in this volume draws on the ecological framework for understanding Contextual Safeguarding.

The ecological framework is traditionally presented by Bronfenbrenner in concentric circles, fitting into each other like Russian dolls. The micro system (the individual's inner world) is situated in the meso system (the individual and their family and close connections) which in turn sits within the exo system (direct community and social network). This was originally surrounded by the macro system (law, culture, policy and procedures) in his work on Ecology of Human Development (for example, Bronfenbrenner 1979) and later by an additional chrono system (for example, Bronfenbrenner and Morris 1998) relating to trends over time.

A major contribution of the ecological theoretical framework is that it provides a way to consider both the inter-familial and extra-familial factors affecting a child (see Bronfenbrenner 1986), and the internal psychological and wider social context within which the child is positioned. Ecological systems can also be seen as bio-ecological on the one hand and socio-ecological on the other. Tudge et al (2009) and Rosa and Tudge (2013) provide very helpful critical analyses of the application and development of the ecological model over time.

Moran et al (2017) have added another useful dimension to this model in that they suggest that often young people – such as those who are in foster care – have, in fact, two overlapping micro and meso systems that they are attempting to manage and negotiate around. This work encourages us to advance the notion of a neatly fitted set of concentric circles to capturing the more dynamic, complex and sometimes contradictory layers of processes and interactions at different levels of the eco-system. Recently, there has also been research that has sought to connect ecological theory more strongly with theories relating to resilience, empowerment and social capital, much of which touches on some of the work on empathy as outlined earlier. For example, Ling and Kwock (2017) consider the general area of working in the field of child abuse and argue that western applications of ecological model pay insufficient attention to resilience. They propose 'An integrated resilience and ecological model of child abuse (REC-model)' and emphasises the importance of taking account of certain cultural parenting values that were mediators against risk of child abuse. Peeters (2012) also associates an ecological approach (referring to sustainable development) with an approach based on strengths, resilience, empowerment and social capital. This is something we come back to later in the chapter.

Moving specifically to the application of the ecological model in relation to CSA, there are a number of relevant publications to note that can guide this work. As Kenny and Wurtule (2012) argue in their introduction to a special issue of the *Journal of Child Sexual Abuse* devoted to addressing CSA via an ecological approach: 'for CSA to be eliminated or reduced, a spectrum of approaches at all levels of the ecology must be employed' (2012:366). Indeed, as shown throughout this book the need for intervention across a range of systems, from psychological to structural, is well established.

Allagia (2010) is one of the main authors who provide an analysis of CSA disclosure specifically from an ecological perspective. She argues that '(m)ulti-level intervention is recommended at the individual, community and macro levels. Future investigations should focus on how to identify and measure the impact of community and macro level factors on disclosure, aspects that have received much less attention'

(2010:32 and see Firmin, Chapter 4 in this volume). Later work, such as Martin and Allagia (2013) highlight how CSA and cyberspace/ internet abuse adds another dimension to the ecological context for children. Collin-Vézina et al (2015) also examine the individual, relational and social factors that have an impact on disclosure and they argue for the importance of using a broad ecological framework:

> to understand the factors that inhibit disclosure of CSA, as barriers to disclosure do not constrain solely the victims. Results are discussed in light of their implications for research, prevention and intervention programs, and social policies and media campaigns, as the burden is on the larger community to create a climate of safety and transparency that makes the telling of CSA possible. (2015:123)

Mooney (2017) has recently applied and adapted an ecological model specifically to look critically at policy and processes for responses to retrospective disclosure of CSA.

Indeed, in the special issue of the *Journal of Child Sexual Abuse* referred to earlier, Kenny and Wurtule (2012) argue that addressing CSA via an ecological approach is very compatible with a public health model. They cover themes focused around prevention that focuses beyond the individual to the wider social context and address interventions focused on youth, parents, community, organisational and policy level. They identify the importance of education for parents, young people and professionals as well as the development of community-based prevention programmes. However, the relationship between understanding disclosures or intervening with CSA, and use of the ecological framework is not straightforward. Pittenger et al (2018), for example, in their longitudinal study of CSA victimisation using ecological theory, found that the most prevalent factors were individual and interpersonal. Limited evidence was found to justify a wider ecological explanation. Ecological theory can helpfully be used to deflect from this continued focus on the individual alone. For example, Terry and Freilich (2012) focus on understanding CSA from a situational and ecological perspective.

In summary, the complexity of CSA is such that while we have had the tools for considering CSA within a wider ecological perspective for some decades now, 'explanations of the etiology of CSA remain focused on isolated cause-and-effect models prioritising interpersonal factors and interactional dynamics' (Martin and Allagia 2013:403). Martin and Allagia go onto refer to other adaptations of

Bronfenbrenner's ecological systems framework. This led to the use of an ecological model to emphasise child abuse as being 'by forces at work from the most proximal (for example, individual and family) to the most distal (for example, community and culture) dimensions of a child's ecology' (cited in Martin and Allagia 2013:403). They emphasis the usefulness of the ecological model, specifically noting how it assists assessing and working with the impacts of child abuse while at the same time reminding us of the complexity inherent with this. They also present an excellent adapted model of the ecological system from micro to chrono with a focus on CSA and cyber abuse and call for the extension of Bronbrenfenner's ecological model to include the level of cyberspace (see 2013:404).

There is clear potential to expand the use of ecological theory beyond offering a tool for mapping levels and relations between individual, relational and social factors. We can look in depth at using this theory to examine how interactions within an ecological system can constrain or enable interventions and responses to CSA. It is important given the scope of the work and range of research developed from it, that we move away from a generalised referencing to the ecological model and are more specific in terms of what aspects specifically are drawn from for certain topics. For example, Bronfenbrenner (1986) considers how this ecological approach can be used to specifically work with families, asking questions of how inter-familial approaches are affected by extra-familial conditions. For CSA, this interaction between inter-familial and extra-familial is highly significant. In the following practice examples, we use this chapter specifically to apply it to responses to CSA.

Two practice case examples

In order to give additional meaning to the theories of social support, social empathy and social ecology, we now provide two case examples as illustrative of how they can be seen and/or utilised in the context of work with children and adolescents who have experienced or are at risk of experiencing sexual abuse and exploitation.

Practice example 1

As discussed earlier, one of the greatest challenges in supporting children and young people who have experienced CSA and exploitation is having an approach that maximises their support network to wrap support around them. This requires those engaging with and supporting the young person to empathise actively with their experience even if that may be distressing for those involved. Taking extra-familial abuse as an example here, this can include working closely in partnership with family and close social networks to build the resilience and supports around the child and young person. The Meitheal model of family support developed recently in Ireland and aimed at preventative practice in child welfare offers a set of principles and approaches that could be adapted to working with children and their families where CSA has occurred using the theoretical approaches discussed here.

As explained in Rodriguez et al (2017) and detailed in the practice toolkit (Tusla 2015) the overall focus of the practice model is that the child and young person is at the centre. While not necessarily specifying the use of an ecological model, the underpinning assumptions and approach draw from the broad ideas inherent in the ecological approach. The 'My World Triangle' is used to ensure a:

> focusing on the child's development, within their family and their wider community, the My World Triangle introduces a mental map which helps practitioners explore a child/young person's experience and identify the strengths, needs and challenges to a child's well-being in partnership with their parents/carers. These are recorded as strengths and needs. (Tusla 2015:20)

This means that all those involved with the child and their family work in partnership to produce the best intervention for the young person in a coordinated and strengths-based manner. The need to identify social supports to highlight strengths and areas within the community and around the family that pose risks (related to the source of the abuse and exploitation) is explicit here and one that can be adapted to support children. To activate this approach in relation to CSA, the value of an in-depth knowledge of social support systems and a critical reflective approach to empathy that recognises the investment and support needed to ensure professionals can do this in cases of CSA is evident. While not exclusively suitable for supporting families where there has been extra-familial abuse, the challenge of supporting a young person where the abuse has come from within the family is greater. This may then benefit from a more systematic use of the ecological model to build on the broad ethos and principles of the approach described here.

Practice example 2

As aforementioned, one guide we propose when using the ecological model is to be specific about which of Bronfenbrenner's periods of work are being focused on and what specific aspects are being applied. We also highlighted the way ecological model works well as a mapping tool and offer deeper development as a specific intervention tool. It works particularly well with social support theory and relies on an underpinning ability to empathise with the situation sufficiently to ensure the identification of dual processes of protection and empowerment for the person in their environment. In the example here, we draw from Bronfenbrenner 1986 specifically where he focuses on three core environmental elements – meso, exo and chrono – and considers how this relates to the micro level encompassing psychological and biological elements. His paper is about how to promote capacity of a family to foster healthy development of their children and is applicable to working with families where the child remains at home as well as with foster families. He asks the question how are inter-familial processes affected by extra-familial processes?

Clearly, depending on the particular case, significant protective measures must be in place with regard to inter-familial abuse and in most instances either the perpetrator or the victim are removed from the physical space if living in a shared home. We suggest here that whatever the internal in-depth judicial, social legal and therapeutic interventions, a number of support strategies can be considered from the wider system context that 'can sustain, enhance, and, where necessary, create environments that are conducive to healthy human growth' (Bronfenbrenner 1986:737). We can use the three elements identified by Bronfenbrenner regarding family work – social networks, family positioning in the community, and the parental workplace – to consider how specific supports may be developed to enhance the wider environmental supports alongside therapeutic trauma focused interventions. It seems we can draw from the theory on social support and linked to this, network analysis, to map out:

• the specific supports that can build strength, resilience and protection and
• the specific elements that are to be avoided and protected from.

It is useful to draw from Moran et al (2017) to suggest that these three elements are not necessarily mapped on to a neat nest of dolls but rather to a set of micro and meso systems that are disrupted, overlapping and possible in conflict or torn. Taking the notion of 'process–context–person' from Bronfenbrenner, we can emphasise that each mapping should be unique to the individual so that it is just not about process (individual) and context (environment), but also taking into account the specific feelings, personality, concerns and wishes of the individual (person) concerned. With this differentiation, we can then take on board the idea of proximal processes that Bronfenbrenner explains in his classic reader *The Ecology of Human Development* (1979) which can carefully map out the important networks and supports that can help a child or young person at a particular moment in time, or during a transition (chrono). This may include one family member being removed from the home, to specify who, what and where the positive supports are. The same process can be used to specify the who, what and where to protect from. Overall, one of the main contributions from an ecological approach is the capacity to emphasise a focus on strengths and capacities. As Bronfenbrenner suggests, 'for every study that documents the power of disruptive environments, there is a control group that testifies to the existence and unrealized potential of ecologies that sustain and strengthen constructive processes in society, the family, and the self' (1986:738).

Discussion and conclusion

Thus far, in this chapter the authors have presented and exemplified a triad of theoretical underpinnings, namely social support, empathy and ecology theories, which they see as having strong resonance to enhance existing approaches to working with young people at risk of or having experienced sexual abuse or exploitation. Essentially it has been argued that the provision of social support can only come from responsive networks and that this is key to coping. This has been contextualised positively as needing to occur within warm and caring relationships from adults who are either informal supporters (family and friends) or formal sources (professionals). These supportive contacts provide empathy, understanding and acts of compassion based, in part, on the social values and sense of social responsibility on the part of the support donor. Furthermore, it has been argued that such support and empathy provision does not occur in isolation but within a set of ecological systems that spans individual responses to active engagement at a societal level. The corrective effect of this contributes to the victim of abuse or exploitation having a sense that they are not being judged in some way but are being helped to become resilient and thrive in the face of adversity. This positive pathway is illustrated graphically in Figure 9.1.

Although helpful, however, theories and models, just like good social policy, are meaningless unless they are usable for practice and implementable in-service development and provision. We now discuss clear barriers which impair support provision.

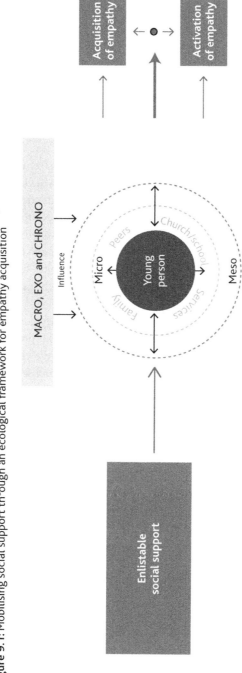

Figure 9.1: Mobilising social support through an ecological framework for empathy acquisition

Whereas, rightfully, much attention is placed on accurate detection and assessment of CSA and exploitation, there are those who have expressed concern in relation to uniformity in assessment methods and judicial systems (Erooga and Masson 1999). For example, recently in an Irish context following a review of CSA cases and their treatment in the court system by the Childcare law reporting project, strong concern has been raised regarding the problem of lack of inter-agency working, complicated and delayed procedures, all resulting in further victimising children and exacerbating their traumatisation (Coulter 2018).

At a wider level this is also problematic in that, even allowing for the limitations of such procedures in CSA cases, the lack of therapeutic services and programmes for victims post assessment is particularly worrying (Waldfogel 2009). The Barnahaus model, based on the childcare advocacy approach, offers a significant step forward in responses to CSA by developing a service that coordinates the judicial, investigatory and therapeutic services in a coordinated way to avoid the major problems of re-victimisation that can occur in the absence of a joined-up approach (see Herbert and Bromfield, 2016). The theories we have discussed here map readily onto such an inter-disciplinary and child focused model.

At a very basic level the matter of family dynamics in relation to CSA and CSE can be complicated, making the provision of support similarly complex. In some cases of CSA for example, many non-offending parents (most typically mothers) feel a sense of guilt in not having adequately protected their son or daughter from abuse. This may impair their capacity to receive the support on offer or more subtly may result in less support being available to them. Conversely, in cases of CSA and CSE there may be a sense of embarrassment or lack of knowledge on how best to approach such a sensitive matter for those familial supporters who want to help. This may result in them feeling inhibited in providing any help at all. Similarly, when children and/or adults are in need of support, other past tensions between family members (negative family history) can act as a barrier to any engagement in support. More obviously it has been well argued that it is easier to provide Family Support in cases of basic health needs such as cancer or following an accident, than in the case of the more sensitive issue of CSA (Canavan et al 2016). Churchill and Sen (2016) have also argued that in cases of CSA the support reaction is more polar. There is either plentiful empathy and support, or none at all. This can have the effect of 'unite or split' in family relationships.

For the tentative model outlined earlier to be effective, these other factors need to be considered. What is important is that levels of burden on the caregiver or 'wear and tear', is a key issue in their ongoing capacity to empathise and turn such compassion into supportive acts. This factor alone is often overlooked by professionals who may assume that willingness to support is constant (O'Reilly and Dolan 2016). Furthermore, the lack of relationships of worth between family members may on the outside appear solid but, once tested under the stressful context of CSA and/or exploitation, they fall apart, resulting in escalating the distress for the victim and his or her immediate family.

Whereas there are both generic programmes who work with CSA as part of what they offer, and those who focus more directly on working with young people who have experienced all forms of abuse including CSA and CSE, they still clearly include ecological-based methods all with a view to resilience building. For example, the Youth Advocacy Programme developed in the US (Fleischer et al 2006) includes a 'wrap around' model advocating direct work but using the young person's social environment to enable him or her overcome adversity which may be wide ranging in terms of its nature, but includes CSA.

For programmes working more directly in assessment and treatment of child maltreatment including CSA – such as the Australian Signs of Safety Programme based on a strengths-based approach to child protection work (Turnell, 2012) – the importance of the worker– client relationship is key and enabling the voice of the young person is strongly promoted. We concur strongly with this approach and advocate for the potential of giving voice to children and youth who experience CSA or exploitation. One could argue that many of the existing approaches, including those discussed in this chapter, derive from a paternalistic positioning of the child as victim and the subject of help rather than the co-producer of the best response to their own situation (see Chapter 2). Just as historically in youth development, generally professionals worked 'for' rather than 'with' young people. This has now changed drastically (Butterbaugh et al 2014), giving actual participation options to young people who experience abuse needs to be actioned (Kennan et al 2018).

Finally, we argue for the importance of taking a strong children's rights approach in responding to CSA through activism that seeks to maximise the support throughout the eco-system to minimise further harm to children and youth and maximise support and legal and social protection for them. This is not just for the children and youth who need protection and support, not just in the interests of those who work with and for them, but for the betterment of all civic society – our global community.

References

Allagia, R. (2010) 'An ecological analysis of child sexual abuse disclosure: Considerations for child and adolescent mental health', *Journal of Canadian Child and Adolescent Psychiatry*, 19(1): 32–29

Ambrosio, F., Olivier, M., Didon, D. and Besche, C. (2009) 'The basic empathy scale: A French validation of a measure of empathy in youth', *Personality and Individual Differences*, 46: 160–165

Barr, J.J. and Higgins-D'Alessandro, A. (2009) 'How adolescent empathy and prosocial behavior change in the context of school culture: A two-year longitudinal study', *Adolescence*, 44(176): 751–772

Benita, M., Levkovitz, T. and Roth, G. (2017) 'Integrative emotion regulation predicts adolescents' prosocial behavior through the mediation of empathy', *Learning and Instruction*, 50, 14–20.

Berkman, L.F. and Syme, S.L. (1979) 'Social networks, host resistance, and mortality: A nine-year follow-up study of Alameda County residents', *American Journal of Epidemiology*, 109(2): 186–204

Bronfenbrenner, U. (1979) *The Ecology of Human Development*, Cambridge, MA: Harvard University Press

Bronfenbrenner, U. (1986) 'Ecology of the family as a context for human development: Research perspectives', *Developmental Psychology*, 22(6): 723–742

Bronfenbrenner, U. and Morris, P.A. (1998) 'The ecology of developmental processes', in W. Damon (series ed) and R.M. Lerner (vol ed) *Handbook of Child Psychology: Vol 1. Theoretical Models of Human Development* (5th edn), New York: Wiley, pp 993–1028

Burnham, J., Moss, L., Debelle, J. and Jamieson, R. (1999) 'Working with families of young sexual abusers: assessment and intervention issues', in M. Erooga and H. Masson (eds) *Children and Young People Who Sexually Abuse Others: Challenges and Responses*, London: Routledge, pp 146–167

Butterbaugh, K., Brennan, M. and Dolan, P. (2014) 'Obstacles to youth civic engagement in Ireland and Pennsylvania', *Youth Studies Ireland*, 7(1): 15–23

Canavan, J., Pinkerton, J. and Dolan, P. (2016) *Understanding Family Support: Policy Practice and Theory*, London and Philadelphia, PA: Jessica Kingsley Publishers

Cassel, J.C. (1976) 'The contribution of the social environment to host resistance', *American Journal of Epidemiology*, 104: 107–123

Churchill, H. and Sen, R. (2016) 'Introduction. Intensive family support services: Politics, policy and practice across contexts', *Social Policy and Society*, 15(2): 251–261

Collin-Vézina, D., De La Sablonnière-Griffin, M., Palmer, A. and Milne, L. (2015) 'A preliminary mapping of individual, relational, and social factors that impede disclosure of childhood sexual abuse' *Child Abuse Review*, 43: 123–134

Coulter, C. (2018) *Child Care Law Reporting Project*, www. childlawproject.ie/

Cutrona, C.E. (2000) 'Social support principles for strengthening families: Messages from America', in J. Canavan, P. Dolan and J. Pinkerton (eds) *Family Support: Direction from Diversity*, London: Jessica Kingsley

Dolan, P. and Pinkerton, J. (2007) 'Family support, social capital, resilience and adolescent coping', *Child and Family Social Work*, 12(3): 219–228

Dolan, P., Kenny, J. and Kennan, D. (2017) 'Activated empathy in child welfare and youth development: A case for consideration', in P. Dolan and N. Frost (eds) *The Handbook of Global Child Welfare*, Abingdon: Routledge

Erooga, M. and Masson, H. (1999) *Children and Young People Who Sexually Abuse Others: Challenges and Responses*, London: Routledge

Feiring, C., Taska, L. and Lewis, M. (2002) 'Adjustment following sexual abuse discovery: The role of shame and attributional style', *Developmental Psychology*, 38(1): 79–92

Ferguson, E. (2016) Empathy: 'The Good, The Bad and The Ugly', in A.M. Wood and J. Johnson (eds) *The Wiley Handbook of Positive Clinical Psychology*, Chichester: John Wiley & Sons, pp 103–123

Fives, A., Canavan, J. and Dolan, P. (2017) 'Evaluation study design: A pluralist approach to evidence', *European Early Childhood Education Research Journal*, 25: 153–170

Fleischer, J., Warner, J., McCulty, C.J. and Marks, M.B. (2006) 'Youth advocacy: Programming justice focused family support intervention', in P. Dolan, J. Canavan and J. Pinkerton, J. (eds) *Family Support as Reflective Practice*, London: Jessica Kingsley, ch 8, pp 118–133

Garbarino, J. (1983) 'Social support networks: RX for the helping professionals', in J.K. Whittaker and J. Garbarino (eds) *Social Support Networks: Informal Helping in the Human Services*, New York: Aldine De Gruyter

Herbert, J.L. and Bromfield, L. (2016) 'Evidence for the efficacy of the Child Advocacy Center Model: A systematic review', *Trauma, Violence, Abuse*, 17(3): 341–357

Howe, D. (2012) *Empathy: What It Is And Why It Matters*, Basingstoke: Palgrave Macmillan

Kennan, D. and Dolan, P. (2017) 'Justifying children and young people's involvement in social research: Assessing harm and benefit', *Social Studies: Irish Journal of Sociology*, 25(3), 297–314

Kennan, D., Brady, B. and Forkan, C. (2018) 'Supporting children's participation in decision-making: A systematic literature review exploring the effectiveness of participatory processes', *The British Journal of Social Work*, 48(7): 1985–2002

Kenny, M.C. and Wurtule, S.K. (2012) 'Preventing childhood sexual abuse: An ecological approach', *Journal of Child Sexual Abuse*, 21(4): 361–367

Kliemann, D. and Adolphs, R. (2018) 'The social neuroscience of mentalizing: challenges and recommendations', *Current Opinion in Psychology*, 24: 1–6

Lewinsohn, P.M., Rohde, P. and Seeley, J.R. (1998) 'Major depressive disorder in older adolescents: Prevalence, risk factors, and clinical implications', *Clinical Psychology Review*, 18, 765–794

Ling, C. and Kwock, S. (2017) 'An integrated resilience and ecological model of child abuse (REC-model)', *Journal of Child and Family Studies*, 26: 1655–1663

Martin, J. and Allagia, R. (2013) 'Sexual abuse images in cyberspace: Expanding the ecology of the child', *Journal of Child Sexual Abuse*, 22(4): 398–415

Masten, A.S. (2015) *Ordinary Magic: Resilience in Development*, New York: Guilford Press

Miller, P.A. and Eisenberg, N. (1988) 'The relation of empathy to aggressive and externalizing/antisocial behavior among Australian adolescents: Testing two competing models', *Journal of Community Psychology*, 32(3): 229–255

Mooney, J. (2017) 'Adult disclosures of childhood sexual abuse and Section 3 of the Child Care Act 1991: Past offences, current risk', *Child Care in Practice*, 1–13, http://dx.doi.org/10.1080/13575279. 2017.1347145

Moran, L., McGregor, C. and Devaney, C. (2017) *Outcomes for Permanence and Stability for Children in Long-Term Care: Practice Guide.* Galway: UNESCO Child and Family Research Centre.

O'Reilly, L. and Dolan, P. (2016) 'The voice of the child in social work assessments: Age-appropriate communications with children', *British Journal of Social Work*, 46: 1191–1207

Peeters, J. (2012) 'Social work and sustainable development: Towards an ecological practice model', *Journal of Social Intervention: Theory and Practice*, 21(3): 5–26

Pinkerton, J. and Dolan, P. (2007) 'Family support, social capital, resilience and adolescent coping', *Child & Family Social Work*, 12(3): 219–228

Pittenger, S.L., Pogue, P.K and Hansen, D.J. (2018) 'Predicting sexual revictimization in childhood and adolescence: A longitudinal examination using ecological systems theory', *Child Maltreatment*, 23(2): 137–146

Richard, L., Gauvin, L. and Raine, K. (2011) 'Ecological models revisited: Their uses and evolution in health promotion over two decades', *Annual Review of Public Health*, 32: 307–326

Rosa, E.M. and Tudge, J.R. (2013) 'Uri Bronfenbrenners theory of Human development: Its evolution from ecology to bio-ecology', *Journal of Family Theory and Review*, 5(6): 243–258

Segal, E.A. (2011) 'Social empathy: A model Built on empathy, contextual understanding, and social responsibility that promotes social justice', *Journal of Social Service Research*, 37: 266–277.

Shrout, P.E., Herman, C.M. and Bolger, N. (2006) 'The costs and benefits of practical and emotional support on adjustment: A daily diary study of couples experiencing acute stress', *Personal Relationships*, 13(1): 115–134

Terry, K.J. and Freilich, J.D. (2012) 'Understanding child sexual abuse by Catholic priests from a situational perspective', *Journal of Child Sexual Abuse*, 21(4): 437–455, doi: 10.1080/10538712.2012.693579

Thompson, N. (2018) *The Social Worker's Practice Manual*, Wrexham: Avenue Media Solutions Publication

Thompson, R.A. (1995) *Preventing Child Maltreatment Through Social Support*, London: Sage

Thompson, S. and Thompson, N. (2018) *The Critically Reflective Practitioner* (2nd edn), London: Palgrave

Tracy, E.M., and Brown, S. (2011) 'Social networks and social work practice', in F. Turner (ed.) *Social Work Treatment* (5th edn), New York: Oxford University Press, pp 447–459

Tudge, J.R., Mokrova, I., Hatfield, B.E. and Karnik, R.B. (2009) 'Uses and misuses of Bronfenbrenner's bioecological theory of human development', *Journal of Family Theory and Review*, 1(4): 198–210

Turnell, A. (2012) 'Building safety in child protection practice: working with a strengths and solution-focus in an environment of risk', Basingstoke: Palgrave-Macmillan

Tusla (2015) *Meitheal Toolkit*, Dublin: Tusla Child and Family Agency, www.drugs.ie/resourcesfiles/ResearchDocs/Ireland/2015/TUSLA_Meitheal_Toolkit.pdf

van Noorden, T.H., Haselager, G.J., Cillessen, A.H. and Bukowski, W.M. (2015) 'Empathy and involvement in bullying in children and adolescents: A systematic review', *Journal of Youth and Adolescence*, 44(3): 637–657

Wadsworth, M.E., Raviv, T., Compas B.E. and Connor-Smith, J.K. (2005) 'Parent and adolescent responses to poverty-related stress: Tests of mediated and moderated coping models', *Journal of Child and Family Studies*, 14(2): 283–298

Wagaman, M.A. (2011) 'Social empathy as a framework for adolescent empowerment', *Journal of Social Service Research*, 37(3): 278–293

Waldfogel, J. (2009) 'Prevention and the child protection system', *Future of Children*, 19(2): 195–210

Will, D. (1999) 'Assessment issues', in M. Erooga and H. Masson (eds) *Children and Young People Who Sexually Abuse Others: Challenges and Responses*, London: Routledge, ch 6, pp 86–103

10

Using an intersectional lens to examine the child sexual exploitation of black adolescents

Claudia Bernard

Introduction

In this chapter I employ intersectionality as a critical lens to interrogate the ways that race, gender, class and sexuality impact black adolescents' experiences of child sexual exploitation (CSE). In particular, the exploration will be anchored in an intersectional analysis to extend understandings of the nuanced ways in which race-constructed otherness is experienced by young black people affected by sexual exploitation. 'Black' is defined here as referring to individuals of African and African-Caribbean origin as well as persons of mixed ethnicity (African or African-Caribbean and another parentage, usually white British). A key reason for focusing on this subgroup of children is that they are disproportionately represented in the care system (Owen and Statham 2009) and the data on CSE suggests that children in the care system are disproportionately affected (Pearce 2009; Beckett et al 2013; Beckett et al 2017). The central argument is that positional and situational inequalities intersect in complex ways which have a negative impact on the everyday realities of black youth, thus rendering them vulnerable to sexual exploitation. Specifically, the chapter discusses the contribution that an intersectional frame of analysis can make to intervening with sexually-exploited black youth. The chapter is organised into three parts: the first section briefly sketches the key messages from the literature on CSE and black children. The second provides an overview of the intersectionality theoretical framework of the chapter. In the final section, using a case study, from the Serious Case Review (SCR) of child R, a 15-year-old black girl in the looked-after system, as an exemplar, I will present ways that an intersectional lens can offer some analytical tools to gain a deeper insight into the challenges for black youths at risk of abusive and exploitative relationships. The chapter concludes with some discussion of the implications for a child-focused approach are also discussed.

Child sexual exploitation and black children

While it is well known that CSE affects children and young people from all backgrounds, little is known about the scale and nature of black children's experiences of CSE. Research indicates that girls are more likely than boys to be the victims of sexual exploitation, though boys are also sexually exploited (Pearce 2009; Berelowitz et al 2013). For Firmin (2018) and Pitts (2013), a number of elements negatively affect young black adolescents' everyday realities to render them a vulnerable population, including being raised in economically-disadvantaged communities and experiencing material hardship and societal racism. Increasingly, attention is being given to the ways in which structural disadvantage can heighten the risk of children being exposed to sexual exploitation (Pearce 2009; Beckett et al 2013; Berelowitz et al 2013; Pitts 2013; Firmin 2018). Consistent findings have highlighted that adverse childhood experiences (ACEs) suffered by children including exposure to domestic violence, intra-familial maltreatment, parental mental health and substance misuse problems, exposes children to greater risks of exploitation (Beckett et al 2013; Berelowitz et al 2013; Pearce 2009; Pitts 2013; Hallett 2015 and 2017). Additionally, research shows that children living in disrupted family environments, or in the looked-after population, as well as those excluded from education (of which black children are over represented), are all at increased risk of sexual exploitation (Beckett et al 2017). Research also suggests that intra-familial sexual abuse trauma is a major risk factor for revictimisation (Firmin 2013; Thomas and D'Arcy 2017). As Firmin et al (2016) reiterate, black youths have multiple contextual factors that coalesce in complex and subtle ways, leaving them more exposed to sexual exploitation.

Additionally, there are gender differences relevant to the way that black adolescents experience sexual exploitation. I argue that a racialised and gendered discourse about black boys and girls exists. Research has brought to light that significant numbers of black girls are sexually exploited by gangs and affected by gang-associated sexual violence (Pearce 2009; 2010; Beckett et al 2013; Berelowitz et al 2013; Pitts 2013; Trickett 2015; Voisin et al 2016). It is also clear that in their lifetimes many black girls experience multiple forms of violence and abuse, invariably racially motivated hate crimes and abuse, which is relevant for understanding the context of their sexual exploitation (Firmin 2017). Research reveals that sexual harassment, teenage relationship abuse, gang rape, sexual violence and physical violence are common facets for black girls living in socially- and economically-deprived urban areas affected by serious youth violence (Pearce 2009; Disley and Liddle 2016; Firmin 2017). Furthermore, it has been argued that misogynist popular culture represents black girls as sexually promiscuous and having loose morals, in contrast to Asian young women who are represented as 'mystical', 'secretive' and 'hidden' (Chesney-Lind and Eliason 2006). Several scholars have brought attention to the negative ways in which devaluing messages about black girls' sexuality and moral worth contribute to the sexual violence that they experience (Stephens and Phillips 2003; Chesney-Lind and Eliason 2006; Miller 2008; Bernard 2015). As Firmin (2017) comments, multifaceted reflections are required to understand how the social location of black girls is crucial in shaping their experiences of exploitation. Here it is imperative to understand how the exploitation experienced by black adolescent girls may result from the marginalised and oppressed positions they inhabit.

While there is a growing literature on boys, much less is known about black boys' experiences of CSE. A Children's Society report highlighted that child protection services struggle to recognise the indicators of sexual exploitation of boys in general (McNaughton et al 2014; Leon and Rawls 2016). Cockbain et al (2014), drawing on data from Barnados' *Not Just a Girl Thing*, noted that out of 1,582 CSE cases involving boys, 6 per cent were black (p 27). It is generally recognised that boys are less likely to disclose sexual exploitation, and service providers may not know how to ask boys questions about exploitation, nor recognise the signs (Becket et al 2017). As a result, we lack knowledge about black boys who are affected by sexual exploitation and the needs and issues of vulnerable and at-risk black boys are little understood. There is increasing awareness that negative stereotypes of black boys as predators serve to exacerbate vulnerabilities and create barriers to identifying and engaging with those black boys who are victimised (West 2008). Some argue that narratives of black masculinity are rooted in racist assumptions about violence and criminality, propagating negative stereotypes about black males which detracts attention from recognising black boys as victims of sexual violations (Curry and Utley 2018).

Intersectionality as a theoretical framework

Intersectionality, a termed first coined by black feminist scholar, Kimberlé Crenshaw (1989), is an analytical approach to interrogate black women's experiences at the intersection of race, gender and class, which has its roots firmly anchored in critical race feminism. Crenshaw broadly conceptualised intersectionality as the interplay between various forms of oppression that affect the lived experiences of black women and the resulting injustices. More recently, the term has been used more expansively and scholars and activists in different fields have used the language of intersectionality as an organising tool to identify and call into question social inequalities (Hill Collins and Blige 2016). Notably, intersectionality allows for the questioning of the interlocking nature of gender, race, class, sexuality, ability and other axes of oppression for groups in oppressed social locations. Essentially, intersectionality advances the notion of interrogating how intersecting forms of oppression converge for racialised and minoritised groups in complex and subtle ways. According to black feminist scholars, to recognise multiple systems of oppression means that we can better understand how black women will experience gender discrimination differently to white women as a result of their racial background, and will also experience racial and ethnic discrimination differently to black men because of their gender (hooks 1984; King 1988; hooks 1989; Hill Collins 1990; Crenshaw 1991). In short, an intersectional theoretical framework helps to conceptualise how categories of difference intersect and interplay in a context of social relations of power, and advances understanding of how divergent groups may experience oppression differently. What is important for black feminist scholars such as Hill Collins and Blige (2016), is that the key tenets of intersectionality are relationality, inequality, power and social context, as well as their interconnectedness. An intersectional lens therefore helps to delineate how multiple marginalised identities coalesce in a social context of power relations. As Hill Collins (1990) asserts, coming from a perspective that is working at the intersection of feminism and anti-racism, an intersectional approach provides the theoretical tools necessary for examining how different groups are affected by inequalities and oppression.

Intersectionality has, however, been criticised for having little substance and specifically, that it lacks a clearly defined methodology (Davis 2008). It is also heavily contested as to whether intersectionality is a theory, a conceptual framework, a paradigm, or a method (Carbin and Edenheim 2013). Indeed, Hill Collins (2015) acknowledges the inherently problematic definitional difficulties of intersectionality. Notwithstanding the criticisms, the strength of an intersectional approach is that it provides necessary tools for being critically attuned to the issues that affect the lives of black adolescents and frame their experiences of sexual exploitation. To this end, I contend that it is thus crucial to locate black adolescents' experiences of sexual exploitation within a broader understanding of intersecting multiple oppressions. Intersectionality is useful as a way of acknowledging how disadvantage and marginalisation differently affect black children's lived experiences and increase vulnerability to exploitative and abusive situations. In essence, an intersectional approach requires us to focus on the complexity of issues that are important for understanding experiences shaped by socially-constructed divisions (Murphy et al 2009; Mehrotra 2010; Mattsson 2014). More specifically, an intersectional perspective can enable the asking of difficult questions that will help inform assessments of the layered experiences of black adolescents which are rooted in relationships shaped by race, (dis)ability, gender and class.

Using intersectional theory concepts of relationality and social context, the next section will analyse a case study drawn from an SCR of child R, a 15-year-old black girl in the looked-after system, to illustrate how an intersectional approach can help make sense of some key issues framing R's experience. An SCR takes place in England when serious or fatal violence or maltreatment of a child has occurred, including when a child or young person dies in custody. Specifically, it involves the Local Safeguarding Children Board commissioning a detailed examination of the case to establish whether there are lessons to be learned about the ways in which professionals and organisations work together to safeguard children and promote their welfare.

Case example

Child R

Child R is a 15-year-old looked-after girl in foster care who was raped by an older man in the context of a history of CSE. In early 2014, R was invited to meet an older, predatory male at a hotel, where he allegedly raped her. The antecedents of this meeting remain uncertain, but R said that a friend of hers had given the man her telephone number, so that he could contact her. R reported the alleged assault to her foster carers the same day, and police action was taken to find and arrest the man. A criminal investigation and court process have now concluded, in which the perpetrator was found guilty of a separate, lesser sexual offence against another young person. The offence of rape against R remains untried, but is held on the man's records as not guilty.

According to the SCR, R had a family history of housing instability, exposure to drug dealing, child neglect and physical abuse. The family had no secure housing or finances and often stayed with relatives or friends. This meant that they moved around a lot, resulting in instability for R and her siblings. Both police and Children's Social Care received referrals about criminality in the household, largely related to drug-dealing and other acquisitive offences, as well as neglect of the children. There was evidence to show a history of R being groomed for drug distribution. The SCR indicates that R suffered emotional rejection, neglect and physical assaults at the hands of her mother. She was neglected and left in charge of her younger siblings and was exposed to many adults who posed a risk to her. R was made subject to a child protection plan in 2009 and taken into care in 2010 at the age of 10, after reporting that her mother had beaten her. While in care, R had periods of going missing, exhibiting highly disruptive behaviour, as well as multiple placements and exclusions from school (Trench 2015).

Using intersectionality to understand vulnerabilities

Drawing on key tenets of Intersectionality, notably relationality, inequality, power and social context, I will illustrate how this approach can help us delve into some of the issues framing R's experiences. Crucially, a common thread running through R's SCR is that the professionals involved lacked an understanding of her particular vulnerabilities. There is no doubt that several unique issues intersected for R and that she had some very complex needs. Most notably, she experienced cumulative adversity, exposure to multiple forms of abuse and neglect, and a dysfunctional home environment, among other issues. R's SCR highlights that she has suffered a number of ACEs defined as experiencing traumatic events such as domestic abuse, intra-familial abuse and neglect, and other early life stressors (Felitti et al 1998). Added to this, she suffered trauma as a result of her 'exposure to witnessing adult violence and being used to prepare and deliver drugs to customers' (Trench 2015:14). The SCR found that R's 'defiant and provocative behavior in schools gave rise to concerns about her vulnerability to sexual exploitation and to "gang activity"' (Trench 2015:10). The SCR also emphasised that 'R was going missing on a regular basis from her foster homes and was often out very late –

sometimes being dropped off by an older man' (Trench 2015:11). In order to appreciate the relational context of R's life, it is important to acknowledge that she is positioned at the intersection of interlocking systems of oppressions (Hill Collins and Blige 2016) which gives rise to some particular vulnerabilities. Specifically, an intersectional lens enables us to better understand that for deeply troubled black girls, like R, the lack of a safe and stable home environment, together with societal racism and gendered power relationships negatively affect their everyday realities; all of which contribute to a context of increased vulnerabilities. An intersectional lens can open ways to re-interpreting the stressful life events and conditions (such as, the trauma resulting from physical and emotional abuse, and a lack of stability in her home life), that negatively affect R's life, potentially contributing to her susceptibility to exploitation. Furthermore, an intersectional approach provides a framework for disentangling the factors that are constraining and shaping R's experiences. Thus, viewing R's experiences of childhood neglect and sexual exploitation through an intersectional lens allows us to make better sense of some of the adversities and obstacles she has to contend with that would have had a significant impact on her psychological wellbeing and coping behaviour. As such, an intersectional lens will be better able to make sense of the factors that come together to affect the experiences of sexual exploitation for young people like R; it can foster the development of a strengths-based approach that can build on R's strengths to engage her in the work. Most notably, a strengths-based approach shifts the focus away from a deficit perspective as it has, as its underlying principle, the idea that most people can change their behaviour when provided with the correct support and adequate resources (Bernard and Thomas 2016). Crucially, for engagement with children like R to happen, it will be important for practitioners to have the skills and awareness to think themselves into the frame of reference of the child to understand the problems that are posed for undertaking nuanced assessments (Bernard and Thomas 2016:67). A strengths-based approach will be essential for harnessing R's resilience and sense of hope, which she will need for navigating the toxic familial and neighbourhood environments that she has to inhabit.

Of relevance here is that, although R's SCR makes no mention that she experienced discrimination, it is important to consider that subtle processes of situational racism and positional racism may have taken their toll. Briefly, situational racism is defined by racist behaviour that is shaped by the social context, which may have had an effect, while positional racism is defined here as the nuanced ways in which race-constructed otherness is experienced by black people (Mirza 2009). For example, some commentators have introduced the concept of adultification to describe the ways that subtle and unconscious race-based bias contributes to the treatment of black children in the child welfare and justice systems: where black children are deprived of 'childhood' as attributed to their white counterparts and treated as if they were adults (Dancy 2014; Goff et al 2014; Epstein et al 2017). As Epstein et al (2017) and Goff et al (2014) observe, black children are often perceived as less innocent than white children and thus less in need of protection; some practitioners may also treat them as if they are older than their actual age and find them more culpable for their actions. These important insights have some relevance in R's case. For example, the SCR notes her patterns of going missing from care, sometimes missing for more than 24 hours; as highlighted earlier, one of the major concerns about children who go missing is their exposure to several risk factors, including sexual and criminal exploitation (Biehal and Wade 2000; Hikkle and Hallett 2016). The SCR also suggests evidence of sexual exploitation, 'R having unexplained amounts of money and being dropped off by an older man' (p 32). Yet, as the SCR points out, the local authority's Multi-agency Missing from Care Protocol was never acted on; for example, having a strategy meeting to discuss a risk management plan and having an independent return home interview with R once she had returned to the placement (DfE 2014). I suggest that the lack of concern for R's wellbeing and the invisibility of her experiences support notions of adultification; an intersectional analysis can enhance our understanding of the subtle processes that may contribute to the adultification of black children affected by sexual exploitation. In short, intersectionality can help us to elucidate many of the underlying issues and dynamics of CSE, as well as to make sense of their coping strategies, help-seeking behaviour and engagement with services.

Intersecting identities: lived experiences

In what follows, I discuss some issues concerning R's intersecting identities. The SCR suggests that R's identity was either ignored or marginalised in assessments of her needs. For example, on page 18 (Trench 2015) the SCR state that, 'a gap has been noted in relation to the attention given to her sense of identity' (Trench 2015:18). However, there is no attempt to reflect upon what this lack of attention may have meant for considering her lived experiences of neglectful and abusive care (Bernard and Harris 2016). Furthermore, on page 32, the SCR points out the lack of awareness by the professional helpers of the risk of sexual exploitation, her 'previous sexualised behaviour', and the risks it posed. Nonetheless, this statement is not subjected to any analysis, so we are not told what her sexualised behaviour consisted of. I contend that an intersectional lens has the potential here to enable the development of counter-narratives to avoid victim blaming and to challenge the dominant perception that girls and young women who are sexually active are participating in transactional sex when in fact they are being manipulated in coercive and exploitative relationships and how this might be affected by racism for black girls and young women. For one thing, an intersectional paradigm enables a more nuanced view of Child R's gendered experiences of sexual exploitation. At the same time, as race and gender oppression coalesce for R, an intersectional lens can help to elucidate the subtle nuances of racialised gendered power dynamics for raising important questions about the set of factors contributing to R's experiences of sexual exploitation. Within this frame, we can appreciate the significance of multiple oppressions, coupled with experiences of trauma and what that means for black adolescent young women, like R, who are socially marginalised, and therefore are at increased risk of victimisation (Miller 1998). To this end, if practitioners are to develop relational practice with R and, especially, to understand the multifaceted dynamics of her whole experience, this has to be informed by an intersectional analysis that can take account of the complexity of the contextual factors framing her lived experiences (Firmin 2018).

To be clear, I am in no way suggesting that engaging highly-resistant young people like R is in any way straightforward. Indeed, how to build up trust with hard-to-engage young people in the statutory child protection system poses a real challenge. The SCR indicates R's 'lack of engagement and her stated mistrust of professionals' (p 19), and in particular her 'mistrust of those in authority' (p 31). The SCR quite rightly points out that, in general, it is not uncommon for looked-after adolescents to have problems trusting and communicating with professionals who are there to help. However, viewed through an intersectional lens, we can consider the additional factors which may act to silence R's voice. For example, 'for black children, the debilitating effects of racism powerfully influence the way traumatic events are experienced and the meaning given to them' (Bernard 2002:241). Additionally, it must be noted that when black young people do ask for help, some may encounter professional helpers who are insensitive, or lack understanding of the key issues affecting their lived experiences. An intersectional perspective therefore provides an entry point to understanding something of the implications this may have on R's ability to give voice to her experiences, as well to recognise her self-efficacy and personal agency and to make sense of help-seeking behaviour (Firmin et al 2016). Therefore, an intersectional lens opens up new ways for considering how R is supported to interpret and make meaning of her experiences as coercive and exploitative (Chung 2005).

Conclusion

This chapter has employed intersectionality as a lens of analysis to explore its possibilities for making sense of black adolescents' experiences of CSE. It has suggested that, as black adolescents experience some unique context-based factors that interplay, an intersectional lens provides the necessary analytical tools for illuminating their lived experiences of sexual exploitation. An intersectional approach allows for seeing how multiple marginalised identities create a context of increased levels of risks for black adolescents. Specifically, an intersectional lens offers scope for pinpointing how structural inequalities resulting in gender, dis(ability), race and class-based oppression are inextricably intertwined facets of black adolescents' lives. Their experiences are likely to be accentuated by these factors when they are victimised by sexual exploitation. Notwithstanding that the case study was but one example of a young woman's individual experiences, it is a powerful story that illustrates the way that black children's complex needs may be overlooked. As the significant role of an SCR is to learn lessons and avoid repeating mistakes, the issues raised are relevant to the broader population of black adolescents affected by sexual exploitation. It is therefore essential to understand that black adolescents' experiences of sexual exploitation take place in a societal context of deficit-thinking that stigmatises their identities and devalues their experiences, which has a significant bearing on how risk is framed. It is evident, then, that an intersectional lens can open up a space for asking important questions about race and racism to make robust assessments that are rooted in an understanding of the complex terrain that shapes risk for black adolescents in particular ways. The intersection of race, (dis)ability, gender and class affects black adolescents significantly, so practitioners must be aware that black adolescents are confronting specific adversities in their lives that need to be disentangled in order to understand the barriers they have to navigate. Intersectional approaches offer critical tools for making nuanced assessments of the risks multiple-disadvantaged black adolescents are exposed to.

References

Beckett, H., Holmes, D. and Walker, J. (2017) *Child Sexual Exploitation: Definition and Guide for Professionals – Extended Text*, Totnes: Research in Practice

Beckett, H. with Brodie, I., Factor, F., Melrose, M., Pearce, J., Pitts, J., Shuker, L. and Warrington, C. (2013) *'It's Wrong...But You Get Used To It': A Qualitative Study of Gang-associated Sexual Violence Towards, and Exploitation of, Young People in England*, London and Luton: Office of Children's Commissioner and University of Bedfordshire

Berelowitz, S., Clifton, J., Firmin, C., Gulyurtlu, S. and Edwards, G. (2013) *If Only Someone Had Listened: Office of the Children's Commissioner's Inquiry into Child Sexual Exploitation in Gangs and Groups*, London: Office of the Children's Commissioner

Bernard, C. (2002) 'Giving voice to experiences: Parental maltreatment of black children in the context of societal racism', *Child and Family Social Work*, 7: 239–251

Bernard, C. (2015) 'Black teenage mothers' understandings of the effects of maltreatment on their coping style and parenting practice: A pilot study', *Children and Society*, 29(5): 355–365

Bernard, C. (2016) 'Child sexual abuse in the lives of black children', in C. Bernard and P. Harris (eds) *Safeguarding Black Children: Good Practice in Child Protection*, London: Jessica Kingsley Publisher

Bernard, C. and Harris, P. (2016) *Safeguarding Black Children: Good Practice in Child Protection*, London: Jessica Kingsley Publishers

Bernard, C. and Thomas, C. (2016) 'Risk and Safety: A strengths-based perspective in working with black families where there are safeguarding concerns', in C. Williams and M. Graham (eds) *Social Work in a Diverse Society: Transforming Practice with Back and Minority Ethnic Individuals and Communities*, Bristol: Policy Press, pp 59–73

Biehal, N. and Wade, J. (2000) 'Going missing from residential and foster care: Linking biographies and contexts', *British Journal of Social Work*, 30(2): 211–225

Boff, A. (2013) *Shadow City: Exposing Human Trafficking in Everyday London*, London: GLA Conservatives, http://glaconservatives.co.uk/wp-content/uploads/2013/10/Shadow-City.pdf

Carbin, M. and Edenheim, S. (2013) 'The intersectional turn in feminist theory: A dream of a common language?' *European Journal of Women's Studies*, 20(3): 233–248

Chesney-Lind, M. and Eliason, M. (2006) 'From invisible to incorrigible: The demonization of marginalisd women and girls', *Crime, Media, Culture*, 2(1): 29–47

Chung, D. (2005) 'Violence, control, romance and gender equality: Young women and heterosexual relationships', *Women's Studies International Forum*, 28: 445–455

Cockbain, E., Brayley, H. and Ashby, M. (2014) *Not Just a Girl Thing: A Large-scale Comparison of Male and Female Users of Child Sexual Exploitation Services in the UK*, London: Barnardo's, https://www.barnardos.org.uk/www.barnardos.org.uk/not-just-a-girl-thing.pdf

Cockbain, E., Ashby, M. and Brayley, H. (2017) 'Immaterial boys? A large scale exploration of gender-based differences in child sexual exploitation services', *Sexual Abuse*, 29(7): 658–684

Crenshaw, K. (1989) 'Demarginalizing the intersection of race and sex: A black feminist critique of antidiscrimination doctrine, feminist theory and antiracist politics', *University of Chicago Legal Forum*, 140: 139–167

Crenshaw, K. (1991) 'Mapping the margins: Intersectionality, identity politics, and violence against women of color', *Stanford Law Review*, 43(6): 1241–1299

Curry, T.J. and Utley, E.A. (2018) 'She touched me: Five snapshots of adult sexual violations of black boys', *Kennedy Institute of Ethics Journal*, 28(2): 205–241

Dancy, T.E. (2014) 'The adultification of black boys: What educational settings can learn from Trayvon Martin', in K.J. Fasching-Varner, R.E. Reynolds, K.A. Albert and L.L. Martin (eds) *Trayvon Martin, Race, and American Justice: Writing Wrong*, Teaching Race and Ethnicity, Rotterdam: SensePublishers, pp 49–55

Davis, K. (2008) 'Intersectionality a buzzword: A sociology of science perspectives on what makes a feminist theory successful', *Feminist Theory*, 9: 67–86

DfE (Department for Education) (2014) *Statutory Guidance on Children who Runaway or go Missing from Home or Care*, London: DfE

Disley, E and Liddle, M. (2016) *Local Perspectives in Ending Gang and Youth Violence Areas Perceptions of the Nature of Urban Street Gangs*, Research Report 88, London: Home Office

Epstein, R., Blake, J.J. and Gonzalez, T. (2017) *Girlhood Interrupted: The Erasure of Black Girls' Girlhood*, Washington, DC: Center on Poverty and Inequality, Georgetown Law

Felitti, V.J., Anda, R.F., Nordenberg, D., Williamson, D.F., Spitz, A., Edwards, V., Koss, M.P. and Marks, J.S. (1998) 'Relationship of childhood abuse and household dysfunction to many of the leading causes of death in adults: The Adverse Childhood Experiences (ACE) Study', *Journal of Preventive Medicine*, 14(4): 245–258

Firmin, C. (2011) *This is It: This is My Life. Female Voice in Violence Final Report: On the Impact of Serious Youth Violence and Criminal Gangs on Women and Girls Across the Country*, London: Race on the Agenda (ROTA)

Firmin, C. (2013) 'Something old or something new: Do pre-existing conceptualisations of abuse enable a sufficient response to abuse in young people's relationships and peer groups?', in M. Melrose and J. Pearce (eds) *Critical Perspectives on Child Sexual Exploitation and Related Trafficking*, Basingstoke: Palgrave Macmillan

Firmin, C. (2017) 'Contextual risk, individualised responses: An assessment of safeguarding responses to nine cases of peer-on-peer abuse', *Child Abuse Review*, doi: 10.1002/car.2449

Firmin, C. (2018) 'Contextualizing case reviews: A methodology for developing systemic safeguarding practices', *Child and Family Social Work*, 23: 45–52

Firmin, C., Warrington, C. and Pearce, J. (2016) 'Sexual exploitation and its impact on developing sexualities and sexual relationships: The need for contextual social work intervention', *British Journal of Social Work*, 46(8): 2318–2337

Goff, P.A., Jackson, M.C., Lewis Di Leone, B.A. Culotta, C.M. and DiTomasso, N.A. (2014) 'The essence of innocence: Consequences of dehumanizing black children', *Journal of Personality and Social Psychology*, 106(4): 526–545

Hallett, S. (2015) '"An uncomfortable comfortableness": "Care", child protection and child sexual exploitation', *British Journal of Social Work*, 46(7): 2137–2152

Hallett, S. (2017) *Making Sense of Child Sexual Exploitation: Exchange, Abuse and Young People*, Bristol: Policy Press

Hikkle, K. and Hallett, S. (2016) 'Mitigating harm: Considering harm reduction principles in work with sexually exploited young people', *Children and Society*, 30. 302–313

Hill Collins, P. (1990) *Black Feminist Thought: Knowledge, Consciousness and the Politics of Empowerment*, Boston, MA: Unwin Hyman

Hill Collins, P. (2015) 'Intersectionality's definitional dilemmas', *Annual Review of Sociology*, 41: 1–20

Hill Collins, P. and Blige, S. (2016) *Intersectionality*, Cambridge: Polity Press

hooks, b. (1984) *Feminist Theory: From Margin to Centre*, Boston, MA: South End Press

hooks, b. (1989) *Talking Back: Thinking Feminist –Thinking Black*, London: Sheba

King, D. (1988) 'Multiple jeopardy, multiple consciousness: The context of black feminist ideology', *Signs: Journal of Women in Culture and Society*, 14(1): 42–72.

Leon, L. and Rawls, P. (2016) *Boys Don't Cry: Improving Identification and Disclosure of Sexual Exploitation of Boys and Young Men Trafficked in the UK*, London: Children's Society

Mattsson, T. (2014) 'Intersectionality as a useful tool: Anti-oppressive social work and critical reflection', *Affilia*, 29(1): 8–17

McNaughton, C., Nicolls, C., Cockbain, E., Brayley, H., Harvey, S., Fox, C., Paskell, C., Ashby, M., Gibson, K. and Jago, N. (2014) *Research on the Sexual Exploitation of Boys and Young Men: A UK Scoping Study: Summary of Findings*, London: Barnardo's, NatCen and UCL

Mehrotra, G. (2010) 'Toward a continuum of intersectionality theorizing for feminist social work scholarship', *Affilia*, 25: 417–430

Miller, J. (1998) 'Gender and victimization risk among young women in gangs', *Journal of Research in Crime and Delinquency*, 35: 429–453

Miller, J. (2008) *Getting Played: African American Girls, Urban Inequality, and Gendered Violence*, New York: New York University Press

Mirza, H.S. (2009) 'Plotting a history: Black and postcolonial feminisms in "New Times"'. *Race Ethnicity and Education*, 12(1): 1–10

Murphy, Y., Hunt, V., Zajicek, A.M., Norris, A.N. and Hamilton, L. (2009) *Incorporating Intersectionality in Social Work Practice, Research, Policy and Education*, New York: NASW Press

Owen, C. and Statham, J. (2009) *Disproportionality in Child Welfare: The Prevalence of Black and Minority Ethnic Children within the 'Looked After' and 'Children in Need' Populations and on Child Protection Registers in England*, London: Department for Children, Schools and Families

Papadopoulos, L. (2010) *An Independent Review into the Sexualisation of Young People*, London: Home Office Publication, www.homeoffice.gov.uk/documents/Sexualisation-young-people

Pearce, J. (2009) *Young People and Sexual Exploitation: It's Not Hidden you Just Aren't Looking*, London: Routledge

Pearce, J. (2010) 'Safeguarding young people from sexual exploitation and from being trafficked: Tensions within contemporary policy and practice', *Sexual Exploitation and Trafficking of Children and Young People: Contemporary Debates*, J. Pearce and M. Melrose (eds), *Special Issue: Youth and Policy*, 104(June): 1–12

Pitts, J. (2013) 'Drifting into trouble: Sexual exploitation and gang affiliation', in M. Melrose and J. Pearce (eds) *Critical Perspectives on Child Sexual Exploitation and Related Trafficking*, Basingstoke: Palgrave Macmillan, pp 23–37

Stephens, D.P. and Phillips, L.D. (2003) 'Freaks, gold diggers, divas, and dykes: The sociohistorical development of adolescent African American women's sexual scripts', *Sexuality and Culture*, 7(1): 3–49

Thomas, R. and D'Arcy, K. (2017) 'Combatting child sexual exploitation with young people and parents: Contributions to a twenty-first-century family support agenda', *British Journal of Social Work*, 47(6): 1686–1703

Trench, S. (2015) *Serious Case Review Report: Child R*, London: Southwark Safeguarding Children Board

Trickett, L. (2015) 'Birds and sluts: Views on young women from boys in the gang', *International Review of Victimology*, 22(1): 25–44

Voisin, D., Takahashi, L., Berringer, K., Burr, S. and Kuhnen, J. (2016) '"Sex is violence": African-American parents' perceptions of the link between exposure to community violence and youth sexual behaviours', *Child and Family Social Work*, 21(4): 464–472

West, C. (2008) '"A thin line between love and hate": Black men as victims and perpetrators of dating violence', *Journal of Aggression, Maltreatment and Trauma*, 16(3): 238–257

11

What's gender got to do with it? Sexual exploitation of children as patriarchal violence

Maddy Coy

Introduction

In the UK and around the globe, victims/survivors of sexual exploitation are disproportionately girls, and those who abuse and exploit them are mostly men and boys. Yet in much policy and public discussion, sexual exploitation is often framed as an issue involving 'children', without attention to the asymmetry between experiences of young women and young men. This does not negate that some boys can be victims, some girls can be perpetrators and either could be victim and perpetrator of sexual exploitation at the same time. What the asymmetric pattern does underscore is that responses to sexual exploitation would benefit from understanding how gender is relevant to victimisation and perpetration. The chapter sets out that gender is critical to talking and theorising about sexual exploitation in two main ways: in understanding patterns of perpetration and victimisation, and in how policy and practice responds to young people. I draw on bell hooks (2000) to suggest that sexual exploitation can be conceptualised as a form of patriarchal violence, an approach reflecting decades of feminist analysis that links sexual abuse and exploitation to patriarchal power. Throughout the chapter, implications for practice are highlighted and are then reiterated in a concluding section.

Defining sexual exploitation

Policy and practice definitions of sexual exploitation across regions of the UK have evolved rapidly over the last two decades (Pearce 2009; Beckett et al 2017). The current government definition for England, introduced in 2017, names sexual exploitation of children under 18 as a form of child sexual abuse, with distinct features involving a) exchange and b) some form of gain for the perpetrator (Department for

Education 2017). This represents a catchup with pioneering feminist analyses that identified sexual exploitation as part of a continuum of child sexual abuse, with 'additional dynamics and realities' (Kelly and Regan 2000:15). Yet the inclusion of 'exchange' has more recently been criticised because sexual abuse can also involve 'exchange' (Kelly and Karsna 2017). As they and Lovett, Coy and Kelly (2018) note, grooming of children in all forms and contexts of child sexual abuse and exploitation can involve attention, affection and gifts, and some reports into sexual exploitation have found little evidence of 'reward'.

The widening out of definitions and understandings of sexual exploitation has been critically interrogated by Margaret Melrose (2013). Tracing the paradigm shift from the 2000 government guidance that identified 'child prostitution' as a form of abuse, she argues that the concept has become so elastic that practitioners struggle with its lack of clarity. At the heart of this debate is whether the separation of sexual exploitation from sexual abuse is a distinction without a difference.

Melrose's analysis also draws attention to another key shift: the decoupling of sexual exploitation from the social institution of prostitution has made a gender analysis less visible in policy and practice definitions. Indeed, the broadening of the concept of sexual exploitation was propelled at least in part by concern about the invisibility of sexually exploited boys. For instance, Lillywhite and Skidmore (2006) argued that a focus on abuse through prostitution led to the exclusion of sexual exploitation of boys, since extant evidence suggested that the contexts in which they are exploited were different, and not so directly connected to the sex industry. Yet as this chapter goes on to discuss, even within these wider dynamics of sexual exploitation, such as 'peer-on-peer' exploitation (Firmin 2011), networks of abuse (Brayley and Cockbain 2014), so-called 'sex parties' (Melrose 2013), the contexts of gangs and groups (Berelowitz et al 2012; Beckett et al 2013), young women are disproportionately likely to be exploited by men and boys.

Globally, data on sexual exploitation of children is scant, and often comprises localised studies that are focused on specific forms (UNICEF 2014). Determining prevalence is beset with difficulties, not least the varying definitions that surround what might be named as sexual exploitation both by victim/survivors and by researchers. In England, sexual exploitation of children 'has yet to be effectively included in prevalence studies' (Kelly and Karsna 2017:51). A recent international report on violence in childhood calls for specialised surveys to measure 'sexual economic exploitation of children' (Know Violence in Childhood 2017:99). Official statistics from data held by organisations are limited because sexual exploitation is consistently under-reported and under-recognised by professionals. Yet a clear pattern emerges from research and practice-based evidence of workers in the field: girls are more likely than boys to be coerced into sexually exploitative practices and more likely to be groomed into doing so by predatory adults or peers, and perpetrators are more likely to be men and boys. This asymmetric pattern also reflects the wider continuum of child sexual abuse, where the majority of victim-survivors are girls and young women, and most perpetrators boys and men (Kelly and Karsna 2017, reporting on data for England).

International human rights approaches recognise this asymmetry. The Optional Protocol on the Sale of Children, Child Prostitution and Child Pornography (United Nations, 2000:247) states 'that a number of particularly vulnerable groups, including girl children, are at greater risk of sexual exploitation and that girl children are disproportionately represented among the sexually exploited'. The point of acknowledging this disproportionality is twofold: to highlight a well-documented reality, and to ask the question of *why might this be so*. This is the question to which this chapter aims to respond, through analysing how gender as a social hierarchy features as a central dynamic in forms and contexts of sexual exploitation.

The entanglement of sex and gender

What the concept of 'gender' means, and its relationship with 'sex', is contested. While the terms gender and sex are often used interchangeably, sex refers to male and female people (with a tiny proportion of intersex conditions), and gender as socio-cultural conceptions of femininity and masculinity (Connell and Pearse 2015; Mackay 2015). Mackay notes that gender refers to a 'set of learnt behaviours; it is the cultural roles and expectations of behaviour, dress, work, appearance and physicality that are attached to males and females' (Mackay 2015:112). Specific forms of masculinities and femininities vary by time and place, shaped by intersections with race/ethnicity, histories of colonisation and class. Commonalties are evident: masculinity is equated with strength, rationality and sexual prowess, and femininity more with submissiveness, emotionality and an expectation to put others before self. These gendered codes are mapped onto embodied sex difference between females and males, built on assumptions about the links between sex, gender and 'natural orders' (Stanley 1984). Connell and Pearse's (2015) definition of gender highlights this interplay between notions of biology and socio-cultural construction: 'Gender is the structure of social relations that centres on the reproductive arena, and the set of practices that bring reproductive distinctions between bodies into social processes' (p 11).

As a structure of social relations, gender is the organisation of society and of power that places more value on attributes associated with men, maleness and masculinity: in feminist terms, patriarchy. As a set of practices, patriarchy involves all the ways in which gendered codes of behaviour are normalised as 'natural' characteristics of female and male people for example, that women are suited to caring for others, men are leaders. These codes are transmitted to children through the embodied practices of adults towards girls and boys, speech-acts, and the gendered use of clothing, toys, characters in books and television and so on (hooks 2000; Fine 2010; Mackay 2015). In turn the interaction between sex and gender creates a socially constructed hierarchy between women and men, evident in a continuing pay gap, a persistent division of labour in the domestic sphere, women's under-representation in political decision-making and limitations on the freedom of women and girls because of fear of violence (for example, Kelly 1988; Walby 2011; Vera-Gray 2016; Heuchan 2017). Constructs of gender are also closely connected to the social construction of heterosexuality. As the chapter will go on to discuss, an equation of masculinity with (hetero) sexual conquest is particularly relevant to sexual exploitation.

How we reproduce, or resist, learned gendered expectations in everyday behaviours (Connell and Pearse 2015; Mackay 2015) is captured by the classic conceptualisation of 'doing gender' (West and Zimmerman 1987). Despite the popularity of the notion that women's and men's behaviours are determined by innately different 'hard-wiring' – a perspective that Cordelia Fine terms 'neurosexism' – research to date does not show connections between sexed differences in brain anatomy and gender stereotypes (Fine 2010; 2017; Connell and Pearse 2015). Behaviourally there is more similarity than variance between women and men (Connell and Pearse 2015), including in attributes that are often understood as products of sex difference such as empathy and spatial skills (Fine 2010; 2017).

Finally, there can be tensions between gender as a social hierarchy and how individuals understand and want to live their sense of self in terms of gendered norms and expressions (Mackay 2015). Greater visibility of transgender identities and gender non-conforming diversity exists alongside persistent unequal social stratification of women and men. Claire Heuchan elegantly articulates how the social and economic conditions of women's lives are different to those of men under the gendered social arrangements of patriarchy:

> Gender is why female sexuality is strictly policed – women called sluts if we allow men sexual access to our bodies, called prudes if we don't – and no such judgements are passed on male sexuality. Gender is why women who are abused by men get blamed and shamed – 'she was asking for it' or 'she provoked him' – while the behaviour of abusive men is commonly justified with 'boys will be boys' or 'he's a good man, really'. Gender is why girls are rewarded for being nurturing, passive, and modest, traits that are not encouraged in boys. Gender is why boys are rewarded for being competitive, aggressive, and ambitious, traits not encouraged in girls. Gender is why women are considered property, passing from the ownership of father to husband through marriage. Gender is why women are expected to provide domestic and emotional labour along with the vast majority of care, yet such work is devalued as 'feminised' and subsequently rendered invisible. Gender is not an abstract issue. (Heuchan 2017)

Any serious attempt to understand phenomena that affect women/girls and men/boys differently must engage with how gender works to produce power inequalities. For sexual exploitation and abuse, gender is acutely relevant because 'it is a social structure of a particular kind – it involves a specific relationship with bodies' (Connell and Pearse 2015:11). The explanation for why men disproportionately exploit women and girls lies in gendered practices that are directed against female bodies.

Yet many acknowledgements of sex and gender in discourse on sexual exploitation are descriptive, rather than linking such exploitation to wider social and sexualised sexism (Coy 2016). In contrast, feminist analysis has extensively theorised and documented the relevance of constructs of gender to violence, abuse and exploitation. For our work in practice, this means that when we are working with young people about sexual exploitation, we need to contextualise their experiences within meanings associated with gender. This offers a deeper route to making sense of their experiences.

Feminist perspectives on gender, violence and exploitation

Violence against women and girls (VAWG), is understood by the United Nations (2006:28) as rooted in 'patriarchy and other relations of dominance and subordination' and includes domestic violence, sexual abuse, assault and harassment, crimes in the name of 'honour', stalking, female genital mutilation, prostitution and trafficking. The impacts of these violations of body and self can be immense and the threat of violence shadows the everyday life of women and girls (Kelly 1988; Vera-Gray 2016). Such forms of abuse are often grouped as 'gender-based violence', although this is a wider and arguably different concept (Boyle 2019). There is also an interaction between sex and gender here, since women and girls' bodies are targeted for violence and exploitation because of female sex. The relevance of gender is perhaps more about perpetrators (Boyle 2019). In terms of gendered norms and practices, the most socially rewarded forms of masculinity equate manhood with (hetero)sexual conquest and entitlement. This, as the chapter will explore, is vital to understanding the gendered dynamics of sexual exploitation and how it can be understood as a form of patriarchal violence. Two main points need developing before I more specifically focus on sexual exploitation.

First, feminists analysed sexual exploitation of children as part of a continuum of child sexual abuse, raising questions about masculinity and men's sexual behaviours (for example, Kelly and Regan 2000; Itzin 2001; Whittier 2011). More recently, others have argued that the gendered asymmetry in victimisation and perpetration of child sexual exploitation, as a form of sexual abuse, should lead to its inclusion in policy definitions of VAWG (Firmin 2011; Brayley and Cockbain 2014). Sexual exploitation of women, for example, often begins in childhood but does not always end there, despite the 18th birthdays representing a line between what is defined as abuse and what as 'choice'. Other forms of VAWG, including rape, domestic violence, sexual harassment and prostitution have all been empirically and conceptually linked to gendered expressions of power (see for example, Kelly 1988; Crenshaw 1991; Coy 2016; Vera-Gray 2016).

Second, as Claire Heuchan clarifies, 'patriarchy is dependent on the hierarchy of gender' (2017). Analysing patriarchy as both a context and power dynamic of child sexual abuse and VAWG is a core tenet of feminist theory (see Kelly 1988; Walby 1990; Crenshaw 1991; hooks 2000; Westmarland 2015). The concept of 'patriarchal violence' captures men's enactment of power through assault, coercion and exploitation (for example, Stark et al 1979; Gill 2006; Erturk and Purkayastha 2012). A version of this concept developed by bell hooks (2000) makes plain the links between perpetrating violence and 'sexism and sexist thinking', 'male domination' and the power that adults have over children. How this framing is useful for making sense of sexual exploitation is discussed in more detail later.

Black feminist theorists highlight the inadequacy of focusing simply on gender as a system of domination. As Kimberlé Crenshaw, bell hooks and Claire Heuchan emphasise, gender as a hierarchy intersects with race/ethnicity, class, sexuality, age, disability, which make a difference to how VAWG is experienced (see also Kanyeredzi 2018). These intersections are under-explored in relation to sexual exploitation of children in the UK, which limits what is possible to discuss here. For victim/survivors, gender and generation (age) are the most widely acknowledged, in terms of children's social, economic and emotional dependency on adults. While UK research has documented the exploitation of young people from minoritised communities (for example, Pearce et al 2003; Ward and Patel 2006), more recently they have been 'missing from discourse' (Sharp 2013). The voices and experiences of young African-Caribbean women are largely absent from discussions in the UK. In short, as noted by Bernard in this volume, alongside the emphasis on minoritised race and culture of male perpetrators (discussed in more detail later), young white women have been more visible as victims (Cockbain 2013; Pearce 2014). There is also limited knowledge about the sexual exploitation of LGBTQ young people, with practice-based evidence of specialist workers indicating that fears of judgements about sexuality and gender identity are barriers to identification and disclosure (Donovan 2014; Fox 2016). Sexual exploitation of young people with disabilities is shrouded in silence. A recent study about young people with learning disabilities found that they faced a 'particular risk' of sexual exploitation, exacerbated by a paradox of professional practice that 'unprotects' by 'over-protecting' (Franklin and Smeaton 2017).

In these studies, gender is rarely explored in an intersectional sense (Crenshaw 1991), that is, in terms of how it is shaped by and in turn shapes race/ethnicity, and/or sexuality and/or disability. The Muslim Women's Network report on sexual exploitation of Muslim women and girls is a notable exception in highlighting specific ways in which constructs of gender, race and faith interlock (Gohir 2013; see also Bernard in this volume). This matters because sexual exploitation as patriarchal violence will vary according to different social locations and identities. In practice, this means talking with young people about how patriarchal practices operate in their peer networks, communities and families. This avoids making assumptions and offers a space for them to reflect on how sexism, racism, classism, homophobia and intersectional discrimination shape their experiences.

The next section turns to perpetrators of sexual exploitation and explores the significance of evidence showing that they are mostly men and boys. This is a conscious choice to make perpetrators visible, rather than maintain their usual position in discussions and debates as the 'and finally'. Highlighting that most perpetrators are men draws attention to the need to interrogate sexual exploitation as a form of patriarchal violence.

Perpetrators of sexual exploitation: making men's abusive practices visible

A recent rapid evidence assessment examined 50 studies about perpetrators of sexual exploitation, 19 from the UK, and concluded that 'perpetrators were generally identified as male, white and aged between 18 and 85 years (with the average age in individual studies ranging from 30 to 46 years)' (Walker et al 2018). Most of the studies reviewed in this assessment focused exclusively on online exploitation, but there is evidence that perpetrators in other contexts are predominantly men: the UK Child Exploitation and Online Protection centre's (CEOP 2011) analysis of 'localised grooming' identified the majority of offenders as men and data gathered for an inquiry into sexual exploitation in gangs and groups in England found the same (Berelowitz et al 2012). Average age varies by study (Walker et al 2018) and in the UK at least, data on race/ethnicity of perpetrators is patchy and often misrepresented (Cockbain 2013; Gill and Harrison 2015). That perpetrators are mostly male is the most consistent finding. The 2009 safeguarding guidance for England acknowledged that 'the predominant evidence is of men sexually abusing children and young people' (DCSF 2009:18), but the 2017 progress report is studiedly silent on this pattern.

Men are the overwhelming majority of perpetrators of sexual exploitation in two ways: those who recruit and control young people, and those who pay for sexual acts. Those who recruit and exploit young women for gain (including status within peer networks) have been more visible than those who pay to sexually abuse young women (O'Hara 2019). Recent prominent convictions in England of perpetrators for offences relating to sexual exploitation include:

- Operation Bullfinch in Oxford, resulting in convictions of seven men in June 2013 for abuse of girls aged 11–15, with offences that included arranging child prostitution[1] and trafficking;
- Operation Brooke in Bristol, with 13 men convicted in November 2014 of offences that included paying for the sexual services of a child and facilitating child prostitution;

- Operation Sanctuary in Newcastle, where 17 men and one woman were convicted in August 2017 of a range of sexual offences against young women aged 13–25, including conspiracy to incite prostitution and trafficking.

That most of the convicted abusers in these cases were men from minoritised communities, with accompanying sensationalist media reporting that emphasised race and/or culture (in contrast to when perpetrators are white men) has been thoughtfully explored elsewhere (Cockbain 2013; Gill and Harrison 2015) and is commented on in Pitt's chapter in this volume. This focus on race, culture and/or religion blocks the possibility of connecting patriarchal power exercised by men in different social locations. Relationships between men, including through friendships and business contacts, can be facilitated by the commodification and exploitation of young women's bodies (Jyrkinen 2012). Yet association between masculinities and sexual conquest in men's abusive practices is a muted aspect of public – or professional – discourse.

For example, despite these cases there has been no spotlight on the men on the other side of the equation. When girls are being sold or traded, there are buyers. Just as the currency for young women may not be hard cash, the trading terms on which they are exchanged by exploiters may also be looser, involving status or favours as payment (Kelly and Regan 2000) and young people may themselves not be aware of an 'exchange'. Yet tackling men who pay for sexual access to young women is the area where policy on sexual exploitation, at least in England, has been most timid (Coy 2016; O'Hara 2019). Serious case reviews note that men come to cities to have sex with girls, and have argued that understanding the motivations of men who exploit young women was beyond the scope of their work and therefore were not discussed (see Oxford and Rochdale reviews 2013 and 2015 respectively in http:///learning. NSPCC. org.uk/case-reviews). This silence is significant because it inevitably limits intervention and prevention to enabling young people to recognise signs of sexual exploitation – for themselves and others – rather than stopping the actions of abusers (Coy 2016).

There is, then, a gap in interventions planned to address abusers that are 'buyers' in a commercial sexual market into which young women are facilitated, arranged and procured. Men who pay for sexual acts reveal much about the dynamics of sexual exploitation. For instance, men's accounts of buying sex demonstrate an uncritical acceptance of the idea that men 'need' regular sexual access to a variety of female bodies (for example, Coy et al 2007; Yonkova and Keegan 2014; Tyler and Jovanovich 2018). The developing work on harmful sexual behaviour with young men is one context in which integration of practices of masculinity, sex and sexuality is essential.[2] Young men may be operating within systems of 'man points', for example, where sexual conquest of young women's bodies is a means of gaining status among peers and where pornography acts as a form of sex education (Coy et al 2013).

In other contexts of sexual exploitation, it is also evident that young women are bought and sold by and between men. That young women who are involved or associated with gangs are viewed as commodities for use, exchange and currency through which to settle scores and enhance male status and authority has been extensively documented (for example, Firmin 2011; Beckett et al 2013). The sexual double standard in these contexts was summed up by one young woman as 'boys get rated, girls get slated' (cited in Beckett et al 2013:21). The expectation that young men are entitled to sex places pressure on young women to consent or comply, and rape of women and girls as a weapon of revenge in gang conflict shows that female bodies are the terrain on and in which men and boys build and bolster a sense of self (Firmin 2011; Beckett et al 2013). Here the 'exchange' in sexual exploitation happens between men. As one young woman reported, 'My ex sold me, well he used me to settle this issue he had with X, and it worked, that is how much I'm worth round here.' (Girl, 17, quoted in Firmin 2011:46).

For practitioners, this suggests that framing sexual exploitation in 'gender-neutral' terms means opportunities are lost to interrogate men's non-consensual sexual practices and their links with notions of masculinity. Many interventions focus on equipping young women with skills to protect themselves under the rubric of 'healthy relationships'. This can reinforce victim-blame, rather than challenging the responsibility and choices of perpetrators.

Hunting gender[3] in professional responses

Professional responses to sexual exploitation have been seriously inadequate and have contributed to the ongoing exploitation of young people and impunity for perpetrators. Research, serious case review and inquiry reports and young women's voices have consistently noted poor professional levels of understanding about impacts of abuse and exploitation (see Lovett et al 2018). The prominence (and as some observe, the dominance) of sexual exploitation in current child protection practice is accompanied by a concern on the ground that austerity measures are undermining interventions, because of the hollowing out and chronic under-funding of both specialised and statutory services.

Interventions are often based on gendered constructions of vulnerability, with young men channelled through criminal or youth justice routes because evidence of sexual abuse or exploitation is read by professionals as 'bad behaviour' (Harper and Scott 2005; Pearce and Pitts 2011). Young women who express understandable and justifiable anger at being abused, neglected and abandoned, are all too often assessed as 'difficult'; their behaviour is not in line with constructs of femininity (Coy 2009; 2017). Some practitioners fail to recognise connections between young women's offending behaviours and the range of abuses to which they are subject by gang-associated men and boys (Firmin 2011; Berelowitz et al 2012). Here 'troubled' is recast as 'troublesome', built on explicitly gendered readings of behaviour and interactions with race and class. As Patricia Yancey Martin (2005) notes, institutions practice gender while claiming that their activities are gender-neutral. The examples given later, discussed by Lovett, Coy and Kelly (2018), illustrate how this dynamic can play out in responses to sexual exploitation.

'Promiscuous girls': a persistent trope

In a recent rapid evidence assessment of literature on discourses about child sexual abuse in England and Wales, 'promiscuous girls' emerged as an implicit feature in professional responses to sexual exploitation (Lovett et al 2018). Beginning in texts about 'child prostitution' as a way of explaining the abuse of girls in the prostitution system from the 1950s onwards (Brown and Barrett 2002), this way of thinking is linked to gendered notions of immorality. For instance, Margaret Melrose (2004) has noted that where abuse of young women through prostitution was acknowledged by professionals in the 1990s, it was attributed to 'bad girls'. These perceptions persist in inquiry reports two decades on. The Office of the Children's Commissioner for England's investigation into child sexual exploitation in the context of gangs and groups (Berelowitz et al 2012) documented examples of case records describing young women as 'asking for it' and 'liking the glamour'. The dictionary definition of 'promiscuity' as 'sexually indiscriminate' has gendered meanings (Lovett et al 2018) which are linked to perceptions by many professionals when sexual exploitation is condoned because young women are viewed as consenting (Pearce 2014).[4]

Analysis of Serious Case Review reports (SCRs) by Lovett et al (2018) revealed that the language of promiscuity in files about sexually exploited young women was explicit and implicit. A review into the sexual exploitation of five young women in Coventry, for example, observed that 'the language used about the children, for example, references to promiscuity, was highly judgemental and demonstrated a lack of understanding of the degree to which they were in control of what was really happening to them' (Lovett et al 2018:78).

This is a coded framing of young women as sexually willing, and therefore not abused. Young women who are sexually exploited are not passive victims, but their survival behaviours can be seen by professionals as evidence of their sexual agency. Lovett and colleagues point to similar implicit references to a discourse of promiscuity in the SCR into Operation Bullfinch in Oxfordshire (Children A, B, C, D, E and F, 2016). Police records include notes such as 'she is a streetwise girl who is wilful' and of a 14-year-old girl who appeared to be 18 or 19, 'by her own admission initiated the sexual intercourse with both named males' (cited in Lovett et al 2018: 78). Similarly, the Centre for Exploitation and Online Protection (2013) note, in a review of barriers to understanding sexual exploitation, that victim/survivors who participated in their consultation reported being discouraged from approaching police, for fear of being judged as promiscuous. The groundbreaking report by the Muslim Women's Network on the sexual exploitation of young Muslim women also highlights perceptions of girls as 'temptresses', which deflect attention from the actions of the men and boys who abuse and exploit (Gohir 2013).

Sexual exploitation of young men: masculinities and victimisation

Lovett and colleagues (2018) also report how boys and young men are often described as 'hidden' victim–survivors (for example, Lillywhite and Skidmore 2006) because of a focus on young women in strategies and approaches to sexual exploitation. While the extent of sexual exploitation of boys is unknown, the same is true of sexual exploitation of girls, and existing evidence suggests that boys are less likely to be targeted for sexual exploitation than girls (Kelly and Karsna 2017). There are also documented differences: boys and young men are often exploited at younger ages than girls, and are more likely to have a criminal record (possibly as a response to previous abuse or as result of criminal exploitation) and some form of disability (Brayley et al 2014).

More useful than a numbers game is to explore barriers to recognition by professionals and young men themselves of boys as victim/ survivors. Notions of what it means to be a man/boy – including constructions of heterosexual masculinity and homophobia – are a barrier to the recognition of exploitation of boys (for example, Harper and Scott 2005; Beckett et al 2013; Gohir 2013; Brayley et al 2014). Lovett and colleagues (2018) extend this observation to argue that a discourse of masculinity as incompatible with victimisation operates to prevent young men, and professionals, from recognising and naming sexual exploitation. They note that this can include an equation of masculinity with sexual prowess (for example, McNaughton-Nicholls et al 2014), and endorsement of stereotypes that men are tough and strong (masculine), in contrast to associations of victimhood as weak and passive (feminine) (McNaughton-Nicholls et al 2014; Fox 2016). Gendered and heteronormative meanings associated with victimisation come into play when young men seek to make sense of their experiences of exploitation and may block professionals from asking questions that would enable their telling. In practice, this means that reflecting on how gendered behaviours influence responses to sexual exploitation is as important as talking with young people about how they navigate meanings of gender. It means being aware that professionals are immersed in patriarchal and sexist ways of thinking too, and may inadvertently reinforce these.

The two examples given earlier suggest that young women invite or want sexual coercion and, somewhat paradoxically, that young men cannot be sexually exploited because to be victimised is to be feminised. This sexist thinking underpins 'patriarchal violence' (hooks 2000).

Sexual exploitation as a form of patriarchal violence

Two examples of international reports on sexual exploitation provide a contrast to how 'gender-neutral' approaches in the UK have developed. ECPAT's international review of the gendered dimensions of commercial sexual exploitation does not flinch from naming men's sexual power and objectification of female bodies that are valued when 'consumed' by men (Altamura 2013). Social, economic and historical contexts that shape prescribed behaviours for women and men are emphasised in the report, including how gendered hierarchies are upheld by families and communities. A vital clue into how the ECPAT report reaches these conclusions is that it draws on multiple qualitative studies of men who pay to abuse children. The men's accounts reveal themes that reflect accounts of men who pay for sex with adult women, in terms of masculine sexual behaviour as entitlement to women and girls' bodies (Altamura 2013). More recently, Promundo's 'gender lens' on sexual abuse and exploitation similarly reiterates that most abusers are men and underscores the need to tackle constructs of masculinity that are exercised as patriarchal power: heterosexual prowess and conquest of female bodies (Heilman and Barker 2018). Understood this way, sexual exploitation is evidence of patriarchal norms and practices, rather than a transgression of them (Ennew 1986).

The value of these international and transnational perspectives is that they indicate that despite variations in constructs of gender, the core of gender as a social hierarchy manifested in who (primarily) abuses and who is (primarily) abused, persists. Theorising sex and gender in relation to sexual exploitation of children in the UK can, with a feminist analysis, flow from the 'who benefits?' question. This question, as Karen Boyle (2019:27) astutely notes, 'allows for a rather different set of connections to be established, conceptualising *men's* behaviour as buyers of women (and men, and children) in relation to broader ideas about men's sexuality, power and sexual entitlement'. Boyle highlights how asking the 'who benefits' question keeps 'the role of patriarchal structures in view' (Boyle 2019:24).

Building on this, I argue that understanding sexual exploitation of children as patriarchal violence is useful because it brings the following into the picture:

- the context of material inequalities between women and men and how adults have powers over children;
- men and boys' sense of entitlement to female bodies, and to a lesser extent to the bodies of young men;
- social constructions of what it means to be a man and the sexual objectification of female bodies in popular culture and pornography;
- intersections between sex, gender, race, class and sexuality under patriarchy, including the racial/ethnic othering of young people from minoritised communities;
- how sexual exploitation can be understood on Liz Kelly's (1988) continuum of violence against women;
- patriarchal power and domination that can be enacted by women (hooks 2000; Westmarland 2015), and perpetrated against boys.

Sexualised sexism in popular culture normalises patriarchal violence. Connections between pornography, perpetration of sexual aggression, attitudes that condone rape, and viewing young women as sexual objects are well-worn themes in empirical research with adults and young people (for overviews, see Flood 2009; Horvath et al 2013). The mainstreaming of a model of sex in popular culture that Tyler and Quek (2016) term pornographification, where women's bodies are represented as sexualised commodities, cannot be separated from practices where men sexually violate women's bodies. As Margaret Melrose (2013) points out, for example, these are the dynamics of 'sex parties' where young women are abused by older men.

hooks' definition of feminism is also useful here, as 'a movement to end sexism, sexist exploitation, and oppression' (2000:viii, drawing on her earlier texts). Sexual exploitation *is* sexist exploitation, rooted in the abuse of female bodies (and, to a lesser extent, of young men), condoned by perceptions that men's sexually abusive behaviour is inevitable because of an uncontrollable sexual drive.

Implications for practice

Why has an analysis of gender not featured prominently in the policy and public debate about sexual exploitation of children? There is more to this than a lack of attention on men that pay to abuse young women. Perhaps it reflects a dilution of feminist analyses, despite a vibrant resurgence in feminist activism (Gill 2016). There has also been a broader unwillingness to address men as perpetrators of VAWG, as prevention and intervention is often limited to work with victims/survivors.

This chapter has proposed that framing sexual exploitation as a form of 'patriarchal violence' clarifies its roots in the power inequalities of gender and generation, with an urgent need to develop an intersectional analysis of race/ethnicity, class, (dis)ability and sexuality.

There are several possible ways to integrate an analysis of patriarchal violence into practice:

- Conversations with young women and young men that explore how they make sense of unequal gendered norms and practices are crucial.
- Focusing on perpetrators and being unafraid to name the empirical reality that most abusers and exploiters are men should be core to these conversations. This can be done in a way that does not alienate boys and young men, but engages them in the debate about gendered norms and practices and the impact that these have on both young men's and young women's behaviours.
- Interventions – in primary prevention and with perpetrators – can and should unpick and challenge how sexual access to young

women's bodies is part of, even central to, doing masculinities (see EVAW 2011).

• Work with young women that explores the connections between sexual exploitation, sexualised sexism in popular culture and inequality between women and men can reframe their experience in such a way as to reduce self-blame (Coy 2017).

Finally, the concept of patriarchal violence (hooks 2000) joins up the dots between sexual exploitation of children and adult women. Girls – and boys – do not stop being victimised by patriarchal violence when or because they turn 18 and are presumed to be consenting to abusive and exploitative sex, despite policy framings that reinforce this distinction. Sexual exploitation is a form of child abuse and VAWG, and integrating this analysis across practice will be a step closer to fully recognising and responding to young people's experiences.

Notes

1   The Serious Crime Act (2015) enacted changes in terminology from 'child prostitution' to 'sexual exploitation'.
2   See www.csacentre.org.uk for an overview of this work.
3   I owe this phrase to Sylvia Walby (2014) who uses it to describe searching crime survey data on violence against women.
4   As Lovett and colleagues (2018) note, it is perhaps unsurprising that this discourse continues to influence professional responses, since landmark 2009 guidance on *Safeguarding Children and Young People from Sexual Exploitation* – the first update since 1999 – included 'promiscuity' on the list of indicators of sexual exploitation (Department for Children, Schools and Families 2009: 43). Links between sexual exploitation and promiscuity became encoded into public policy.

References

Altamura, A. (2013) 'Understanding demand for CSEC and the related gender dimensions: A review of the research in ECPAT International, in M. Capaldi (ed) *Examining Neglected Elements in Combatting Sexual Exploitation of Children*, Journal Series 7, Bangkok: ECPAT International, https://resourcecentre.savethechildren.net/node/7712/pdf/ecpat_journal_jul_2013_eng.pdf.

Beckett, H., Holmes, D. and Walker, J. (2017) *Child Sexual Exploitation: Definition and Guide for Professionals*, Luton: University of Bedfordshire

Beckett, H. with Brodie, I, Factor, F, Melrose, M, Pearce, J, Pitts, J, Shuker, L. and Warrington, C. (2013) '*It's Wrong…But You Get Used To It': A Qualitative Study of Gang-associated Sexual Violence Towards, and Exploitation of, Young People in England*, London and Luton: Office of Children's Commissioner and University of Bedfordshire

Berelowitz, S., Firmin, C., Edwards, G. and Gulyurtlu, S. (2012) *'I Thought I Was the Only One. The Only One in the World': The Office of the Children's Commissioner's Inquiry into Child Sexual Exploitation in Gangs and Groups*, London: Office of the Children's Commissioner

Brayley, H. and Cockbain, E. (2014) 'British children can be trafficked too: Towards an inclusive definition of internal child sex trafficking', *Child Abuse Review* 23: 171–184

Brayley, H., Cockbain, E. and Gibson, K. (2014*) Rapid Evidence Assessment: The Sexual Exploitation of Boys and Young Men*, Essex: Barnardo's

Boyle, K. (2019) 'What's in a name? Theorising the inter-relationships of gender and violence', *Feminist Theory* 20(1): 19–36.

Brown, A. and Barrett, D. (2002) *Knowledge of Evil: Child Prostitution and Child Sexual Abuse in Twentieth Century England*, Cullompton: Willan

CEOP (Child Exploitation and Online Protection Centre) (2011) *Out of Mind, Out of Sight: Breaking Down the Barriers to Understanding Child Sexual Exploitation*, London: CEOP

Cockbain, E. (2013) 'Grooming and the "Asian sex gang predator": The construction of a racial crime threat', *Race and Class* 54(4): 22–32

Connell, R.W. and Pearse, R. (2015) *Gender: In World Perspective* (3rd edn), Cambridge: Polity Press

Coy, M. (2009) 'Moved around like bags of rubbish nobody wants': How multiple placement moves make young women vulnerable to sexual exploitation, *Child Abuse Review* 18(6): 254–266

Coy, M. (2016) 'Joining the dots on sexual exploitation of children and women: Gaps in UK policy approaches', *Critical Social Policy* 36(4): 571–592

Coy, M. (2017) *'All Fired Up Now': The Safe Choices Leaving Care and Custody Project Programme on Sexual Exploitation. Final Evaluation Report*, London: Child and Woman Abuse Studies Unit (CWASU)

Coy, M., Horvath, M.A.H. and Kelly, L. (2007) *'It's Just Like Going to the Supermarket': Men Buying Sex in East London*, London: Child and Woman Abuse Studies Unit (CWASU)

Coy, M., Kelly, L., Elvines, F., Garner, M. and Kanyeredzi, A. (2013) *'Sex Without Consent, I Suppose That is Rape': How Young People in England Understand Sexual Consent*, London: Office of the Children's Commissioner

Crenshaw, K. (1991) 'Mapping the margins: intersectionality, identity politics, and violence against women of colour', *Stanford Law Review* 43(6): 1241–1299

DCSF (Department of Children, Schools and Families) (2009) *Safeguarding Children and Young People from Sexual Exploitation: Supplementary Guidance to Working Together to Safeguard Children*, London: DCSF

DfE (Department for Education) (2017) *Child Sexual Exploitation: Definition and a Guide for Practitioners, Local Leaders and Decision Makers Working to Protect Children from Child Sexual Exploitation*, London: Department for Education

Donovan, C. (2014) *The Ace Project: Developing an Agenda for Change in the North East and Beyond on Young LGBTQ People and Child Sexual Exploitation*, Newcastle: Northern Rock Foundation

Ennew, J. (1986) *The Sexual Exploitation of Children*, Basingstoke: Palgrave Macmillan

EVAW (End Violence Against Women) (2011) *A Different World is Possible: Promising Practices to Prevent Violence Against Women and Girls*, London: EVAW

Erturk, Y. and Purkayastha, B. (2012) 'Linking research, policy and action: A look at the work of the Special Rapporteur on Violence against Women', *Current Sociology* 60(2): 142–160

Fine, C. (2010) *Delusions of Gender: The Real Science Behind Sex Differences*, New York: Norton

Fine, C. (2017) *Testosterone Rex: Myths of Sex, Science and Society*, New York: Norton

Firmin, C. (2011) *This Is It. This Is My Life…: The Female Voice in Violence Project Final Report*, London: ROTA, www.rota.org.uk/content/rota-march-2011-female-voice-violence-project-final-report-it-my-life

Flood, M. (2009) 'The harms of pornography exposure among children and young people', *Child Abuse Review* 18: 384–400

Fox, C. (2016) *'It's Not on the Radar': The Hidden Diversity of Children and Young People at Risk of Sexual Exploitation in England*, Barkingside: Barnardo's

Franklin, A. and Smeaton, E. (2017) 'Recognising and responding to young people with learning disabilities who experience, or are at risk of, child sexual exploitation in the UK', *Children and Youth Services Review* 73: 474–481

Gill, A. (2006) 'Patriarchal violence in the name of "honour"', *International Journal of Criminal Justice Sciences* 1(1): 1–12

Gill, A. and Harrison, K. (2015) 'Child grooming and sexual exploitation: Are South Asian men the UK media's new folk devils?', *International Journal for Crime, Justice and Social Democracy* 4(2): 34–49

Gill, R. (2016) 'Post-postfeminism?: New feminist visibilities in postfeminist times', *Feminist Media Studies* 16(4): 610–630

Gohir, S. (2013) *Unheard Voices: The Sexual Exploitation of Asian Girls and Young Women*, Birmingham: Muslim Women's Network

Harper, Z. and Scott, S. (2005) *Meeting the Needs of Sexually Exploited Young People in London*, Barkingside: Barnardo's

Heilman, B. and Barker, G. (2018) *Masculine Norms and Violence: Making the Connections*, Washington, DC: Promundo-US

Heuchan, C. (2017) 'Sex, gender, and the new essentialism', 7 February, https://sisteroutrider.wordpress.com/2017/02/07/sex-gender-and-the-new-essentialism/

hooks, b. (2000) *Feminism is for Everybody: Passionate Politics*, Cambridge, MA: South End Press

Horvath, M.A.H., Alys, K., Massey, K., Pina, A., Scally, M., Adler, J.R. (2013) *'Basically, Porn is Everywhere…': A Rapid Evidence Assessment on the Effects that Access and Exposure to Pornography has on Children and Young People*, London: Office for the Children's Commissioner

Itzin, C. (2001) 'Incest, paedophilia, pornography and prostitution: Making familial males more visible as the abusers', *Child Abuse Review* 10(1): 35–48

Jyrkinen, M. (2012) 'McSexualisation of bodies, sex and sexualities: Mainstreaming the commodification of gendered inequalities', in M. Coy (ed) *Prostitution, Harm and Gender Inequality: Theory, Research and Policy*, Farnham: Ashgate

Kanyeredzi, A. (2018) *Race, Culture, and Gender: Black Female Experiences of Violence and Abuse*, London: Palgrave Macmillan

Kelly, L. (1988) *Surviving Sexual Violence*, Cambridge: Polity Press

Kelly, L. and Karsna, K. (2017) *Measuring the Scale and Changing Nature of Child Sexual Abuse and Child Sexual Exploitation*, London: Centre of Expertise on Child Sexual Abuse

Kelly, L. and Regan, L. (2000) *Rhetorics and Realities: Sexual Exploitation of Children in Europe*, London: Child and Woman Abuse Studies Unit (CWASU)

Know Violence in Childhood (2017) *Ending Violence in Childhood: Global Report 2017*, New Delhi: Know Violence in Childhood

Lillywhite, R. and Skidmore, P. (2006) 'Boys are not sexually exploited? A challenge to practitioners', *Child Abuse Review* 15: 351–361

Lovett, J., Coy, M. and Kelly, L. (2018) *Deflection, Denial and Disbelief: Social and Political Discourses about Child Sexual Abuse and their Impact on Institutional Responses: A Rapid Evidence Assessment*, London: Independent Inquiry into Child Sexual Abuse

Mackay, F. (2015) *Radical Feminism: Feminist Activism in Movement*, Basingstoke: Palgrave Macmillan

McNaughton-Nicholls, C., Harvey, S. and Paskell, C. (2014) *Gendered Perceptions: What Professionals Say About the Sexual Exploitation of Boys and Young Men in the UK*, Barkingside: Barnardo's

Melrose, M. (2004) 'Young people abused through prostitution: Some observations for practice', *Practice: Social Work in Action* 16(1): 17–29

Melrose, M. (2013) 'Twenty-first century party people: Young people and sexual exploitation in the new millennium', *Child Abuse Review* 22(3): 155–168

O'Hara, M. (2019) 'Making pimps and sex buyers visible: Recognising the commercial nexus in "child sexual exploitation"', *Critical Social Policy* 39(1): 108–126.

Pearce, J. (2009) *Young People and Sexual Exploitation*, London: Routledge

Pearce, J. (2014) 'Moving on with Munro: Child sexual exploitation within a child protection framework', in M. Blyth (ed) *Moving On From Munro: Improving Children's Services*, Bristol: Policy Press

Pearce, J. and Pitts, J. (2011) *Youth Gangs, Sexual Violence and Sexual Exploitation: A Scoping Exercise for the Office of the Children's Commissioner for England*, Luton: University of Bedfordshire

Pearce, J., Williams, M. and Galvin, C. (2003) *It's Someone Taking a Part of You: A Study of Young Women and Sexual Exploitation*, London: National Children's Bureau

Sharp, N. (2013) 'Missing from discourse: South Asian young women and sexual exploitation', in M. Melrose and J. Pearce (eds) *Critical Perspectives on Child Sexual Exploitation and Related Trafficking*, Basingstoke: Palgrave Macmillan

Stanley, L. (1984) 'Should "sex" really be "gender" – or "gender" really be "sex"?', in S. Jackson and S. Scott (eds) *Gender: A Sociological Reader*, London: Routledge, pp 31–41

Stark, E., Flitcraft, A. and Frazier, W. (1979) 'Medicine and patriarchal violence: The social construction of a "private" event', *International Journal of Health Services* 9(3): 461–493

Tyler, M. and Quek, K. (2016) 'Conceptualizing pornographication: A lack of clarity and problems for feminist analysis', *Sexualization, Media and Society* 2(1): 1–14

Tyler, M. and Jovanovski, N. (2018) 'The limits of ethical consumption in the sex industry: An analysis of online brothel reviews', *Women's Studies International Forum* 66: 9–16

UNICEF (2014) *Hidden in Plain Sight: A Statistical Analysis of Violence Against Children*, New York: UNICEF

United Nations (2000) *Optional Protocol to the Convention on the Rights of the Child on the Sale of Children, Child Prostitution and Child Pornography*, New York: United Nations, https://treaties.un.org/pages/ViewDetails.aspx?src=IND&mtdsg_no=IV-11-c&chapter=4&lang=en

United Nations (2006) *The Secretary-General's In-depth Study on all Forms of Violence Against Women*, New York: UN General Assembly

Vera-Gray, F. (2016) *Men's Intrusion, Women's Embodiment: A Critical Analysis of Street Harassment*, London: Routledge

Walby, S. (1990) *Theorizing Patriarchy*, Oxford: Basil Blackwell

Walby, S. (2011) *The Future of Feminism*, Cambridge: Polity Press

Walby, S. (2014) 'How is domestic violence changing?', Paper presented at the *Social Exclusion Seminar*, London School of Economics, 18 June

Walker, C., Pillinger, K. and Brown, S. (2018) *Characteristics and Motivations of Perpetrators of Child Sexual Exploitation: A Rapid Evidence Assessment of Research*, London: Centre of Expertise on Child Sexual Abuse

Ward, J. and Patel, N. (2006) 'Broadening the discussion on "sexual exploitation": Ethnicity, sexual exploitation and young people', *Child Abuse Review* 15(5): 341–350

West, C. and Zimmerman, D. (1987) 'Doing gender', *Gender and Society* 1(2): 125–151

Westmarland, N. (2015) *Violence Against Women: Criminological Perspectives on Men's Violences*, London: Routledge

Whittier, N. (2011) *The Politics of Child Sexual Abuse: Emotion, Social Movements, and the State*, Oxford: Oxford University Press

Yancey Martin, P (2005) *Rape Work: Victims, Gender and Emotions in Organization and Community Context*, London: Routledge

Yonkova, N. and Keegan, E. (2014) *Stop Traffick! Tackling Demand for Sexual Services of Trafficked Women and Girls*, Dublin: Immigrant Council of Ireland

12

Understanding models of disability to improve responses to children with learning disabilities

Emilie Smeaton

Introduction

The sexual abuse of children and young people with disabilities has been highlighted in high profile cases such as Rochdale Borough Safeguarding Children Board's Serious Case Review (Griffiths 2013) and investigations into the sexual abuse perpetrated by Jimmy Savile. This chapter will explore the differences between a medical and a social model of disability to support application of these models to children with learning disabilities who experience, or are at risk of, child sexual exploitation (CSE). The chapter will include an overview of how disability intersects with abuse in general and CSE in particular. In addition, the chapter will draw upon evidence-based learning to consider how theory-informed services can identify children with learning disabilities affected by CSE and implement accessible services that deliver preventative and responsive practice to meet their needs.

Child abuse and disability

Children with disabilities are more likely to be abused than their non-disabled peers. A meta-analysis of 17 studies of violence against disabled children representing over 18,000 individuals (Jones et al 2012) illustrates that this group are between three and four times more likely to experience violence than non-disabled children with one study estimating that as many as 15 per cent of children with learning disabilities[1] experience sexual violence. A 2012 review of literature (Stalker and McArthur) identified that children with communication needs, learning disabilities, behavioural disorders and sensory impairments are more likely to experience higher levels of neglect and violence. Miller and Brown (2014) highlight how those children at greatest risk of abuse are those with behaviour/conduct conditions but that other high-risk groups include those with learning difficulties/disabilities, children with health-related conditions, deaf children and those with speech and language difficulties. There is some evidence that the abuse of disabled children differs to the abuse of their peers, starting at an earlier age (Sullivan and Knutson 2000) with boys disproportionately represented among abused disabled children (Sullivan and Knutson 2000; Kvam 2004). The quality and quantity of information about the abuse and protection of disabled children in the UK has been highlighted as being poor (Cooke and Stanton 2002). The NSPCC note that little has been known about the experiences of children with disabilities in the child protection system (Miller and Brown 2014).

A small number of research studies undertaken in the UK report that children with learning disabilities are vulnerable to CSE (Smeaton 2009; Beckett 2011; Brodie and Pearce 2012; Smeaton 2013; Franklin et al 2016). The Office of the Children's Commissioner for England report (Berelowitz et al 2013) addressing CSE in gangs and groups identified how learning disabilities are a typical vulnerability in a child prior to abuse. A UK-wide research study addressing the sexual exploitation of children and young people with learning disabilities (Franklin et al 2016) provide evidence that those with learning disabilities are more vulnerable to CSE than their non-disabled peers and that professionals working in specialist CSE services estimate that between 10 and 50 per cent of the children with whom they work have a diagnosed or undiagnosed learning disability.

Medical and social models of disability

The medical and social models of disability have been dominant in framing how disability is viewed and addressed in the UK. Understanding key elements of these two models, including criticism of these models, is important for professionals working to address CSE to enable consideration of their own and others' responses to children and young people with disabilities and meet this group's needs.

The medical model is the traditional model of disability in which the disadvantage faced by those with disabilities is a consequence of their individual impairments. This model outlines how the impairment causes the disability. Responses to disability include viewing an individual's disability as 'a problem', looking at 'what is wrong' with an individual and 'curing' the impairment:

At its most fundamental, a medical model view of disability considers disability to be something 'broken' inside a person. From this perspective, the required response is therefore to 'fix' the person, to try to change the person in ways that make it easier to 'fit in' with society, or to seek to eliminate the 'disability'. (Cologon and Thomas 2014:29)

The social model of disability locates disability in the social, cultural, material and attitudinal barriers that exclude people with impairments from mainstream life, as opposed to looking at the individual in terms of 'deficit'. As noted by Franklin et al (2016), the social model of disability promotes assets and what those with disabilities can do and encourages researchers, practitioners and policymakers to view disabled children as children first. There are criticisms of the social model of disability relating to the model being simplistic and a political doctrine (Shakespeare and Watson 2010; Thomas 2010) alongside prioritising the social dimension over physical and psychological aspects of impairment (Corker 2002; Terzi 2004). The separation of impairment from disability within the social model of disability is viewed as a major difference between the medical and social model of disability: 'From a social model perspective disability is imposed upon someone who has been labelled as "impaired", while a medical model holds that disability is caused by, or equates to, impairment' (Cologon 2016).

While there is no doubt about the contribution of medical science in supporting the health and wellbeing of those with disabilities, the social model usefully points to how attitudes towards those with disabilities and physical barriers are themselves disabling. The separation of impairment from disability that forms a key criticism of the social model of disability (see, for example, Thomas 1999; Barnes et al 2002; Shakespeare 2004; Tremain 2005; Thomas 2007; Barnes 2012) reinforces that, while there is need to remove both social prejudices towards those with disabilities and physical barriers, it is important to retain a focus upon an individual's lived experience of disability. So, while the promotion of positive social attitudes and availability of aids and approaches, including design of physical environments, can support the participation and integration of those with disabilities, it is important to recognise that barriers can also be caused by an individual's condition such as chronic pain, fatigue, cognitive functioning and communication. To meet an individual's needs and consideration of the actual or potential barriers they face, it is necessary to consider their identity not only in relation to their disability but also, for example, their ethnicity, gender and sexuality.

Factors contributing to the increased vulnerability to CSE of children and young people with learning disabilities and other impairments

As the present evidence base is currently limited in scope, the remainder of this chapter will focus upon research addressing CSE and children and young people with learning disabilities, and working with theory and practice-based learning to meet their needs.

Franklin et al (2016) describe how a number of elements contribute to the increased vulnerability of children and young people with learning disabilities to CSE. Impairment related factors, linked to the impact of a disability, include: a lack of cognitive ability to recognise exploitation or risk; impulsive behaviours and needs associated with a different understanding of social interaction and communication; and limited capacity to consent to sexual activity. Drawing upon arguments presented by the social model of disability, it is clear that societal treatment of children and young people with learning disabilities also plays a part in this increased vulnerability (Franklin et al 2016). This societal treatment includes overprotection of children and young people with learning disabilities, isolation, disempowerment and failing to see young people with learning disabilities as sexual beings who are interested in relationships. This all leads to little attention being given to informing children and young people with disabilities about healthy sexual relationships. To add to the foregoing, Franklin et al (2016) also identify how this increased vulnerability is also a result of: a lack of knowledge, understanding and awareness of the sexual exploitation of children and young people with learning disabilities among professionals, parents and carers and the wider community; the lack of training received by professionals addressing CSE and learning disabilities; and the low priority generally given to children and young people with learning disabilities by service providers. To avoid imposing further disability upon children and young people with learning disabilities who experience, or are at risk of, CSE, it is necessary for national and local policies and practice to ensure that attitudes and responses to this group reduce vulnerability to CSE.

Case study: Leon[2] (part one)

Leon is a 15-year-old male who has a global learning disability. Leon attends a mainstream secondary school with a unit for those with additional learning needs. Leon receives additional support which meant that he missed out on PSHE lessons, including those addressing online safety, consent and sexual relationships.

Leon found it difficult to make friends, was isolated at both school and home and spent a lot of time chatting to others online. One man, called Tony, seemed particularly friendly. Leon was very happy to accept Tony's invitation to come to his house to play on his X-Box. Tony told Leon to tell his parents that he was going to a schoolfriend's house. Leon's parents were pleased he had a friend and did not ask for information about this friend. Tony offered Leon cider and Leon enjoyed feeling drunk and laughing with Tony.

One weekend, after being given vodka, Leon began to feel unwell and was told to lie down on Tony's bed. Tony subjected Leon to a serious sexual assault which was very frightening. Tony told Leon that this is what friends did and that, if Leon wanted to keep Tony as a friend, he had to not tell anyone about what they had done. Tony also told Leon that he would be in a lot of trouble because he had been playing violent video games and drinking alcohol. Leon later explained that fears of losing Tony as a friend and being in trouble stopped him from telling anyone what had happened to him.

Learning from theory and responding to children with learning disabilities who experience, or are at risk of, CSE

Reinforcing arguments presented by the social model of disability, UK research focusing upon improving responses to children and young people who experience, or are at risk of, CSE (Franklin et al 2016) emphasises the importance of ensuring that disability is not imposed upon individuals. In line with critiques of the social model of disability that emphasise recognising an individual's lived experiences of disability, the findings of the research also highlight promoting understanding of the impact of an individual's impairment and the interplay between this impact and vulnerability to CSE. This research, and that conducted by others, provides the following evidence-based learning, outlined later in the chapter, to support practice with this group of children and young people and ensure their needs are met.

Understanding children's communication and learning needs

Understanding a child or young person's communication and learning needs is key when supporting children and young people with disabilities who experience, or are at risk of, CSE. This can be achieved by: asking children and young people themselves, their parents and carers, volunteers and professionals who are familiar with the child about what works best for the individual in relation to communication, understanding and learning styles (Smeaton et al 2016); listening to children and young people with learning disabilities who have experienced, or are at risk of, CSE; and facilitating their understanding by breaking information into smaller parts and frequently checking understanding (Smeaton et al 2016).

It is also important to make an effort to understand children and young people who may have difficulties with communication. Much can be learned directly from disabled children to improve their protection (Jones et al 2012). Many children and young people with learning disabilities may want to please others and, for a variety of reasons, say that they understand something when they do not. It is important to be mindful of this and not assume that they have understood information or the issue being explained. Frequent repetition and review is particularly helpful with meeting the needs of children and young people with learning disabilities.

Supporting disclosure of CSE among children with learning disabilities

Many children and young people experience a range of difficulties in recognising that their experiences are abusive and in disclosing abuse (see, for example, Allnock and Miller 2013; Smeaton 2016; Franklin et al 2016). Allnock and Miller (2013) identify how disclosure often leads to a sequence of events that are out of a child or young person's control and often entail talking to numerous professionals about sensitive matters. Hershkowitz et al (2007) suggest that disabled children and young people are more likely to delay disclosure of abuse than non-disabled peers for a range of reasons including: lack of awareness of abuse, difficulties communicating their experiences and fear. Disclosing CSE can be particularly challenging for children with learning disabilities who may find it difficult to process and respond to questions (Smeaton et al 2016). In line with arguments advocated by the social model, this highlights the importance of ensuring that professionals, and volunteers, working with children and young people with learning disabilities are informed about possible indicators of CSE to enable them to proactively identify that a child with learning disabilities is experiencing, or at risk of, CSE. This would remove the burden placed on children with learning disabilities to recognise that they are being sexually exploited, or are at risk of being so, and disclose CSE.

Disabled children often make clear disclosures of abuse but their expressions of distress are often assumed to be due to their disability and not an indicator of abuse (NSPCC 2015). Franklin et al (2016) found that some children with learning disabilities are not believed when they disclose CSE. As the initial response to disclosure of CSE is very important, it can be very distressing for children with learning disabilities when they are not heard and it is important that they receive an appropriate and positive response when they disclose CSE or risk of CSE. To support disclosure of CSE, children with disabilities should be assured that they will not get into trouble if they disclose and professionals should ensure that they ask this group of children about their relationships and potential risks and be genuinely interested in their lives. There are a number of positive outcomes that stem from professionals responding well to disclosure including children and young people feeling relieved and becoming aware that it is safe to tell someone what is happening to them (Franklin et al 2016). Disclosure also enables responses to be set in place to meet the needs of children with learning disabilities and prevent risk of CSE escalating.

Recognising and responding to individual children's needs

Responses to CSE require a focus upon the individual needs of a child (see, for example, Smeaton 2018). In line with Shakespeare and Watson's (2010) critique of the social model of disability and emphasis upon the importance of the individual aspect of impairment, Franklin et al (2016) highlight that it is critical to not treat all children and young people the same because they share an impairment label, as the spectrum of learning disabilities means that children and young people can have diverse needs and experience the world in very different ways. This points to the necessity to consider the impact of a child's disability or impairment when assessing their needs, understanding their particular vulnerability to CSE and/or experiences of CSE and designing a needs-based response to effectively support them. Addressing diversity is a core consideration and needs relating to gender identity and sexual orientation should be considered and appropriately addressed (Franklin et al 2016). Focusing upon ensuring service provision is accessible to children and young people from black and minority ethnic communities is similarly important as is sensitive consideration to cultural, gender, sexuality and ableism.

Recognising the challenging and complex nature of work to support children with learning disabilities affected by CSE

Supporting children and young people with learning disabilities who experience, or are at risk of, CSE can be immensely rewarding and enjoyable but there are challenges in meeting the needs of this group (Smeaton et al 2016). For example, there may be tensions between protecting this group of children and young people from those intent upon harming them and ensuring, in line with social models of disability, that they have the right to independence and to have appropriate sexual relationships. This entails due consideration of individual needs and circumstances, and a balance between child protection and children's rights in order to avoid harm. This, in turns, requires ensuring that professionals are supported to develop a sound understanding of child protection and the rights of those with disabilities. The lack of identification of a child or young person's learning needs at referral, or an incorrect diagnosis or assessment also causes challenges for ensuring appropriate support is put in place for a child or young person. In addition, there may also be crossover between symptoms of trauma and identification of learning disabilities. Learning disabilities can sometimes be hidden due to difficulties faced by children and young people, including childhood abuse. As noted by Franklin et al (2016), some children and young people are diagnosed with a medical condition or learning disability when childhood abuse has resulted in them missing key developmental milestones, having impaired cognition, experiencing difficulties with empathy and/or easily-triggered fight or flight responses. The crossover of presentation and symptoms of experiential trauma and learning disabilities can result in a diagnosis not being clear which, in turn, may result in care plans that do not effectively meet children and young people's needs. Awareness of the social model of disability plays a crucial part in supporting how a lack of understanding of the impact of trauma and abuse can result in misdiagnosis. While, as noted previously, recognising abuse can be difficult for any child or young person, the lack of recognition of sexual exploitation can be intensified for those with learning disabilities. Some children and young people with learning disabilities and/or other impairments are not always able to retain and transfer their learning or experiences to other situations and, as a consequence, it can be unrealistic to expect them to remember general ideas about what is 'unsafe' or 'risky', even when they have had a bad experience.

Preventing, and responding to, the sexual exploitation of children with learning disabilities

Case study: Leon (part two)

Tony was arrested for accessing online child pornography. The police also found evidence that Tony had arranged to meet young males including Leon. A referral was made to a specialist CSE service who was able to support Leon and his family. Leon's worker, Kate, spent time getting to know Leon and found out how Leon's learning disability affected him to ensure that she worked with him in a way that met his needs and ensured his understanding of the work they do together. Kate knows that she has to work with Leon at a slow pace and that she needs to regularly repeat information to enable Leon to understand. The CSE service has flexibility in their approach to work with children and young people with learning disabilities as there is understanding that meeting the needs of a child or young person with learning disabilities can take longer than with their non-disabled peers. Kate is aware that some existing CSE resources are not appropriate to use with Leon and is working with pictorial resources due to Leon's difficulties with the written word. By taking this approach Kate has found that Leon is able to think and talk about safe sex and relationships, for example, and about his experience of abuse.

Kate also works with Leon's parents and has explained the importance of Leon being informed about sex and relationships and steps to take to keep Leon safe online and offline. Leon's parents' initial response was to prevent Leon from going online by taking his phone and laptop away from him but Kate has worked with them to understand that a more effective approach is to ensure safe access to the internet. Leon's parents now know that some young people with learning disabilities are vulnerable to sexual exploitation as they move into adulthood and that they need to continue to support Leon to develop healthy relationships.

Kate outlined to the police about how Leon could give a statement and the police agreed to take the suggested approach. Leon has also been supported to attend a group for young people with disabilities and enjoys the friendships and activities this group provides.

Drawing on a social model of disability, Franklin et al (2016) emphasise the importance of undertaking a variety of preventative work on an individual basis with children and young people with learning disabilities who are identified as being at risk of CSE. Also, wider preventative and CSE awareness-raising work can take place with groups of children and young people in, for example, children's homes, educational establishments and secure training units. Providing accessible sex and relationships education is crucial to prevent the sexual exploitation of children and young people with learning disabilities and other impairments (Smeaton et al 2016). Draft guidance issued in England (DfE 2019) emphasises how relationships and sex education (RSE) must be accessible for all pupils and that the provision of 'differentiated and personalised' (DfE 2019:11) high quality teaching will ensure accessibility for pupils with special educational needs and disabilities (SEND). This draft guidance also notes that: those with SEND may be more vulnerable to exploitation; that relationships education can be a 'particular priority' (DfE 2019:12) for this group; and the importance of ensuring RSE content is tailored to meet the specific needs of children and young people.

Franklin et al (2016) present a number of suggestions that practitioners can focus on to support their practice with children and young people with learning disabilities who experience, or are at risk of, CSE. These include the following:

Planning sessions

To effectively meet the needs of children and young people with learning disabilities, it is necessary to pay particular attention to planning a session addressing CSE to ensure that it is effectively tailored to meet their individual needs. This could include:

- the need for consistency in time and location of session;
- providing lower intensity shorter sessions to aid concentration;
- provision of toys, games or gadgets to alleviate anxiety and promote relaxation at the start of a session;
- breaking information into smaller sections and allowing for repetition and review;
- consideration of use of CSE resources (discussed in more depth at a later point in the chapter).

Focus of intervention

As previously noted, responses to children and young people with learning disabilities who experience, or are at risk of, CSE should focus upon individual needs and circumstances. However, Franklin et al (2016) found that some generic, socially informed interventions are particularly pertinent with this group of children and young people including:

- teaching about sex, relationships and consent as many children and young people with learning disabilities do not have a basic understanding;
- improving awareness of CSE to increase understanding of, and reduce risk of, CSE;
- supporting recognition of safe and abusive relationships, including friendships, to aid reduction of associations with risky peers and adults and aid positive relationships;
- addressing self-esteem and self-blame to prevent escalation of risk of CSE and facilitate recovery from CSE;
- where children and young people have experienced CSE, enabling them to recognise that they have been sexually exploited, address its impact and recover as far as possible.

Resources to support practice

Resources often provide an important aid to support understanding of CSE by children and young people with learning disabilities and address issues relevant to them. However, it may be necessary to try a range of materials and resources before finding out what works well with individual children and young people and meet their communication and learning needs. Creative resources including games, plasticine and sand work are often used with children and young people with learning disabilities to create a comfortable atmosphere and enable them to 'open up'. As touched upon previously, toys or gadgets to fiddle with can assist learning as some children and young people find it easier to process information when doing other things and can help with expressing or controlling feelings and emotions.

While there is presently a lack of CSE resources specifically for children and young people with learning disabilities, professionals often successfully adapt existing CSE resources to work with individuals and meet their communications and learning needs. There are, however, some resources that can be particularly confusing for some children and young people with learning disabilities including those based upon metaphor or complex plots of ideas. Graphic CSE resources can be particularly problematic for some children and young people with learning disabilities and cause, for example, fright or anxiety.

Supporting the transition to adults' services

Finally, considerable thought should also be given to supporting young people with learning disabilities and other impairments when they leave specialist CSE services and make the transition to adults' services. This can be very difficult for young people who may have a number of worries about leaving a specialist CSE service, particularly when they have built trust-based relationships with professionals who understand the individual impact of their disability or impairment. Ensuring a smooth transition can be facilitated by, for example, joint working sessions involving both children's and adults' service and holistic transition planning. As young people over the age of 18 can continue to be vulnerable to sexual exploitation, there is a need for a sex and relationships education to form part of a lifecourse approach from an early age and be a significant focus in transition planning.

Conclusion

The medical and social models of disability, along with their critiques, offer useful elements that, along with learning from evidence-based findings, can support services and professionals addressing the sexual exploitation of children and young people with learning disabilities. Medical knowledge about learning disabilities can support with assessment and understanding the physical symptoms that accompany a learning disability. The social model reinforces how social, cultural, material and attitudinal barriers also form a disability and, in relation to children and young people with disabilities who experience, or are at risk of, CSE, highlight the importance of ensuring that this group, along with their non-disabled peers, have the support and opportunities to develop safe and healthy relationships. Learning from the social model also emphasises that professionals require support including training to understand the needs of children and young people with disabilities and ensure that they are able to both prevent risk to CSE and respond when a child or young person has experienced abuse. Significantly, critiques of the social model emphasise the need to understand the impact of a learning disability on the individual and support evidence-based learning that focuses upon the importance of meeting individual needs and ensuring consideration of how disability intersects with other elements of individual identity such as gender, race and sexuality.

Notes

[1] While it is recognised that several definitions of learning disability are use in the UK and internationally, the Department of Health (DH 2001) state that a learning disability meets three criteria: a significantly reduced ability to understand new or complex information, to learn new skills (impaired intelligence), with a reduced ability to cope independently (impaired functioning) which started before childhood, with a lasting effect on development.

[2] Leon (not his real name) is a young person who has participated in consultation activity to support development of specialist services for young people who have experienced CSE.

References

Allnock, D. and Miller, P. (2013) *No One Noticed, No One Heard: A Study of Disclosures of Childhood Abuse*, London: National Society for the Prevention of Cruelty to Children (NSPCC), www.nspcc.org. uk/services-and-resources/research-and-resources/2013/no-one-noticed-no-one-heard/

Barnes, C. (2012) 'Understanding the social model of disability: Past, present and future', in N. Watson, A. Roulstone and C. Thomas (eds) *Routledge Handbook of Disability Studies*, London: Routledge

Barnes, C., Oliver, M. and Barton, L. (2002) *Disability Studies Today*, Oxford: Blackwell Publishing Company

Beckett, H. (2011) *Not a World Away: The Sexual Exploitation of Children and Young People in Northern Ireland*, Belfast: Barnardo's

Berelowitz, S., Clifton, J., Firmin, C., Gulyurtlu, S. and Edwards, G. (2013) *'If Only Someone Had Listened': The Office of the Children's Commissioner's Inquiry into Child Sexual Exploitation in Gangs and Groups*, Final Report, London: Office of the Children's Commissioner, www.thebromleytrust.org.uk/files/chidrens-commission.pdf

Brodie, I. and Pearce, J. (2012) *Exploring the Scale and Nature of Child Sexual Exploitation in Scotland*, Edinburgh: Scottish Government, www.nls.uk/scotgov/2012/9781782561439.pdf

Cologon, K. (2016) '"What is disability? It depends whose shoes you are wearing": Parent understandings of the concept of disability', *Disabilities Studies Quarterly*, 36(1), http://dsq-sds.org/article/view/4448/4212

Cologon, K. and Thomas, C. (2014) 'Ableism, disablism and the early years', in K. Cologon (ed) *Inclusive Education in the Early Years: Right from the Start*, South Melbourne: Oxford University Press, pp 27–48

Cooke, P. and Stanton, P. (2002) 'Abuse and disabled children: Hidden needs...?', *Child Abuse Review*, 11: 1–18

Corker, M. (2002) 'Deafness/disability – problematising notions of identity, culture and structure', in S. Riddell and N. Watson (eds) *Disability, Culture and Identity*, London: Pearson

DfE (Department for Education) (2019) *Relationships Education, Relationships and Sex Education (RSE) and Health Education Guidance for Governing Bodies, Proprietors, Head Teachers, Principals, Senior Leadership Teams, Teachers*, https://consult.education. gov.uk/pshe/relationships-education-rse-health-education/ supporting_documents/20170718_%20Draft%20guidance%20 for%20consultation.pdf

DH (Department of Health) (2001) *Valuing People: A New Strategy for Learning Disability for the 21st Century*, London: DH

Franklin, A. and Smeaton, E. (2017a) 'Listening to young people with learning disabilities who have experience, or are at risk of, child sexual exploitation', *Children and Society*, doi:10.1111/chso.12231

Franklin, A. and Smeaton, E. (2017b) 'Recognising and responding to young people with learning disabilities who experience, or are at risk of, child sexual exploitation in the UK', *Children and Youth Services Review*, 73: 474–481

Franklin, A., Raws, P. and Smeaton, E. (2016) *Unprotected, Overprotected: Meeting the Needs of Young People with Learning Disabilities who Experience or are at Risk of, Sexual Exploitation*, Barkingside: Barnardo's

Griffiths, S. (2013) *The Overview Report of the Serious Case Review in Respect of Young People 1, 2, 3, 4, 5 and 6*, Rochdale: Rochdale Borough Safeguarding Children Board, www.rochdaleonline.co.uk/ uploads/f1/news/document/20131220_93449.pdf

Hershkowitz, I., Lamb, M. and Horowitz, D. (2007) 'Victimisation of children with disabilities', *American Journal of Orthopsychiatry*, 77(4): 629–635

Jones, L., Bellis, M.A., Wood, S., Hughes, K., McCoy, E., Eckley, L., Bates, G., Mickton, C., Shakespeare, T. and Officer, A. (2012) 'Prevalence and risk of violence against children with disabilities: A systematic review and meta-analysis of observational studies', *Lancet*, 380(9845): 899–907

Kvam, M. (2004) 'Sexual abuse of deaf children: A retrospective analysis of the prevalence and characteristics of childhood sexual abuse among deaf adults in Norway', *Child Abuse and Neglect*, 28: 241–251

Miller, B. and Brown, J. (2014) *'We Have the Right to be Safe': Protecting Disabled Children from Abuse*, London: National Society for the Prevention of Cruelty to Children (NSPCC), www.nspcc.org. uk/globalassets/documents/research-reports/right-safe-disabled-children-abuse-report.pdf

NSPCC (National Society for the Prevention of Cruelty to Children) (2015) 'Disabled children have an equal right to protection from abuse', www.nspcc.org.uk/what-we-do/news-opinion/disabled-children-equal-right-protection-abuse/

Shakespeare, T. (2004) 'Social models of disability and other life strategies', *Scandinavian Journal of Disability Research*, 6(1): 8–21, http://dx.doi.org/10.1080/15017410409512636

Shakespeare, T. and Watson, N. (2010) 'Beyond models: understanding the complexity of disabled people's lives', in G. Scambler and S. Scambler (eds) *New Directions in the Sociology of Chronic and Disabling Conditions: Assaults on the Lifeworld*, London: Palgrave Macmillan, pp 57–76

Smeaton, E. (2009) *Off the Radar: Children and Young People on the Streets in the UK*, Sandbach: Railway Children

Smeaton, E. (2013) *Running from Hate to What you Think is Love: The Relationship Between Running Away and Child Sexual Exploitation*, Barkingside: Barnardo's

Smeaton, E. (2016) *Going the Extra Mile: Learning from SECOS' Child Sexual Exploitation Service*, London: Barnardo's, www.barnardos.org.uk/17561_going_the_extra_mile_23_5_16.pdf

Smeaton, E. (2018) 'Assessing children who experience, or are at risk of, child sexual exploitation', in J. Horwath and D. Platt (eds) *The Child's World*, London: Jessica Kingsley Publishers

Smeaton, E., Franklin, A. and Raws, P. (2016) *Practice Guide: Supporting Professionals to Meet the Needs of Young People with Learning Disabilities who Experience, or Are At Risk Of, Child Sexual Exploitation*, www.barnardos.org.uk/cse_ld_practice_guide.pdf

Stalker, K. and McArthur, K. (2012) 'Child abuse, child protection and disabled children: A review of recent research', *Child Abuse Review*, 21(1): 24–40

Sullivan, P. and Knutson, J. (2000) 'Maltreatment and disabilities: A population-based epidemiological study', *Child Abuse and Neglect*, 24: 1257–1273

Terzi, L. (2004) 'The social model of disability: a philosophical critique', *Journal of Applied Philosophy*, 21(2): 141–157

Thomas, C. (1999) *Female Forms: Experiencing and Understanding Disability*, London: Open University Press

Thomas, C. (2007) *Sociologies of Disability and Illness: Contested Ideas in Disability Studies and Medical Sociology*, Basingstoke: Palgrave Macmillan

Thomas, C. (2010) 'Medical sociology and disability theory', in G. Scambler and S. Scambler (eds) *New Directions in the Sociology of Chronic and Disabling Conditions: Assaults on the Lifeworld*, London: Palgrave Macmillan, pp 37–56

Tremain, S. (2005) 'Foucault, governmentality and critical disability theory: An introduction', in S. Tremain (ed) *Foucault and the Government of Disability*, Ann Arbor, MI: The University of Michigan Press

13

Some concluding thoughts

Jenny Pearce

The chapters in this book aim to help us think about the relationship between theory and practice in our work with children and young people affected by CSE. In the opening introductory chapter, I was suggesting that we encourage ourselves to also think about when and why certain theories make sense to us, how they emerge in different political and economic environments and how our understanding of different theoretical perspectives may change according to our own lifecourse events, employment opportunities and geographical/environmental locations. Subsequent chapters then focused on a number of different theoretical perspectives that influence how CSE is defined, understood and responded to.

While the sexual exploitation of children is the focus of this book, the ideas within it can be used to explore a range of forms of exploitation and abuse of children. For example, the earlier chapters in the book look at how definitions have shifted away from children being 'blamed' for prostitution-related offences towards them being understood as victims of sexual offences perpetrated by others. Such changing constructions are now emerging for young people who might hitherto have been seen as young offenders, arrested for drug related offences. The current shift towards awareness of these young people's vulnerability to exploitation by organised criminal networks is, rightfully, taking referrals away from the criminal justice system and towards referral for family and community-based support and diversion. But some questions, also explored in the book, follow this change. Is the shift in definition being informed by a better understanding of the nature of adolescence as a stage in the lifespan and by the increasing awareness of the impact of trauma on children's development? Are we sophisticated enough to embrace the perspectives of young people who do not want to be perceived solely as 'vulnerable' and focus on them as both 'victims' of criminal exploitation and 'agents' of their own destiny, trying to survive poverty through action within the informal economy? If we do create a plethora of 'vulnerable' children in need of welfare-based support, do our children's services have the resources and capacity to respond through a lens informed by Contextual Safeguarding that asks child protection agencies to address the environment outside of the family home? It is certain that responses will be limited and partial when youth services, and detached youth work services in particular, have been cut back, sometimes to the point of nonexistence. While these perspectives and political and economic concerns are explored in this book with sexually exploited children in mind, they are transferable to other exploitative contexts facing a range of children and young people.

I also hope that the chapters in the book are relevant both to those thinking about how to set up or perhaps reshape a service for children and young people, and to those currently working within a fixed, established service context. I hope that the chapters raise questions not only about how we understand children and young people but about how these understandings are translated into service provision to address perceived need. Do we know which theoretical perspectives are informing our work and why? Are we incorporating awareness of developing theoretical perspectives into our work and how do we ensure that our current engagement with children and young people and the contexts within which they live inform the development of theory, making sure that we have practice informed theory as well as theory informed practice (Factor 2017).

I also hope that the book will support trainers, lecturers and teachers who are developing or delivering coursework to students and interested practitioners. As noted in the introduction, the idea for the text was promoted by my own teaching of students who raised important questions about the use and applicability of theory to their work with children. It could be argued that it is through teaching and learning activities that theories become alive and useful or, indeed, further developed and refined. The questions remain for me as to whether I fully embrace this within the scope of my teaching and learning activities. Do I make this alive by openly explaining my 'leaning' towards particular theoretical perspectives, encouraging my students to do the same, as a mechanism for understanding if, how and why certain perspectives inform certain approaches to practice? This embraces the need to consider what is taught to trainee teachers, police, social workers, youth workers and others holding responsibility for children. If nothing else, I hope that the book encourages us not only to think about what we do, but why we do it and how that 'why' is conveyed into teaching, learning and practice.

Finally, while the content of the book is mainly UK focused, these questions are applicable to the international agendas driving responses to children affected by all forms of exploitation. I'd be interested in thinking more about this with colleagues working as, what Cloward (2016) calls 'international moral entrepreneurs'. As discussed in the introduction to the book, Cloward's particular focus is on exploring the relationships between theories driving international change and local agendas to prevent early and forced child marriage and female genital mutilation. While chapters in this book are UK focused, the questions of how, when and why these interact with work taking place at both local, national and international levels are important (see www. end-violence.org/).

While this book has not been able to fully cover or address the breadth and depth of different perspectives informing work with children and young people affected by CSE, I hope that it has promoted some thinking about what we do know and encouraged further thought about how our ongoing practice can continue to inform and develop theoretical perspectives of the future.

References

Cloward, K. (2016) *When Norms Collide*, Oxford: Oxford University Press

Factor, F. (2107) *Practice Informed Theory*, Unpublished PhD, Luton: University of Bedfordshire

Index

Made in the USA
Coppell, TX
03 June 2020

26915831R00155